SOCIAL CONSTRUCTIONISM, DISCOURSE AND REALISM

INQUIRIES IN SOCIAL CONSTRUCTION

Series editors
Kenneth J. Gergen and John Shotter

Inquiries in Social Construction is designed to facilitate across disciplinary and national boundaries, a revolutionary dialogue within the social sciences and humanities. Central to this dialogue is the idea that all presumptions of the real and the good are constructed within relations among people. This dialogue gives voice to a new range of topics, including the social construction of the person, rhetoric and narrative in the construction of reality, the role of power in making meanings, postmodernist culture and thought, discursive practices, the social constitution of the mental, dialogic process, reflexivity in theory and method, and many more. The series explores the problems and prospects generated by this new relational consciousness, and its implications for science and social life.

Also in this series

SOCIAL CONSTRUCTIONISM, DISCOURSE AND REALISM

EDITED BY

IAN PARKER

SAGE Publications
London • Thousand Oaks • New Delhi

Foreword © Rom Harré 1998
Chapter 1 © Ian Parker 1998
Chapter 2 © Vivien Burr 1998
Chapter 3 © Jonathan Potter 1998
Chapter 4 © Andrew Collier 1998
Chapter 5 © Ruth Merttens 1998
Chapter 6 © Steven D. Brown, Joan Pujol
and Beryl C. Curt 1998
Chapter 7 © Carla Willig 1998
Chapter 8 © Don Foster 1998
Chapter 9 © Maritza Montero 1998
Chapter 10 © Bronwyn Davies 1998
Chapter 11 © Kenneth J. Gergen 1998

First published 1998

SAGE Publications Ltd
6 Bonhill Street
London EC2A 4PU

SAGE Publications Inc.
2455 Teller Road
Thousand Oaks, California 91320

SAGE Publications India Pvt Ltd
32, M-Block Market
Greater Kailash – I
New Delhi 110 048

British Library Cataloguing in Publication data

A catalogue record for this book is
available from the British Library.

ISBN 0 7619 5376 0
ISBN 0 7619 5377 9 (pbk)

Library of Congress catalog card number 98–060145

Typeset by M Rules
Printed in Great Britain at the University Press, Cambridge

Contents

Contributors

Steven D. Brown is a lecturer in social and organizational psychology at Keele University and a member of the Centre for Social Theory and Technology. He has published articles on critical social psychology, STS and organization studies. Research interests include the role of technics in discourse and the organization of emotion. He is currently carrying out work (around Groupware and the mediation of memory) as part of the Economic and Social Research Council's Virtual Society programme.

Vivien Burr is Senior Lecturer in Psychology in the department of Behavioural Sciences at the University of Huddersfield. Her current areas of interest include social constructionism, personal construct psychology and gender. She is the author of *An Introduction to Social Constructionism* (1995), and *Invitation to Personal Construct Psychology* (with Trevor Butt, 1992). Her most recent book, *Gender and Social Psychology*, was published in 1998.

Andrew Collier is Reader in Philosophy at the University of Southampton, and author of *R.D. Laing: The Philosophy and Politics of Psychotherapy* (1977), *Scientific Realism and Socialist Thought* (1989), *Socialist Reasoning* (1990) and *Critical Realism: An Introduction to Roy Bhaskar's Philosophy* (1994). He has recently completed a book on Marxism and Christianity, and is working on realism in ethics.

Beryl C. Curt is author of *Textuality and Tectonics: Troubling Social and Psychological Science* (1994). She holds numerous baccalaureate degrees in psychology and sociology as well as a number of PhDs. She has been married several times and also otherwise-related. Her work is all the more remarkable as she has congenital acorporeality, and her writings have been made possible through the efforts of a group of devoted amanuenses. One of the bases for her work is the Mount Effort Foundation in Oxfordshire, England.

Bronwyn Davies is Professor of Education at James Cook University, Australia. Her research involves analysing the ways in which individual and collective gendered identities are constructed through text and talk. Her latest research aims to theorize the particular relations between new texts, embodied subjectivity and social action within the Asia–Pacific context. In June

1996 her latest book, *Power/Knowledge/Desire: Changing School Organisation and Management Practices*, was published. Later this year the *Encyclopedia of Language and Education* will be published in which she co-edited with David Corson *Volume 3 Oral Discourse and Education*.

Don Foster is Professor of Psychology at the University of Cape Town, South Africa, and author/editor of *Detention and Torture in South Africa* (1987), *Perspectives on Mental Handicap* (1990), *Social Psychology in South Africa* (1991) and *Towards Peaceful Protest in South Africa* (1992). His current interests are identity politics, racism, collective psychology, and mental health policy. Most recently he has completed a piece on perpetrators of gross violations of human rights for the Truth Commission.

Kenneth Gergen is the Mustin Professor of Psychology at Swarthmore College, USA. He is the author of *Toward Transformation in Social Knowledge* (1992), *The Saturated Self* (1991) and *Realities and Relationships* (1994). He is Associate Editor of *Theory and Psychology*, and *The American Psychologist*, and co-founder of the Taos Institute, an organization working at the intersection of social construction and societal practice.

Rom Harré graduated in mathematics and physics and then in philosophy and anthropology at the University of Auckland. He did postgraduate work in Oxford under J.L. Austin. His published work includes studies in the philosophy of both the natural and human sciences, such as *Varieties of Realism* (1986) and the trilogy *Social Being* (1979), *Personal Being* (1983) and *Physical Being* (1991). His current research interests have concerned the ways that language enters into all aspects of human life, including the sense of self (reported in *Pronouns and People*, 1990, with P. Muhlhausler) and the emotions. His most recent book in this area is *The Discursive Mind*, with G. Gillett (1994). He has also been involved in theoretical studies of the computational model of mind popularized as Artificial Intelligence. He is currently Professor of Psychology at Georgetown University, Washington, DC, and Emeritus Fellow, Linacre College, Oxford, UK.

Ruth Merttens is currently a professor of primary education at the University of North London. She is the director of the IMPACT Project, a research centre which coordinates a programme of research in the areas of parents in education, early numeracy/literacy, parenting practices and pedagogies. Ruth teaches one morning a week in a local primary school and is the mother of six children. Her current interests include the relations between ideology, pedagogy and psychoanalytic concepts.

Maritza Montero is a professor of social psychology at Universidad Central de Venezuela, where she is also a member of the Psychology Doctorate Academic Council. She is Vice-President for South America of the Interamerican Society of Psychology, as well as a member of the Radical

Psychology Group. Her main interests are community social psychology and politics. She has published several books about these subjects in Spanish (of which *Psicologia de la accion politica*, co-edited with O. D'Adamo and V. Garcia-Beaudoux, 1995, is the most recent), and has published widely in Spanish, French, English and Portuguese journals.

Ian Parker is Professor of Psychology at Bolton Institute, and co-director of the Discourse Unit. His recent work has been on the intersection of Marxism and psychology (*Psychology and Society: Radical Theory and Practice*, co-edited with Russell Spears, 1996), the production and circulation of psychoanalytic explanation (*Psychoanalytic Culture: Psychoanalytic Discourse in Western Society*, Sage, 1997), and critical exploration of therapeutic practices (*Deconstructing Psychotherapy*, forthcoming). He is a member of Psychology Politics Resistance.

Jonathan Potter has researched science, riots/uprisings, current affairs television, racism and relationship counselling. He is the third author of the (constructed as) notorious paper 'Death and furniture' (*History of the Human Sciences*, 1995) which is a celebratory reformulation of relativism. His most recent book (*Representing Reality*, 1996) is a rigorous, analytically grounded study of the rhetoric of grounding. He is also Professor of Discourse Analysis at Loughborough University.

Joan Pujol is Lecturer of Psychology at the Universitat Antònoma de Barcelona. His main interest has been the analysis of the techno-scientific discourse, and his present area of concern combines discursive and material perspectives in the analysis of social issues. His recent work has been on the perception of negatively defined social categories (*The Non-Delinquent: How Citizens Understand Criminality*, with P. García-Borés, M. Cagigós, J.C. Medina and J. Sánchez, 1995), the technological discourse applied to Reproductive Technologies ('Assisted reproductive technologies as techno-scientific phenomena', in A. Gordo López, J.L. Linaza Iglesias, *Psicologías, Discursos y Poder (PDP)*, 1995), and the analysis of techno-scientific discourse ('Understanding the rhetoric of techno-scientific discourse', *Anthropos*, forthcoming).

Carla Willig is Lecturer in Psychology at Middlesex University. Her research is concerned with the relationship between discourse and practice. She has published papers and book chapters exploring the ways in which discursive constructions can facilitate the practice of unsafe sex within the context of HIV/AIDS. She has also published, with Martin Roiser, on the history of the Authoritarian Personality research and working-class psychology. She is currently editing a book on the relationship between deconstruction and application, and the possibility of an applied discourse analysis.

Foreword

Rom Harré

Catch-all terms like 'realism', 'constructionism' and so on, invite endless and distracting debates, most of which can be resolved just by attending to the varieties obscured by excessive generality. How can one who espouses social (linguistic) constructionism avoid slipping into relativism? How can a realist avoid slipping into essentialism? Surely the answer is 'By making enough distinctions'! The authors of the chapters in this book are hard at work in just this enterprise. There will be no resolutions to the *big questions* posed above, good in all circumstances and for all occasions. Context by context the balance between constructionism and essentialism and between realism and relativism, and how each pair maps on to the other, will be decided in different ways in different contexts.

If anything is a hard fact about human beings it is their embodiment. But how many people ought there to be per body, and how many bodies might there be needed to sustain a person? Reflection on this question in the light of glimpses into other cultures than our own, makes this question exemplary. Universally humanity is embodied, yet how bodies and persons are mapped on to one another is provided for discursively, not least in the grammars of pronoun systems. The mappings are matters of how things ought to be rather than how they are.

Again, while we all have natural and acquired powers, 'agency' is a defeasible claim, manifested in accounts and positions. To ask 'Is every human being an agent? Answer Yes or No!' invites the riposte 'What's the story-line on this occasion?'

How to combat the relativism that these social constructionist ripostes seem to imply? 'Agency' cannot be a non-relative category if the question of whether I am one or not is answered in different ways depending on which story the events in question are embedded in, and even whether there are any story-free 'events in question'. I think there are two ways of resisting relativism, both of which are represented in and also challenged by discussions in this collection. The move implicit in Collier's critical realism is to invoke the concept of practice and its correlative, project, in response to the shifting focus of the various discourses available at some moment. Not all projects can be brought to fruition. Partly because of the intransigence of the material substrate of life, and partly because the reach of discourse extends beyond the individual speaker/actor in indeterminate ways. True, there are no atomic psychological individuals, and true, most psychological phenomena are attributes of the flow of semantically significant interactions, yet individuals are fenced in by material forces and barriers of incomprehension. Try getting an early morning cup of coffee in Budapest! Potter's observation that material nature enters life only as it is described is close to the fallacy of actualism. Undertaking a project on the basis of some such description depends on a material exploitation of what nature affords.

We *must* separate the world from our knowledge of it. We live in an *Umwelt*, beyond which there are currently unimagined material possibilities. We must assume that the world is richer than we know. And, I would argue, the same should be our attitude to people. Why should we assume that the possibilities of the human world are exhausted by our current discursive resources? But to think that we must break with the strict claims of hard-line social constructionists. Something exists outside the reach of symbolic systems. Language must be reaching beyond itself. Systems of metaphor are mentioned but metaphor as a topic ought to be high on the list of topics that interest those of us who try to strike the balance between the paired dichotomies that we have tried to put in place of the positivism from which we all dissent. How can symbolic systems reach beyond themselves?

But there is a second line of argument, one which we owe at least as much to Holiday as to Habermas. If any of the texts collected here are to come to life, the conditions for the possibility of language must be met. And this must be a non-relativist truth about non-relativist matters. Some of these necessary conditions are material, that print should have some temporal stability. Some are social, that we share, *ceteris paribus*, a common language. Some are moral, that not all occasions of speech and writing are deceptive. It is here, I believe, that the tie to a political dimension can be tied quite tightly. Modes of action, forms of discourse and so on, that are addressed to other members of our species and yet undercut the conditions of their own intelligibility, violate the only categorical imperative, the preservation of persons.

As one who has personally faced the challenge: 'How can you be a social constructionist in psychology and a realist in physics?' I welcome these chapters. Yet, I would like to add another pair of 'positions' to the double dichotomy explored here. It seems to me that the way forward opens up by introducing the ontological distinction between a dynamical, potentialist, account of the world and a static, actualist view. This dichotomy plays a subsidiary role in some of the chapters that follow. I would hope that it would come to the fore as at least as important a contribution to all the good things the authors of this volume hope for.

1

Realism, Relativism and Critique in Psychology

Ian Parker

This book explores disputed claims about what we can know of reality in social constructionist and discursive research in psychology. Among the questions the contributors address are the following: should pragmatic and relativist views of meaning and the world necessarily be adopted by discourse analysts?; where is 'the real' in contemporary critical research in psychology?; and how does the turn-to-language affect, encourage or inhibit perspectives for change? The book explores connections between theory, method and politics in social research, with particular reference to social constructionist and discursive debates in psychology.

Context for the Debates

The last ten years have seen an increasing interest in social constructionist perspectives in psychology in general, and in approaches which locate the stuff of psychology in discourse in particular (Gergen, 1985, 1994; Harré and Gillett, 1994; Potter and Wetherell, 1987; Shotter, 1993, Wetherell and Potter, 1992). This represents a critical reflexive movement away from mental paraphernalia in each individual's head towards a socially mediated and historically situated study of action and experience. Social constructionism makes it possible to conceptualize human psychology as an 'ensemble of social relations', and the turn to discourse helps us to reflect on the discipline as part of the powerful 'psy-complex' in modern culture which helps constitute and regulate subjectivity (Burman et al., 1996).

There are also, however, serious risks in this social constructionist reworking of psychological concepts. The theoretical resources that critical and discursive researchers have drawn upon are part of a wider discursive turn in the human sciences that carry conservative as well as progressive prescriptions for social activity. At the same time as deconstruction, discourse theory, pragmatism and postmodernism cut away the positivist ground from beneath traditional psychology and relativize their claims about the nature of human nature, these theoretical currents also relativize the truth claims of the critics and sabotage principled resistance to abuses of power in the discipline (Burman, 1990; Gill, 1995). Relativism in social constructionism or discourse analysis could make it difficult for us to sustain the project of a critical psychology.

Realism would appear to provide the solution to this problem, for it both exposes positivist psychology's pretensions to model itself on what it imagines the natural sciences to be, and it grounds discursive accounts of mentation in social practices whose underlying logic and structure can, in principle, be discovered (Harré, 1983, 1986). Realism and critical realism run alongside the social constructionist attacks on the discipline while preventing a wholesale collapse into discourse idealism (Bhaskar, 1986; Collier, 1994). This solution is not as clear-cut as it seems, however, and 'realism' of different varieties is already being mobilized by those sympathetic to mainstream psychology to warrant it as a science and to rebut social constructionist critiques (e.g., Greenwood, 1989, 1991; Rantzen, 1993). It would seem, in this light, that even 'critical' realists may end up falling into the arms of science as they look for certainties in this confusing landscape, and only critical relativists who go all the way can really resist the truth claims of psychology (e.g., Curt, 1994; Stainton Rogers et al., 1995).

Many researchers in psychology now perceive a two-fold threat to critical work in the discipline. On the one hand, too many colleagues in the human sciences now assume that a discursive or social constructionist approach necessarily entails a thorough relativist suspicion of radical political engagement in psychology, in and out (Callinicos, 1995; Eagleton, 1991; Geras, 1995; Norris, 1996). On the other hand, too many colleagues in psychology now assume that a realist approach to research necessarily entails our participation in the accumulation of a corpus of knowledge in the discipline and of at least some of the 'facts' psychologists think they know about individuals and culture. Our engagement with relativism and realism in this book, in contrast, looks to an account of how psychological facts are socially constructed, how subjectivity is discursively reproduced within present social arrangements, *and* for an analysis of the underlying historical conditions that gave rise to the 'psy-complex' (Burman et al., 1996; Rose, 1989).

The contributors to this book do not represent the whole spectrum of relativist and realist positions that psychology now houses and uses to buttress its disciplinary practices. We have not included conservative relativists who care nothing for the social implications of their arguments or who imagine that everything in the world and human nature can be made and remade at will, or conservative realists who simply care for the scientific status of psychology and for the philosophical arguments that can be recruited to support it against those who wish to change it. Our contributors' starting point is a critical, or what some would prefer to term 'reflexive' inquiry into psychology which is sympathetic to radical research and which would want to situate critical debates in the broader context of debates occurring in the human sciences. There is between them, though, a range of arguments and disagreements about how best to be critical or reflexive. The structure of the book provides *one* way of making sense of the differences.

The book also explores the way the range of positions represented is also cross-cut by a number of different preferences and aversions. The different degrees of acceptance of a social constructionist argument or a critical realist position also entail a series of contrasting positions over, for example, the integrity of the self (whether constructed or given), the role of psychoanalysis as an interpretative system (whether as corrigible or empirically grounded) which may undermine psychology, or the extent to which psychology reflects or constitutes the ways in which individuals as members of social classes (imaginary or real) understand themselves. The stakes of the realist/relativist debate for a critical perspective in psychology (warranted, perhaps, by realism), or for a multiplicity of critical perspectives (warranted, perhaps, by relativism) are high, and entail a review of many of the positions that traditional psychology takes for granted. One of the tasks of the book is to disambiguate and explore some of the overlaps and confusions of perspective that provoke and then inhibit critique in the discipline.

Mapping the Terrain

Various metaphors are deployed in the following chapters to divide the advocates of different positions (most often the game-plan in Part I) or to bring them together (the main rhetorical strategy in Part II), so that we then see our task as being able to distinguish 'truth' from 'fiction', for example, or 'absolutism' from 'pluralism'. One of the virtues of social constructionism in general and discourse analysis in particular is that systems of metaphors are revealed to be the stuff of psychology and the social world, they furnish the places where we study the mind and provide us with ways of speaking about what we find (Danziger, 1997; Soyland, 1994). When we remember this, we are then able to step back and understand that we are actually presented with three tasks.

First, we should notice that these distinctions construct particular maps of the problem and perform distinct functions as they attempt to win us to a certain vantage point. If we imagine that relativism is concerned only with fictions as accounts which are patently false, for example, we may then be tempted to find something more certain in 'truth', and if realism is presented as a form of absolutism, we may well prefer to opt for something more open in 'pluralism'. This advice applies as much to those who generously open up a place where the different positions could live alongside each other happily as those who are determined to fight their corner. What sense, for example, would a realist or a relativist make of the possibility of a plurality of truths? Critical realists are happy to accept that scientific inquiry operates in a climate of 'epistemic relativism' in which knowledge is always provisional, open to challenge (Bhaskar, 1986; Collier, 1994), and relativists see many varieties of truth as constituted within different discourses or narratives (Burr, 1995; Gergen, 1994).

Secondly, we need to view the various sets of distinctions between realism and relativism made by the contributors, and the lists of associations, pre-cursors and consequences that are grouped under each side as themselves *making* something when they appear to be clearing something away. Discourse analysis in psychology has been concerned with how systems of terms and turns of phrase are mobilized to make it seem as if things are inside the head as psychological mechanisms or properties rather than func-tions of discourse (Burman and Parker, 1993; Harré and Gillett, 1994) and to make it seem as if things are 'out there' with an uncontestable factual status (Edwards and Potter, 1992; Potter, 1996). It is difficult sometimes to uncou-ple some of the connections made between terms, in phrases like 'liberal pluralism' and 'fixed truth' for example, and it can seem as if they go natu-rally together. That decoupling effort – in a refusal to take existing forms of knowledge for granted, for realist or relativist ends – is something that drives many of the contributors to this volume.

Thirdly, we should appreciate that 'realism' versus 'relativism' is itself one of those metaphorical constructions, it is not the baseline which the others obscure as they depart from it. Many of the contributors in Part I of the book point out that the opposition between the terms does not accord with the way debates over the nature of reality and conditions of change have been conducted in other disciplines, and contributors in Part II comment on the false dichotomies that are set up if we feel we must view the issue using these terms. This attention to the socially constructed, thoroughly discursive char-acter of the debates should not of itself lead us to one side or the other (or indeed induce us to collapse them both together). While relativists will emphasize the way in which these sets of debates could have been different, realists would want to understand how the terms have come to be fixed and how they position us when we use them.

The commentators in Part II have had to move into this strange terrain from outside. Their contributions are so valuable because they help us re-orient ourselves in the debates and find different paths through these competing definitions. Discourse analysis sometimes seems to those outside Britain to be a peculiar local phenomenon and to have a strange grip on social psychology here, even though there are now a good number of exam-ples of discourse analysis in other countries (e.g., Gordo-López and Linaza, 1996; Levett et al., 1997) and the main textbooks here are still firmly wedded to a laboratory-experimental paradigm. Because they are 'outsiders' and are concerned with the social consequences of psychological knowledge, the commentaries in Part II have been able to draw attention to the way some of the contours of this terrain are really rather peculiar, and even though all the contributors would think of themselves as being 'critical', the debates in Part I of the book are themselves 'outside' the strongest currents of critical psy-chology internationally (e.g., D'Adamo et al., 1995; Fox and Prilleltensky, 1997; Montero, 1987; Nicholas, 1993; Tolman and Maiers, 1991).

To talk about negotiating the terrain here is a metaphor, of course, and it is useful to help us set out realistic expectations as to what we can hope to accomplish. This collection will not 'solve' the problem or persuade us once and for all that one side is right. Rather, it helps us see better what the lie of the land is, so that when we meet the different combinations of arguments again we can make judgements about how far down the road we might want to go with them. Let us move into another metaphor, that of framing.

Framing the Debates

The arrangement of the chapters in the book reveals something of the history of these specific debates, located at a particular place and point in time and preoccupied with particular disciplinary concerns. Part I comprises worked-up contributions to a meeting in April 1996 organized by the Discourse Unit, and we have been able to make use of that opportunity for the contributors to set out their positions, discuss agreements and objections from the others and present here a reasoned case which anticipates a range of possible responses. Vivien Burr, who was discussant at that meeting, provides an overview of the different perspectives in which 'the basis upon which moral and political choices are made' is her main cause for concern, and she traces her own route from personal construct psychology to worries about how we should decide between a multiplicity of perspectives and where agency might be found in social constructionism. Despite her helpful review of the three ways 'reality' seems to function in the debates – as 'truth', 'materiality' or 'essence' – we might also notice an underlying sense in her account that 'reality' might serve as a source of *certainty*, and that the 'agency' she wants to save would be a sure point of reference in the uncertain world created by relativists.

As Jonathan Potter's contribution makes clear at the outset, these arguments are occasioned by that day conference, and a sub-text perhaps is an awareness of what the social, 'politically acceptable' stakes might be for these arguments. His description of the variety of rhetorical devices that construct 'realism' to persuade us that it is something 'out there' and his plea for detailed transcription of everyday talk to represent accurately different kinds of 'reality construction business' returns to the question of the social consequences of these debates at the end of his chapter to argue that a more plural politics may be built out of relativism. Andrew Collier also foregrounds political implications, but from a realist perspective, and his defence of realism is taken further with an account of 'critical realism' in which explanation does not function simply as another description (which a social constructionist may then be happy to lay alongside other descriptions) but simultaneously as a *critique* (Bhaskar, 1986). Here Collier introduces a critical realist argument that may rebut relativism's political quietude and radicalize accounts of how socially constructed things come to be the way they are.

Politics and critical realism recur as motifs in many of the following chapters, including in Ruth Merttens's chapter. Although Merttens claims that the two stories she tells us about children, schooling and power are 'explanation-free', she carefully constructs them as part of a narrative about the way narratives are always embedded in practices and laced through with the injunction that we should always connect theory and practice in our accounts of educational practices. Steven Brown and Joan Pujol with Beryl Curt also connect theory and practice, but by unravelling the critical realist argument that we need to be 'epistemic relativists' (that is, perpetually sceptical about forms of knowledge) in order better to be ontological realists (that is, to better understand what real things we have knowledge about). Instead, they argue that 'relativist ontology' could be one of the most helpful prerequisites for a 'realist epistemology'. In this way, forms of knowledge are regarded as constitutive, much in the way that a form of discourse analysis derived from Foucault (1972) would argue it to be (see Henriques et al., 1984).

Carla Willig pursues the connection with discourse analysis and argues that this is an approach which is both 'historically and linguistically reflexive' and also 'capable of guiding active intervention in ideological and material struggles'. When discourse analysts choose certain topics and challenge dominant constructions of the world, they are necessarily operating within the orbit of critical realism, and, as Willig points out, to abstain from following through the consequences of analysis is itself a politically situated choice. When Willig returns, at the end of her chapter, to ally herself explicitly with critical realism, she has already framed 'choice' as something contrary to, or complicit with, existing forms of discourse and power. The arguments in these chapters have all been framed, of course, and to conclude with Willig's realist perspective affects the picture we construct as we look back over the contributions so far.

Part II reframes that collection of arguments. The four commentaries were solicited when we had written versions of all the chapters in Part I, and the task of these authors was to make sense of a series of claims and counter-claims that newcomers feel so lost in when they first come across social constructionism and its critics.

Don Foster tackles this by focusing on the distinction that Saussure (1974) makes between 'signifier' (the sound or written image of a word) and 'signified' (the concept associated with that sound or written mark). Foster suggests that 'the core difference between realists and relativists is (i) their location in and across this divide, and (ii) the conflation of two separate meanings of discourse'. While realists are often tempted to make each signifier directly and immediately represent each signified, relativists simply reverse that relation so that signifieds obediently follow the rule of the signifier. Foster then offers an example of an empirical study, of racist rhetoric in South Africa, which negotiates its way through that relation by tracing the way the discourse was organized *and* the way its organization was located in structures of power and ideology.

Maritza Montero focuses on the dualism between the knowing subject and the object of knowledge which bedevils many of the self-characterizations and critiques levelled at enemies in both social constructionism and critical realism. This dualism is, she argues, too often buttressed by a form of 'linguistic imperialism' which forgets that meanings are interwoven with practices, with things in the world (like rocks) and with ethical activity around notions of truth and human interests. While Montero argues strongly both for the things that relativism seems unable to reach and the capacity to act that realism sometimes seems unable to warrant, she is certainly not trying to bring relativists and realists together in some kind of fixed 'absolute coherence'. Like Foster, she also gives examples of research which is committed to understanding and changing the world and the rhetoric of relativism and realism is deployed as part of a critical practice.

Bronwyn Davies clarifies the way in which contributors construct an opposition which is invested with such power that they can then only avoid terms they dislike by finding refuge in the 'other' side. Part of the problem here is, she points out, in treating the use of certain discourses as necessarily defining what kind of person you must be. This is crucial, for 'underestimating both the constitutive power of discourse and the extraordinary difficulty and fragility of deconstructive moves' is, she argues, 'an inevitable side effect of maintaining the individual as the central conceptual device of psychology'. If we can take seriously the notion of subject position *and* conceive of ourselves as using different competing discourses tactically on different occasions, then we can avoid this trap. Does this line of argument mean that others must then see her as a relativist? She thinks not.

Ken Gergen focuses on the way 'isolation and subterranean warfare' seem so often to mark the activities of relativists and realists, and he wants to step aside from the very process of 'argumentation' which freezes advocates into opposing positions and prevents them from moving on. Here he is concerned with the way we may be trapped in realist and constructionist discourses such that argumentation always turns into confrontation. Like Davies, he argues that discourse should not be seen as an expression of the essence of a person but as a 'communal tool', and it may thereby be possible to develop 'new forms of relationship'. Although Gergen is often positioned as a relativist and will often celebrate that position himself, there is an ethical tactical movement around different forms of language and practice here that makes his critique of traditional psychology coincide with realists at many points.

Closing and Opening

The chapters in both parts of the book are framed, of course, by this introduction, and I have had two, sometimes competing, demands to meet. One has been to set the debates in the context of *critical* conceptual and methodological research in psychology. As many of the contributors have commented, these debates matter because we do not take the facts presented by the discipline of psychology as given and self-evident, but as constructed within culturally-specific narratives, regimes of truth, patterns of power or forms of ideology. Although there is disagreement over the best terms to use, and some degree of misunderstanding between us when one of us may refer to 'narrative' and another to 'ideology', the debates make sense enough by virtue of our dislike of reification (a risk in realism) and value-neutrality (a risk in relativism) in traditional psychology. We each understand, then, the relativist argument against fixing descriptions as if they cannot be changed and the realist attempt to comprehend the conditions of change.

The other demand has been to moderate these different perspectives without being intrusive, for this has not been the place for me to complain and intervene (but see Parker, 1992, 1996, 1997, 1998). Only by understanding how the discipline of psychology reproduces notions of individuality and human nature, a realist endeavour, will it be possible to transform it, and to socially construct it as something different. Discourse analysis tries, but does not necessarily succeed in this task (Parker and Burman, 1993). The way I have laid out the perspectives here has already ordered them, and you will no doubt detect covert agreement and disagreement smuggled in along the way. And the foreword to the book, the cover, the advertising, the place it occupies in a library and the position it is allocated as a course text will each frame, and subtlely change the way in which it is read. Each of these frames is socially constructed, fabricated within the discursive conditions of modern psychology, and each is real, operating within the material structures of teaching and transmission of knowledge in the discipline. There is room for movement of course. This is part of it.

References

Bhaskar, R. (1986) *Scientific Realism and Human Emancipation*. London: Verso.

Burman, E. (1990) 'Differing with deconstruction: a feminist critique', in I. Parker and J. Shotter (eds), *Deconstructing Social Psychology*. London: Routledge.

Burman, E., Aitken, G., Alldred, P., Allwood, R., Billington, T., Goldberg, B., Gordo-López, A.J., Heenan, C., Marks, D. and Warner, S. (1996) *Psychology Discourse Practice: From Regulation to Resistance*. London: Taylor and Francis.

Burman, E. and Parker, I. (eds) (1993) *Discourse Analytic Research: Repertoires and Readings of Texts in Action*. London: Routledge.

Burr, V. (1995) *An Introduction to Social Constructionism*. London: Routledge.

Callinicos, A. (1995) *Theories and Narratives: Reflections on the Philosophy of History*. Cambridge: Polity Press.

Collier, A. (1994) *Critical Realism: An Introduction to Roy Bhaskar's Philosophy*. London: Verso.

Curt, B. (1994) *Textuality and Tectonics: Troubling Social and Psychological Science*. Buckingham: Open University Press.

D'Adamo, O., García Beaudoux, V. and Montero, M. (eds) (1995) *Psicología de la Acción Política*. Buenos Aires: Paidos.

Danziger, K. (1997) *Naming the Mind: How Psychology Found its Language*. London: Sage.

Eagleton, T. (1991) *Ideology: An Introduction*. London: Verso.

Edwards, D. and Potter, J. (1992) *Discursive Psychology*. London: Sage.

Foucault, M. (1972) *The Archaeology of Knowledge*. London: Tavistock.

Foucault, M. (1977) *Discipline and Punish: The Birth of the Prison*. Harmondsworth: Penguin.

Fox, D. and Prilleltensky, I. (eds) (1997) *Critical Psychology: An Introduction*. London and New York: Sage.

Geras, N. (1995) *Solidarity in the Conversation of Humankind: The Ungroundable Liberalism of Richard Rorty*. London: Verso.

Gergen, K.J. (1985) 'The social constructionist movement in modern psychology', *American Psychologist*, 40 (3): 266–75.

Gergen, K.J. (1994) *Realities and Relationships: Soundings in Social Construction*. Cambridge, MA: Harvard University Press.

Gill, R. (1995) 'Relativism, reflexivity and politics: interrogating discourse analysis from a feminist perspective', in S. Wilkinson and C. Kitzinger (eds), *Feminism and Discourse: Psychological Perspectives*. London: Sage.

Gordo-López, A.J. and Linaza, J.L. (eds) (1996) *Psicologías, Discursos y Poder (PDP)*. Madrid: Visor.

Greenwood, J. (1989) *Explanation and Experiment in Social Psychological Science*. New York: Springer.

Greenwood, J. (1991) *Relations and Representations: An Introduction to the Philosophy of Social Psychological Science*. London: Routledge.

Harré, R. (1983) *Personal Being: A Theory for Individual Psychology*. Oxford: Blackwell.

Harré, R. (1986) *Varieties of Realism: A Rationale for the Natural Sciences*. Oxford: Blackwell.

Harré, R. and Gillett, G. (1994) *The Discursive Mind*. London: Sage.

Henriques, J., Hollway, W., Urwin, C., Venn, C. and Walkerdine, V. (1984) *Changing the Subject: Psychology, Social Regulation and Subjectivity*. London: Methuen.

Levett, A., Kottler, A., Burman, E. and Parker, I. (eds) (1997) *Culture, Power and Difference: Discourse Analysis in South Africa*. London and Cape Town: Zed Books and University of Cape Town Press.

Montero, M. (ed.) (1987) *Psicología Política Latinoamericana*. Caracas: Editorial Panapo.

Nicholas, L.J. (ed.) (1993) *Psychology and Oppression: Critiques and Proposals*. Johannesburg: Skotaville Publishers.

Norris, C. (1996) *Reclaiming Truth: Contribution to a Critique of Cultural Relativism*. London: Lawrence and Wishart.

Parker, I. (1992) *Discourse Dynamics: Critical Analysis for Social and Individual Psychology*. London: Routledge.

Parker, I. (1996) 'Against Wittgenstein: materialist reflections on language in psychology', *Theory and Psychology*, 6 (3): 363–84.

Parker, I. (1997) 'Against relativism in psychology, on balance'. Paper presented to the conference on Critical Realism and the Crisis in the Human Sciences, Warwick, August.

Parker, I. (1998) 'Against postmodernism: psychology in cultural context', *Theory and Psychology*, 8.

Parker, I. and Burman, E. (1993) 'Against discursive imperialism, empiricism and constructionism: thirty-two problems with discourse analysis', in E. Burman and I. Parker (eds), *Discourse Analytic Research: Repertoires and Readings of Texts in Action*. London: Routledge.

Potter, J. (1996) *Representing Reality: Discourse, Rhetoric and Social Construction*. London: Sage.

Potter, J. and Wetherell, M. (1987) *Discourse and Social Psychology: Beyond Attitudes and Behaviour*. London: Sage.

Rantzen, A.J. (1993) 'Constructivism, direct realism and the nature of error', *Theory and Psychology*, 3 (2): 147–71.

Rose, N. (1989) *Governing the Soul: Technologies of Human Subjectivity*. London: Routledge.

Saussure, F. de (1974) *Course in General Linguistics*. London: Fontana.

Shotter, J. (1993) *Cultural Politics of Everyday Life: Social Constructionism, Rhetoric and Knowing of the Third Kind*. Buckingham: Open University Press.

Soyland, A.J. (1994) *Psychology as Metaphor*. London: Sage.

Stainton Rogers, R., Stenner, P., Gleeson, K. and Stainton Rogers, W. (1995) *Social Psychology: A Critical Agenda*. Cambridge: Polity Press.

Tolman, C. and Maiers, W. (eds) (1991) *Critical Psychology: Contributions to an Historical Science of the Subject*. Cambridge: Cambridge University Press.

Wetherell, M. and Potter, J. (1992) *Mapping the Language of Racism: Discourse and the Legimation of Exploitation*. Hemel Hempstead: Harvester Wheatsheaf.

PART I: DEBATES

2

Overview: Realism, Relativism, Social Constructionism and Discourse

Vivien Burr

The central theme of the contributions to this book, the realism/relativism debate, revolves around methodological and moral questions. These questions are about the social sciences, about their contribution to the social construction of people and social life, about what ought to be the focus of social science inquiry and about if and how the social sciences could or should be used to benefit humankind.

In this chapter, I have drawn out a number of issues which I think have attained the status of problems for those who have adopted a critical or social constructionist approach, and then discussed where I believe some of the other contributors stand with respect to these problems, offering some critical commentary of my own along the way. This has been a somewhat artificial organizing strategy to some extent, given the very varied aims and emphases of the different writers, and I hope that I have done no great disservice to any of them here.

When I first began to read about social constructionist ideas in the late 1980s, I was attracted, as I believe were many others, by the liberatory promise of its anti-essentialism. I had come from a background in personal construct psychology, and had originally been attracted to this by its key concept of constructive alternativism, the idea that there exists a potentially infinite number of alternative constructions of events. The focus was therefore not upon some objective reality but upon the different meanings with which our worlds become invested. Once this principle is accepted, the liberatory message becomes clear: if what we take ourselves and others to be are constructions and not objective descriptions, and if it is human beings who have built these constructions, then it is (at least in principle) possible to re-construct ourselves in ways which might be more facilitating for us, and social constructionism seemed to me to offer the same basic message but on a wider social scale. This does not necessarily mean that we have limitless choice in how we may construe ourselves, and it certainly does not mean that we can simply decide to dispense with oppressive and limiting constructions just by 'changing our minds' about how we think about people. Nevertheless, it becomes possible to think not only of individuals re-construing aspects of themselves, but of re-thinking whole social categories, such as gender, sexuality, race, disability and illness.

In addition, social constructionism offered a critical reading of psychology itself. The discipline of psychology has in the past been at pains to claim to be a-political. This claim, it has been argued, is in itself highly political since it serves to legitimate questionable social practices, representing them as derived from value-free social or psychological 'facts'. Social constructionism radically questioned the idea of the 'objective fact' and at the same time characterized the discipline and practice of psychology as partial, value-ridden and driven by implicit vested interests.

However, after a while I, like others, began to feel frustrated with constructionism and somewhat disillusioned. The extreme relativistic views that were often espoused under the banner of social constructionism seemed to lead down a road to social and personal paralysis, for at least two reasons. First, if we must abandon any notion of a reality which bears some relation, no matter how this relation is conceived, to our constructions, then we are left with a multiplicity of perspectives which become a bewildering array of alternative (and, it could be argued, equally valid) realities in themselves. Abandoning the idea of an ultimate truth appears at first a liberatory move, but brings with it the question of how one is then to decide between alternative perspectives. In wishing to advocate some change for ourselves or for others, the usual foundation on which to base this is removed. How can we say, for example, that certain groups are oppressed, if these 'groups' and their 'oppression' are constructions which can have no greater claim to truth than any other? How can we claim that some groups and not others should be given a social 'voice'? If our concern is to give greater social space to marginal groups, does this include, for example, the National Front and if not, why not? And who is in a position to arbitrate such choices?

Secondly, the notion of 'agency' slips between our fingers in the same way. 'Agency' becomes transformed into a language game, a way of talking which in itself is part of the social construction of the western individual, and the 'self' to which it relates becomes an effect of discourse. The rug is pulled out from under our feet once more as the basis of a claim to the capacity of persons to reconstruct themselves and their world is removed. If we abandon all attempts to theorize human beings in ways which allow room for some notion of the 'choosing person', then it is hard to see what the point of our attempts to persuade each other can possibly be.

The issues fuelling the current realism/relativism debate in social constructionism therefore seem to me to be these. First, without some notion of truth or reality, how can we justify advocating one view of the world over another, and one way of organizing social life over another? Can we avoid moral relativism if we take a relativistic stance as academics? Do we need to take some form of realist stance in order to make these justifications? Secondly, if the answer is that we must build back into our theorizing some notion of a reality which underpins social and psychological phenomena, then what kind of reality is this? What kinds of things do we want to give the status of 'real' to and what does this mean? Thirdly, how should we think of the relationship between language and reality? Is there a 'real' beyond the text, or is language and discourse all there can be? Just how much importance should we place upon discourse in our attempts to understand and change the social world? And fourthly, how should we understand the self and agency in all this? If our aim is change, then we must have some notion of whether our intentions and efforts towards re-construction, either social or personal, finally make a difference. How can we conceive of the person as some agent and director of change without falling back upon our old humanistic notions of the pre-social, free-thinking individual?

Moral Relativism and Taking Action

Edwards, Ashmore and Potter (1995) argue that what are sometimes referred to as 'naive realists' don't really exist in the social sciences any more, except as 'straw men'. What we have instead is a continuum of acceptance of social constructionist and relativist ideas, and people vary in the distance along that continuum that they are prepared to travel. And the decision about where to get off the constructionist wagon seems prompted by the fear of losing our critical edge on important social phenomena, such as inequality or oppression, which threaten to become casualties of relativism and turn into just another story, just another way of interpreting the social text.

Willig expresses this fear. She begins by declaring her problematic positioning as both a social constructionist academic and a revolutionary socialist, which appear to require a relativist and a realist epistemology respectively. However, she argues that since both relativists and critical realists recognize the historical and cultural constitution of knowledge, our arguments should not be about whether or not knowledge can be objective and unmediated, but how we are going to deal with and respond to that epistemological relativity.

She points out that the power of discourse analysis and deconstruction is in showing that 'things could be different'. But she argues that discourse analysts often stop at this point, afraid of reifying alternative constructions, and remain 'observers and commentators', leaving the action for others to take. Although they may talk of discourse operating ideologically and are certainly aware of the effects of talk in constituting individuals and groups in particular ways, discourse psychologists seem wary of following this through in terms of recommendations for social change.

Furthermore, Willig asserts that we can never not act, since things are constantly in motion and inaction is a form of action. We can only ever argue for or against, accept or resist the positions in discourse on offer to us, but we cannot abstain. If we do, then by default we end up legitimating the *status quo* and feeding the argument that relativism leads to conservatism.

Willig's approach is helpful in recasting the issue away from arguing over epistemological relativity and the status of reality, towards how we are going to deal with that relativity and ontological insecurity. Willig reminds us that realism does not readily provide us with a vision of possible social change, and at least relativism gives us the possibility of this – in principle we can construct a form of social life that we want. In this respect, her view appears similar to that of Potter, who also points out that relativism has a moral and political strength in its capacity to provide a lever of resistance against reality claims. For Potter, academic and political issues are not in conflict. He characterizes relativism as a kind of 'non-position', a radical scepticism that provides the only way of challenging all truth claims, of resisting any move to have reality pinned down and described once-and-for-all as the social sciences have always tried to do. But Willig argues that the power to 'veto' all other claims to truth is not sufficient. If we limit our action to the deconstruction of existing discourses, for fear of reifying alternative constructions that may turn out to be as bad or worse, she says we may as well leave our dominant constructions unchallenged. She argues that discourse analysts must rely upon politics to inform their choice of which discursive objects to deconstruct and what to put in their place.

But on what basis do we argue for the legitimacy of our position? Without the familiar and comfortable presence of truth behind the scenes to back up our claims we must find other criteria by which to justify our moral choices. If we argue that a position is justifiable if it leads to the improvement of conditions for certain people, what do we mean by improvement, and can we be satisfied that our understanding would be the same as theirs? The celebration of 'difference' that deconstruction has brought leaves us in the difficult position of problematizing the categories and groups of persons whose interests we might wish to serve, so that we can no longer allow ourselves to talk about 'women', 'blacks' or 'gays' and the basis for collectivity begins to disappear.

Merttens expresses a related dilemma. Once we have used our social constructionist framework to reveal potentially oppressive practices, what version of events do we choose to put in their place and how do we justify privileging this account over others? She demonstrates the difficulties experienced by those trying to put social constructionist ideas into practice for the purpose of benefiting human beings. Social constructionism provides us with little guidance for how we should choose a course of action, what 'discourses' we should support, which marginal voices we should allow to speak, and this can lead to a frustrating impotence. On what basis, then, do we make such decisions? And how can we defend them? She asks upon what theoretical basis do we advise at all? Perhaps all we can do is to adopt those practices or perspectives which appear to create possibilities for increasing freedom, choice and quality of life for those who seem to need it. Since we cannot ever step outside our own culturally and historically located value systems, perhaps we must (and can only) make such judgements from within this system and defend them regardless of their inevitable relativism. With regard to the child with a 'reading problem', perhaps all that can be done is to ask whether alternative constructions of the situation might produce practices which are likely to be more facilitating for the child, or to provide them with alternative constructions of their difficulty with which they can 'resist' their position.

Some clinical practitioners have examined the way that prevailing constructions of mental health and pathology produce social interactions in which their clients are constructed as pathologized individuals. Harper (1995) describes how one of his own clinical interviews constructs his client as 'paranoid', and recommends that practitioners aim to provide their clients with alternative constructions of their experience which do not necessarily position them in unhelpful ways. For example, the Hearing Voices Network (see Parker et al., 1995; Romme and Escher, 1993) aims to help people to re-construe their experience in ways which do not characterize them as 'sufferers' or 'victims'.

In this context Merttens, drawing on her work with children, emphasizes the power of stories to allow people to enter into a 'dialogue' with alternative values and ways of life through imaginatively casting ourselves into the storied scenario. By experimenting with different narratives, by telling different stories of who we are, we search for a narrative which empowers us to deal more effectively with our circumstances (Burr and Butt, forthcoming).

However, for some social constructionists the problem of difference arises again here. Part of the power of social constructionist accounts is that they deconstruct categories and classifications and urge us to recognize the diversity, fragmentariness and localness of experience and subjectivity. Thus, for example, it may be argued that feminists, when they believe they are speaking for 'women' are actually silencing and invalidating the very different experience of black women, working-class women or disabled women. And these 'sub-categories' also mask vital differences.

When we take this view to its logical conclusion, however, we find that in the process of making space for marginal voices to be heard, we are in danger of losing a collective base from which to proceed. Social constructionism makes us conscious of the diversity and difference in humanity. I believe that it rightly cautions us against assuming that 'we' (whoever 'we' are) can legitimately speak on behalf of 'them' (whoever 'they' are). This recognition of difference and diversity is in general a positive feature, since it rightly reminds us that when our common-sense discourse leads us to speak of, for example, 'men', 'lesbians' or 'the deaf' we may be taking part in the accomplishment of collective identities for people which may not be in their interests and which they may wish to resist. Nevertheless, if we insist upon difference and diversity to the extent of denying the possibility of identifying collective interests, we again paralyse ourselves. The extreme view of denying collectivity in the desire to proclaim diversity and difference is potentially dangerous since it threatens our capacity for collective action. Foucault (Gordon, 1980) was emphatic about the dangers of 'totalizing discourses', but he was also heavily criticized for refusing to commit himself to any positive recommendations for action (Habermas, 1986; Sedgwick, 1982). We must therefore tread a very fine and delicate line so as not to ignore the multiplicity of power relations that operate, making the issues of 'oppression' and 'disadvantage' very complex ones indeed.

Collier, whose view is explicitly realist, does not consequently find these questions troublesome. For Collier there is a material reality which pre-dates both language and our experience. Language does not constitute either reality or our subjective experience. Although he acknowledges the constructive tendencies of language, in the end he sees both language and experience as contingent upon the nature of reality. In our practical engagement with the world, we are brought up against its nature and are forced to recognize which constructions it will and which it will not bear. Collier's political and moral concerns therefore revolve around discovering social truths or facts upon which to base one's beliefs and consequent political action, and around ensuring that our practices are not 'closed' to invalidating evidence. Within this view, Merttens's difficulty over how to avoid perpetuating the iniquities of expert discourses disappears, since the learning difficulties she encounters would be seen as described by and not as constituted by language. For Collier, therefore, there is again no conflict between academic and political issues, since he sees political choices as (ideally) flowing from our understanding of reality as revealed by our academic study of it.

What is Real?

Despite the differences of opinion, outlined above, as to the existence of some (in principle knowable) reality 'behind' social phenomena, it is not necessarily the case that those who adopt a more explicitly relativist position retain no concept of 'that which is real'.

For Collier, there is a real world which pre-dates our experience of it and the language we use to describe it. Reality is 'given' to us through our different modes of engagement with it, only one of which is language. In our practical engagement with the world we also come to know reality, through our experience of the limitations which reality places upon what we are able to do; in practice, reality 'hits you in the face'. He therefore recommends that we focus upon practice, which, he argues, constantly reveals to us the nature of reality (although we don't always hear what it is trying to tell us). Collier shows a concern for practice, then, as a form of engagement with the world which stands outside discourse.

Brown and Pujol with Beryl Curt take a stance with respect to what we should regard as real, and again adopt a generally relativist position. Realist views tend to see real structures as existing prior to or behind and producing manifestations in the social world. This reality is not contingent, it exists independently of human efforts to experience or know it. For Brown and Pujol with Curt, this model is reversed. What is real *is* what is manifested. Subjectivity, consciousness and experience constitute the real, and are the products of a structure lying prior to or behind them. But that structure is language, which is contingent. It is historically and culturally local and dependent upon human practice. In contrast to Collier, then, Brown and Pujol with Curt see language as prior to social reality. Furthermore, Brown and Pujol and Curt's view of discourse and materiality asserts that discourse and materiality are part of the same process – they are only separable analytically.

So that which underlies and produces social reality is an 'assemblage' of discourses, practices and structures that cannot be disaggregated.

Language and Reality

Potter argues for a thoroughgoing relativist position. Here, the world is seen as textual and discursive. The problem with talking about a reality that exists beyond language is that as soon as you begin to talk about it, it immediately enters the discursive realm as a *representation* of events, and there would seem to be no way out of this. Presumably, even if there were some ultimate or fixed reality behind discourse and social constructions, we could never describe it, since to do so would inevitably mean to offer an account of it, thus transforming it into a discursive event. Since we cannot escape these effects of language, Potter argues that we should therefore dispense with the question as to what might lie behind discourse and concentrate instead on how accounts are constructed and what they achieve.

The approach of this relativist discourse psychology has been attacked as morally relative and a-political. Again, we are back to the problem of how you can take a stance for or against a state of affairs without some notion of a material reality that lies behind it. Potter claims that the debate between realism and relativism is not relevant to our decisions about our political practice, and that we should instead focus our efforts upon the everyday accomplishment of reality in the course of social relationships and interaction. Realism becomes just another story, another way of accounting and making claims in the world. He therefore to some extent side-steps the question of whether there *is* a reality behind discourse (whether or not we can in principle know it) and claims that the question itself is irrelevant. He maintains that we do not need to believe in a reality lying behind social phenomena in order to see that certain social relationships and accounts have ideological functions.

Nevertheless, the ideological functions and effects of accounts have not been the focus of discourse psychologists' work, and it perhaps remains to be seen whether the theoretical framework informing this position is in fact compatible with recommendations for action or change.

Collier's view is sharply contrasted with that of Potter. For Collier, there is certainly a material reality which pre-dates both experience and language. Though language clearly sometimes has a performative and constructive function, which is where Potter's focus lies, for Collier language is also about something; our descriptions of the world in some way derive from the nature of reality itself. But Collier further questions the privileged position that language has been granted in social constructionism, so that not only does he claim that things like experience, consciousness and language can only be understood in so far as they tell us something about reality, but also that language bears a more distant relationship to reality than other forms of our engagement with the world. Our practical encounters with the world pre-date language and are therefore a more reliable route to understanding the nature of reality.

Collier's critical realism therefore draws upon Bhaskar's assertion that social practices, though to some extent shored-up by concepts or discourses, always have a material dimension and cannot be described in conceptual or discursive terms alone. The world is much more than textual. However, is such a critical realism significantly different from a structuralist view in its implications? From the perspective of critical realism, we do not necessarily need to study language or discourse in order to identify the structures lying behind social reality (though we might choose to do so) and the focus of our efforts is upon uncovering and finding ways to change those structures. If language and discourse do not play a major constitutive role in the production of forms of social life, then it is not really necessary to study them or to incorporate them into our theorizing.

For Brown and Pujol with Curt also, discourse and the material world cannot be separated, they are but different manifestations of the same thing. This discourse/material 'assemblage' is what constitutes our social reality, our subjectivity, consciousness and experience. Using the example of reproductive technologies, the 'assemblage' of discourses (e.g., those surrounding family life, gender, etc.) and materiality (reproduction and the technology associated with it, such as pregnancy testing, ultrasound scanning, AID, IVF, etc.) produces real psychological processes (e.g., the desire for a child, the meaning of becoming a parent, the subjective experience of birth and interventions in it, etc.).

If we accept this view of the unity of discourse and materiality, then it becomes possible to challenge or resist social reality through changes in discursive practice. Language is not privileged but neither is it relegated to the status of an outcome or effect of social structure.

Agency and Change

Like many social constructionists, Brown and Pujol with Curt take an anti-humanist position, and are deeply suspicious of talk of individuals or human agency. The reason for this is that agency, as it is traditionally characterized, involves locating the source of action within the individual, and often within private cognitive processes, a view which locates the self-contained individual as prior to society. For Brown and Pujol with Curt, action does not originate in this way; it cannot be traced back to the ideas or intentions of the person, but arises from multiple sources. Brown and Pujol with Curt do offer some conception of agency, however, arguing that agency is 'real in its effects'. In a culture where social and discursive practices revolve around the notion of agency, then social and psychological reality will be constructed accordingly.

This is something like Harré's (1989) argument that agency can be thought of as a language game prevailing in societies influenced by the Judaeo-Christian tradition and its emphasis upon personal choice. However, convincing though this argument is, it seems to leave a question mark over the issue of the capacity of persons to take action to change their lives or that of others. In deconstructing the concept of agency, the 'authorship' of ideas and actions becomes problematized and we are left without any clear conception of the relationship between personal intention or action and change. Nevertheless Brown and Pujol with Curt retain the possibility of conceptualizing political action and justice. This possibility lies in what we can say about the likely consequences of certain courses of action or social practices.

This is also the position adopted by Potter, who says that this is the reason why our attention should be focused upon the construction of accounts and what they achieve. He contends that, rather than arguing about the nature of reality, we can study it as a topic, as something locally managed and accomplished by people in interaction. However, the focus is very firmly upon the content and function of the accounts themselves, not upon the persons doing the accounting. In line with other social constructionists, Potter rejects intrapsychic structures and processes such as attitudes and motivations, preferring to see accounts as constructed from social resources, interpretative repertoires (Potter and Wetherell, 1987), which are not located inside people's heads. While this re-location of the centre of gravity away from the individual and into the inter-personal realm is to be welcomed, the absence of 'the person' in any form makes it difficult to see how we might harness such analytic work for the purposes of personal or social change. Even if we can point to the likely effects of representations and accounts, without any idea of what processes (psychological and social) might be involved in their production, we cannot put this understanding to use.

For Collier and Willig, the individual human actor makes moral and political judgements which guide action, and therefore human beings are agents in the usual sense. For Collier, action is guided by our beliefs about how the world works (and we should do what we can to ensure that those beliefs are consistent with what the world really is like). For Willig, although social reality does not pre-date discursive practices, so that the world gets constructed through these, nevertheless she sees human beings as capable of making judgements about which constructions and practices are oppressive and in need of challenging through deconstruction and discourse analysis.

Despite assertions that practice can be challenged or changed once we have identified oppressive relations and shown how they are enshrined in discursive practice, this is perhaps where the difficulties begin. Merttens takes as her starting point the constructionist view that language is constitutive of reality, and follows this through in terms of its practical implications in one particular field, that of the child with a 'learning difficulty'. Her description of the difficulties she encountered in applying constructionist ideas in her own practice raises this issue. She deconstructs the notion of 'learning difficulty', seeing it as a construction of the discursive practices which operate in an oppressive educational system. Her problem is then both how to legitimate alternative 'readings' of the child's experience, and how to put this into practice as someone who is already positioned as an 'expert' within that discourse. In the absence of 'truth' or guidance from theory, she asks upon what basis can we legitimately make recommendations. Must our judgements simply come down to an act of faith? And even if we can confidently make such judgements, can we really escape the power relations in which we are enmeshed as 'experts' in the system? She doubts this, since any advice or recommendations we would have to offer are necessarily produced within the expert discourse of education which has itself constructed the 'problem of learning difficulty'. In a different context, Marks (1993) has also noted the difficulties involved in trying to challenge prevailing discursive practices. In her research she found that, despite her best efforts at 'democratization', her own reading of events as 'researcher' was the one that appeared to carry greater weight.

Concluding Comments

Is the dichotomy between realism and relativism a fruitful one? Does saying that something is socially constructed necessarily mean that it is not real? Do we need to take a realist view in order to defend our actions and choices?

To me, one of the clearest things to emerge from this discussion of the other contributions to this book is that they agree on the importance of values and upon the necessity of making moral and political choices. The debate between realism and relativism has often been set up as if it were primarily about moral relativism or nihilism. But it is becoming clear that those who adopt a relativist view of the world are no more likely than realists to recommend or defend an 'anything goes' morality. The differences between the contributors are more about the basis upon which moral and political choices are made, and there may be as much difference of opinion between realists on this question as between them and relativists. Also, while the certainty furnished by a realist position may indeed provide a basis for choice and action which relativists may envy, the radical scepticism of the relativist is in the end, I believe, indispensable.

Aside from the issue of moral and political choice, debates between realist and relativist positions have at their centre the realist's claim to be able to establish a discoverable reality and the relativist's assertion of the impossibility of doing so. The debates often end in a stalemate, the arguments seeming intractable. It seems to me that these intractable arguments over realism and relativism, like agency and structure, self and society and mind and matter, are intractable precisely because they are dichotomous constructions which have limited usefulness, a limited capacity to furnish us with useful ways of viewing the world and our place in it. One of the reasons for our problems, I believe, is that 'reality' and its contrast term have at least three different meanings, and this means that the arguments are not always premised on the same assumptions. The three dimensions which I believe have become confounded in the debate are:

1 Reality (truth) versus falsehood.
2 Reality (materiality) versus illusion.
3 Reality (essence) versus construction.

I think that social constructionist arguments, which tend to take a relativist stance, are sometimes rejected because the reality–construction dimension (dimension 3) gets 'mapped on to' the other two, so that constructionism is taken as also implying illusion and/or falsehood. There is therefore a tendency to talk of things being either real or 'merely constructed'. The constructed world thus construed is somehow less tangible, less trustworthy. It is a sham. I think that this is in part what is going on in the 'table banging' disputes described by Potter. Critics of constructionism here appear to be contesting the idea that the world is a figment of our imaginations and has no materiality (dimension 2), which was never constructionism's claim.

Edwards, Ashmore and Potter (1995) and Wetherell and Still (1995) show clearly the mistake here, and I think that the way out of this problem is to transcend these three misleading dichotomies so that we can talk of things being at one and the same time socially constructed *and* real. This is what I like in the position of Brown and Pujol with Curt.

The phenomenological idea that objective reality is impossible for humanity to perceive (intellectually only possible from God's view, since God is everywhere at all times) is a very powerful one since it leads us to the conclusion that all our perceptions and knowledges are necessarily imbued with value. Our perception has 'intentionality', so that we can only ever perceive something in terms of what it can matter to us, or do for us. In this way our relationship with the world and with each other necessarily transforms things and others because of the intentionality of thought. To this extent, our discourses, systems of signs that in no way represent an objective reality, are manifestations of this intentionality.

If we follow through this argument, then 'knowledge' and practice cannot exist independently, as Foucault has convincingly argued (Foucault, 1972), and practices are social structures in action. For example, the individual is a construction that is practised daily and is given life and validation in our legal system. It is more than real in its effects, since it informs all our daily practices, our deliberations about who we are and what we should do, and our thinking about conflicts, moral dilemmas, choices of jobs and so on. As I have argued elsewhere (Burr, 1995), social practice and discourse sustain each other. Together with social structure, they form a unit and are only separable analytically (the term 'discursive practice', for me, does not simply refer to our use of language, but signals the way that practices are always framed by and given meaning by language). Practice is the realm in which discourse has real effects upon people, so that perhaps social and personal change may begin with changes in practice, as Collier suggests.

It therefore seems to me that our concepts and knowledges must in the end be inseparable from practices and structures, the material conditions of everyday life (and this will include bodily conditions as well as economic ones and conditions of power). But if we accept an epistemology/ontology dichotomy, as realism does, we separate the world from our knowledge of it and our talk about it. If we do this, we are likely to 'discover' that social problems have their feet planted in the material world of social structure rather than in the world of discourse, and we therefore slide back into traditional structural 'top-down' accounts which privilege the status of social structure. The outcome of this is that we may as well abandon our attention to language and discourse and its constructive effects and look only to transforming material power relations through changing our social structure or economy.

This, of course, is a legitimate argument, and it is possible that the implications for action and change are in the end not all that different from some of those taking a constructionist, relativist stance. The claim that its quarrel with constructionism is about moral relativism cannot, I think, really be sustained. Although it is true that a relativist position offers no guidance as to which constructions of the world we should adopt, which 'discourses' we should support or what choices we should make in our actions and recommendations for change, social constructionists, as it turns out, have not espoused an 'anything goes' philosophy and, as far as can be judged, appear to be just as committed to defending their own moral and political choices as are realists. Arguments between realists and relativists are more likely to be about the basis upon which our choices are made. The relativist must accept that, like everything else, our values and beliefs are culturally and historically located and produced. Since we cannot ever step outside our own culturally and historically located value systems, perhaps we must (and can only) make such judgements from within this system and defend them regardless of their inevitable relativism. Having said this, some critical realists are also able to accommodate this relativism. The argument here is that, while we must acknowledge that our values are culturally and historically specific, we are nevertheless able to examine them critically and to make an informed judgement about the appropriateness of our values based upon our knowledge of the reality that lies behind social phenomena.

This argument that we are necessarily locked inside our value system and must inevitably make and defend our judgements from within it is a feature of pragmatism, and it turns on a 'danger signal' for those who, like Collier, see pragmatism as a way of justifying self-serving, convenient beliefs about the world. The attraction of pragmatism is that it at least gives one a basis on which to make some choices – to adopt those practices or perspectives which 'work', which appear to create possibilities for increasing freedom, choice and quality of life for those who seem to need it. It is reflexive in that it cautions us to be always critical of our own constructions and aware that our judgements may have unintended consequences. Its critics, however, argue that there can be no a priori grounds upon which one could decide what will 'work' and that our recommendations for action are therefore dangerously likely to be hedonistic ones masquerading as social conscience.

Pragmatism therefore currently has a bad press, but I'm not convinced that this is totally justified. Just as relativists are no more likely than anyone else to advocate the moral relativism or nihilism of which they have been accused, pragmatists are no more hedonistic or self-serving than other theorists. There seems to me to be no good reason to suppose that pragmatism is more likely to lend itself to iniquitous practices than any other theory or philosophy, and it is worth pointing out that realism has a poor track-record in this respect (I think Foucault had it right when he said that nothing is necessarily bad, but everything is dangerous).

Despite the above, it still seems to be the case in practice that constructionists and discourse analysts, afraid of reifying any particular constructions, remain 'observers and commentators' leaving the action to others. Willig points out that the power of discourse analysis and deconstruction is in showing that 'things could be different' but although discourse analysts talk of discourse operating ideologically and are certainly aware of the effects of talk in constituting individuals and groups in particular ways, they seem particularly wary of following this through in terms of recommendations for change and I agree with her that they have a responsibility to do this.

References

Burr, V. (1995) *An Introduction to Social Constructionism*. London: Routledge.

Burr, V. and Butt, T.W. (forthcoming) 'Psychological distress and postmodern thought', in D. Fee (ed.), *Pathology and the Postmodern: Mental Illness as Discourse and Experience*. London: Sage.

Edwards, D., Ashmore, M. and Potter, J. (1995) 'Death and furniture: the rhetoric, politics and theology of bottom-line arguments against relativism', *History of the Human Sciences*, 8 (2): 25–49.

Foucault, M. (1972) *The Archaeology of Knowledge*. New York: Pantheon Books.

Gordon, C. (ed.) (1980) *Power/Knowledge: Selected Interviews and Other Writings 1972–1977*. New York: Pantheon.

Habermas, J. (1986) 'Taking aim at the heart of the present', in D. Couzens Hoy (ed.), *Foucault: A Critical Reader*. Oxford: Blackwell.

Harper, D.J. (1995) 'Discourse analysis and "mental health"', *Journal of Mental Health*, 4: 347–57.

Harré, R. (1989) 'Language games and the texts of identity', in J. Shotter and K.J. Gergen (eds), *Texts of Identity*. London: Sage.

Marks, D. (1993) 'Case-conference analysis and action research', in E. Burman and I. Parker (eds), *Discourse Analytic Research: Repertoires and Readings of Texts in Action*. London: Routledge.

Parker, I., Georgaca, E., Harper, D., McLaughlin, T. and Stowell-Smith, M. (1995) *Deconstructing Psychopathology*. London: Sage.

Potter, J. and Wetherell, M. (1987) *Discourse and Social Psychology: Beyond Attitudes and Behaviour*. London: Sage.

Romme, M. and Escher, S. (eds) (1993) *Accepting Voices*. London: MIND.

Sedgwick, P. (1982) *PsychoPolitics*. London: Pluto Press.

Wetherell, M. and Still, A. (1995) *Issues for Social Psychology*, D317 Social Psychology Book 4. Milton Keynes: Open University Press.

3

Fragments in the
Realization of Relativism

Jonathan Potter

Rë'aliz | e, –is | e (-ïz), v.t. **1.** Convert (hope, plan, etc.) into fact (usu. pass.). **2.** Give apparent reality to, make realistic, present as real . . . **3.** Convert (securities, property) into money (often abs., = sell one's property); amass (fortune, specified profit); fetch as price. (*Concise Oxford Dictionary*, 1964)

28 May 1995

Dear Jonathan,

I am writing about a day conference we are planning for 20 April 1996 called 'Social Constructionism, Discourse and Realism' which will be advertised with the following blurb: 'Should pragmatic and relativist views of meaning and the world necessarily be adopted by discourse analysts? Where is 'the real' in contemporary critical research in psychology? How does the turn-to-language affect, encourage or inhibit perspective for change? This conference will explore connections between theory, method and politics in social research, with particular reference to social constructionist and discursive debates in psychology.'

Would you be willing to speak at this conference?

We are also approaching, at this early stage, Beryl Curt, Norman Geras, and Viv Burr (as discussant).

All best wishes,

Ian.

Some time (and talk) later . . .

Date: Mon, 28 Nov 1995 02:49
To: Ian Parker
From: J.A.Potter@lut.ac.uk
Subject: Reality

Hi Ian

OK, I am going to stop farting around and say yes, I will speak at your workshop next year (assuming it doesn't clash with any teaching at Loughborough – I assume it will fall in the Easter vacation). As long as it does not turn into a competition for who is the most politically acceptable I am happy to speak on realism, construction, and social analysis, that kind of stuff (rhetorics of the real). I will give you a title proper when you need it, preferably a bit closer to the time.

That is assuming, of course, that I have not put you off too much by prevaricating and twitching!

Regards

Jonathan

Hence:

This text comprises a series of fragments as a way of resisting the ordering implied by traditional philosophical argument. It seems appropriate that a relativist textual form might be disorderly, promiscuously moving between different kinds of discourse, and speaking in a range of different voices and experimenting with alternative subject positions. I will be providing a range of sometimes inconsistent *realizations* of relativism. The aim is to use a set of comments and interventions based around rhetoric rather than to draw directly on the discourses of philosophy. So, in (almost) no particular order, some fragments . . .

The 'Realism/Relativism Debate' is a Literary Construction

The realism/relativism debate is a literary construction. That is, it is produced in narratives which invoke a range of tropes and produce a set of characters: realists, materialists, constructionists, relativists. The trouble is that when a debate gets going it is hard to sustain disbelief in the solidity of these characters. On any particular occasion of argument the characters appear solid, coherent and timeless and the argument slips the clutches of the indexical now and turns into something abstract and universal. Philosophical discourses tug us towards the timeless and abstract; a rhetorical corrective (*doing* rhetoric, of course, in the process) stresses the situated and practical nature of such arguments.

So am I claiming that we should avoid the debate because it is a literary construction? Yes and no. *Yes*, the debate should be resisted, because the very taking part starts to reify its elements (even writing like this does it: writing of 'the debate', as if 'it' has an existence projecting back to Protagoras (say) rather than being something worked up locally for a conference at Manchester Metropolitan University (say)). But also *no*, in the sense that these discursive processes are a generic and omnipresent part of debates; the specific constructions can be resisted and commented upon, but there is no ideal world of debate insulated against such processes.

Highlighting the Literary Nature of 'the' Debate (1: With History)

One way of emphasizing the locality and literality of debates about realism is to look to history. If we take just the recent history of social psychology and some of its border zones, we can see the way that there is not one single realism/relativism debate carrying on like a piece of trench warfare with new troops arriving at the front when others get exhausted, shot down or just plain bored. Rather there is a range of debates with their own rhetorical targets and moral heroes based around issues such as rationality, positivism, and naturalism. Realism has been constructed in particular ways and directed at specific targets: for example, in the 1970s Rom Harré (e.g., Harré and Secord, 1972) took on experimental social psychologists while Roy Bhaskar (e.g., Bhaskar, 1978) defended Marxism and psychoanalysis against Popperian critiques, while, more recently still, John Greenwood (e.g., 1994) uses realist philosophy to rework social constructionist developments into a more conventional experimental fold. In this historical story, then, realism is constructed according to its rhetorical targets.

Highlighting the Literary Nature of 'the' Debate (2: With Sociology)

Sociologists of science (another literary construction) have produced analysis which can highlight the literary nature of this debate in another way. Instead of being concerned with the rhetorical nature of broad debates in philosophy of social science, they have been more interested in considering the practical ways that scientists use notions of reality in the course of doing their jobs. On the one hand, they have emphasized that scientists – and this is 'proper', 'hard nosed' scientists – *cannot fail* to move between realist, constructionist and conventionalist discourses as they do different things (Latour and Woolgar, 1986). It is wrong, therefore, to think of physicists, say, simply as realists; as wrong as it would be to think of theologians, say, simply as constructionists. On the other hand, some sociologists have suggested that different areas of science gravitate towards different philosophies, as they make the best general sense of their findings and theories. For example, Knorr Cetina (1995) suggests that while molecular biologists tend towards a philosophical realism, the high energy physicists working on the massive particle detector at CERN tend towards a form of relativism.

Too Many Cooks – An Analogy Emphasizing Rhetoric and Context

Here is an analogy to help think about the potential importance of rhetoric and context to 'the' (now established as really fictional) debate. Consider this. We are faced with a piece of paper with 'too many cooks spoil the broth' written on it. What are we to do?

One course would be to set up immediately a study to see if it is right. We might have some philosophers working on the logic of 'too many', or we might have some experimentalist scientists setting up studies of cooking with three, four or even five cooks who are all producing broth which is tasted and rated from 1 (totally spoiled) to 7 (not at all spoiled) by both experts and 'blind' members of the public. The aim of this line of research would be to assess whether 'too many cooks spoil the broth' is true or not. If it checks out, this will be a green light for people to go on saying it with confidence; if not, it will be a licence for these researchers to intervene whenever this claim is wrongly made and point out the error.

The other course would be to treat what is written on the paper as a piece of transcript; that is, as a record of something said on a particular occasion as a part of a particular activity. This would pay attention to the context-dependent ('indexical') nature of the utterance (note: *utterance*, not just a *sentence* now) and what it is doing rhetorically. For example, is it part of an argument against, or justification of, limiting the people involved in some task. This is the approach to proverbs taken by Michael Billig (1987) and Harvey Sacks (1992) – and it is very much *not* the approach taken by numerous writers of introductory social psychology textbooks. If we follow through the example with the case of realism, the implication would be to say that we need not be concerned with the truth or falsity of realism; instead we can identify a whole variety of different language games in which the word real is used to do particular tasks.

So What is Realism?

Here are four kinds of realism (with examples) which appear in debates in, around, and against relativism (and constructionism) in the mid-1990s.

1   *Realism as a philosophical cum social theory about the ontology of social science, how it should be conceived and, perhaps, how it should be investigated.* Andrew Collier (this volume) provides some arguments in this discourse.
2   *Realism as another way of describing empirical work in social psychology.* For example, Brown and Pujol with Curt (this volume) get close to this.
3   *Realism as an alternative formulation of the Marxist notion of materialism (the social theory of base and superstructure, economic determinants on social change, class conflict and so on).* Parker (this volume) sometimes implies this equivalence.
4   *Realism as a rhetorical commonplace in a range of more or less everyday, non-technical discourse.* Slippage to this sense is endemic in realist argument against relativism.

In much of the writing on the realist side in this book, however, these four kinds of realism are somewhat blurred together. Indeed, together they can provide a flexible set of argumentative resources to do a range of different tasks. (Look, it is happening again: having developed an argument against formulating a debate with sides, it then cannot resist wading in as if you could describe the sides in a realistic way, and enter the debate. Realist discourse is so seductive, so inevitable.)

Why the Realism/Relativism Debate Makes No Difference
(1: Philosophy is not Politics)

Carla Willig quotes Terry Eagleton on philosophy and politics. He is complaining that proper political questions (should troops be withdrawn from Northern Ireland?, should industrial production be socialized under workers' self-management?) need to be addressed in terms of their politics. Their answers generally do not follow from methodico-ontological arguments about the nature of tables, or from the decision to treat realism as a set of more or less helpful stories rather than being just true.

Let me put this another way. Various kinds of more or less abstract, philosophical even, positions might be drawn on when addressing some more or less specific political question. To take one of Eagleton's examples, workers' self-management and its relation to capitalism and liberation might be rather differently understood under some constructions of post-structuralism, postmodernism and the self. So while I think Eagleton's constructions of postmodernists and relativists are (wilfully?) misleading I agree with his emphasis that the *political* business needs to be *done* rather than simply flowing from some set of epistemological commitments. However, I do not think that this is an issue for relativists alone; practical politics in specific domains flows neither from relativism nor realism.

For this reason (among others), I disagree with Ros Gill who *attacks* (and I think that is the right word) relativists for offering 'no principled alternative to realism by means of which we might make *political interventions*' (Gill, 1995: 171; original emphasis). Political interventions should come from political argument and commitment – relativism is neither claiming nor excluding either of these things.

Why the Realism/Relativism Debate Makes No Difference
(2: Ideological Dilemmas)

If there is one really solidly established empirical finding from work in discourse analysis it is that discourse is highly fragmented. Studies of people's practical reasoning about social issues show a huge amount of variation and considerable flexibility. They have identified wide discontinuities between theory and practice in different realms and found that ideological arguments tend to have a dilemmatic form (Billig, 1992; Billig et al., 1988; Wetherell and Potter, 1992). For example, Ros Gill's (1993) study of radio controllers' accounts for the low representation of female DJs, found a general pattern of support for *principles* of equality combined with *practical* reasons for failures to appoint more women. When the controllers were describing and justifying their own recruiting practice it was notable that they constructed accounts that presented the lack of women as a product of external factors rather than their own desires; for example, few women apply, or listeners do not like women's 'shrill' voices.

The important point is that this dilemma between egalitarian principle and unequal practice is not something that is a *problem* for the controllers, something to be resolved; rather it is a *resource* that they use to sustain current practices. The contradictions are not a problem for the stability of the institution; quite the reverse, they can help sustain its current organization.

The study that Margaret Wetherell and I did of ideology, accounts and racism in New Zealand (Wetherell and Potter, 1992) found a rather more complex pattern. Notably, it traced the use of around ten rhetorical commonplaces – brief arguments, generally treated as clinching or beyond question – such as 'everyone should be treated equally', 'you have to live in the modern world', 'you cannot turn the clock backwards', 'injustices should be righted'. They are unproblematic and unexceptional notions that encompass many of the ideas of modern liberal thinking. It is not a list to raise eyebrows, let alone hackles. However, note the way they pull in different directions: how should injustices be righted without turning the clock backwards? The list has the same mix of principles and practical considerations that the radio controllers use to such good effect. The upshot is that it provides a highly flexible resource for doing a range of delicate activities such as arguing against Maori land claims being handled in the courts or attacking the teaching of Maori language to Pakeha (white) pupils.

The point of this jog through some areas of recent discourse analysis is its implication for the relation between the realism/relativism debate and particular political positions and actions. It suggests that it is rather hard to tell what kind of politics will go with broad principled claims about the metaphysical nature of the objects of science or the fallibility of knowledge. Politics does not fall out of principles, ideals, epistemologies or philosophies ready formed; rather it is, and has to be, worked up from these things.

Why the Realism/Relativism Debate Makes No Difference (3: Religion, Politics and the Internet)

Another way of conceiving the relationship between abstract positions and political theories and practices is that it is something to be worked up; it is constructed and made to seem apparently obvious, straightforward and unproblematic in particular settings. It is not a fact of nature that forces itself on all comers.

A good place to look for such constructions is on the Internet. In the period of writing this chapter I have done several searches using AltaVista™, an engine which looks for words and strings within Web pages. Searching for the term 'relativism' generates what is described as 'about 800 matches'. The patterning of these is fascinating. Taking the first 100 (which AltaVista™ judges the most relevant), discussion between anthropologists of 'cultural relativism' is heavily represented, as are postings from (apparently) philosophers on relativism and ethics. Many of these pages include reading lists designed for particular courses. There are some science studies pages, a couple of entries on social constructionism and management science, and a page on Zen and Relativism. However, what interests me here are two kinds of pages that are also well represented: pages addressed to Christianity and relativism, and pages on relativism and political correctness.

The Christian pages vary. There is one that seems to be trying to produce a postmodern account of Christianity. Most, however, are more or less extreme attacks on relativism. A not untypical page (*Two Worldviews on Collision Course*, by Dr K. Alan Snyder) starts:

> Two worldviews are in conflict in America. That conflict is becoming more evident. On one side is the Biblical worldview that emphasizes God's absolute moral standards, man's sinfulness, and the forgiveness that God wishes to bestow on all who truly repent of their sins. On the other side is the humanistic worldview that stresses moral relativism, man's basic goodness (although how 'goodness' can be defined under the umbrella of moral relativism is an open question) and the total acceptance of all types of behavior.

From this beginning it moves on to attack the humanistic worldview for failing to condemn homosexuality ('We should discriminate – that is, discern the difference – between proper sexual conduct and a perversion of sexuality'), for perpetuating the myth that 'normal' people are at risk from AIDS, and for allowing homosexual adoption: 'Sodom and Gomorrah offer a poignant testimony of the ruinous effects on societies engaged in rampant homosexual behavior.' And so it goes on . . .

The relativism and political correctness pages also vary. As an unsophisticated outsider to US politics, I suspect that they are produced by people with allegiance to various elements of new right thinking. The general complaint is that young people in America are increasingly succumbing to the malaise of moral relativism, and this prevents them being able to make judgements about (US) cultural superiority, or concerning the superiority of particular (often white) practices over other (often black) ones. For example:

> Are Relativists really successful in modern society?
> Oh, yes. Anywhere you see 'multiculturalism', 'conflict resolution' or 'political correctness' mentioned somewhere you can be sure a Relativist is around somewhere.

The blending of relativism and political correctness is fascinating as it is a complaint that people are both excessively unevaluative and over-ready to exclude particular practices and descriptions; of course, this is treated as a problem of the (alleged) victims of the (alleged) malaise rather than a confusion in the diagnosis.

The construction of relativism and political correctness on the Internet deserves some serious study beyond these preliminary observations. There are three points I will pick out here. First, I am not wanting these views to be taken as the sort of thing that 'nutcases' write. Ideas change and minority views now can become the orthodoxies of the future. I want to take them seriously as possible (but certainly malign) constructions on relativism and politics. Secondly, relativism is being treated as a threat by cultural authoritarians and supremacists and by more or less fundamentalist Christians. This may (or may not) be reassuring to those who are concerned that relativism is at odds with the kind of materialism needed for a systematic social critique. Thirdly, it is notable that it is full of people constructing versions for the purposes of criticism rather than versions produced by advocates. As Barbara Herrnstein Smith (1988) notes, much of the time the version of relativism that is used in discussion, and has become taken for granted, is that produced by realists. Perhaps the most pervasive such misconception is: 'anything goes'.

Anything Goes

No! Please! How many times does it have to be repeated that 'anything goes' is a realist slur on relativism, probably resulting from a (disingenuous?) misreading (or a failure to read?) Feyerabend's *Against Method* (1975). Anything goes is an *extraordinarily* realist claim, which no relativist has any business espousing. It is a fundamental, timeless, contextless statement about the nature of causal relations, not all that dissimilar from the laws of physics or psychology. For the relativist, what 'goes' is at stake for people; it is what is constructed and argued over. Different positions, cultures and theories have different (any)things which go, or don't go, or go a bit.

Reflexivity is the Key

Why is reflexivity the key? It is all to do with authoring. Somewhere embedded in realists critiques of relativism is generally a 'knock down' example that demonstrates the unavoidable effect of 'the real' on some part of human life. For example, in the paper 'Death and furniture' (on which, more below) Derek Edwards, Malcolm Ashmore and I (1995) discuss the (almost) relativist Harry Collins's bottom-line case – the case where 'the real' obtrudes beyond any negotiation – which happens 'as we stumble against a rock' (Collins, 1990: 50). Whatever else can be questioned and reconstructed (neutrinos, gravity waves, the Health Service), the rock is a brute physical event, in which 'our actions are caused directly by the rock rather than by our interpretations of what the rock is' (Collins, 1990: 50). The point is that it is easy to miss how Collins's example is not a brute bit of reality: it is authored, and the authoring produces the brutality of the reality impingement. Actual cases tend to escape the clutches of single sovereign authors and everything may be up for grabs.

Stumbling is wonderful, with its aura of happenstance and unintentionality; it is surely no accident that 'stumbling over' is both a description of an action/behaviour and a more idiomatic gloss on finding something by chance. Such things are often *precisely* what is at issue in practical situations, whether the concern is how come baby Duncan broke his toy or how come Sue circulated *that* memo. And *rock* is brilliant too, with its generic, uncultured quality; it is a prototypical thing; what could be more real than that? A real (that is, not (yet) produced in a literary narrative) rock might, ironically, be

more open to the usual range of interpretative questions: is it actually an arte-
fact?, a bit of tree?, hard mud?, a stage prop?, something invented to account
for a nasty bruise got in a fight with the boy over the road?, the door to a
secret tunnel? Authoring the example is a reality-defining practice, and as
such, authored examples of this kind are ideal for arguing the case for realism;
they have their realism built in.

Some examples from the conference and the book of the conference:

- Andrew Collier's open door, and his version of Estersen's version of a
  dysfunctional family.
- Ruth Merttens's problems in disciplining her unruly children.

Oh, and am I not authoring quite a lot in this chapter? Yes indeed; but I am
embracing authoring, and accepting its pervasiveness, not pretending it is not
happening and disattending to its consequences. Authoring is the biz.

Reflexivity, Authoring and Experimental Social Psychology

Ironically, perhaps, the closest analogy I can find to the kind of reality-presupposing practice used in realist arguments against relativism is the use of
imaginary invented vignettes in experimental social psychology. In our critical discussion of work on attribution theory one of the things that Derek
Edwards and I (1992, 1993) stumbled across was the way attribution theory
research is overwhelmingly done using vignettes ('John laughs at the comedian', 'Sue is afraid of the dog') which are reality-presupposing. The
real-world issues about whether John is laughing or sneering, or whether it is
at the comedian or not, or, more significantly, what someone is *doing* by
telling us that John laughs at the comedian, are defined out of existence. The
participants in such studies do not encounter reality with all its relativizing
doubts and uncertainties, but a vignette where much of the business is already
authored. The authoring itself is never examined – reflexivity is as corrosive
for experimental social psychology as it is for realist philosophy.

Goodbye Agency, Hello Person Talk (etc.)

One of the concerns expressed by some of the sorts of social psychologists
who care about constructionism is that a proper, psychological, notion of
agency is lost in newish postmodern, post-structural, relativistic, discourse
analytic, ethnomethodological, constructionist work (Burr, 1995, this volume;
Madill and Doherty, 1994). These concerns are well justified. This strand of
work raises very deep problems with many of the standard ways in which persons have been constructed in a wide range of psychological and social
psychological perspectives. That idea of a solid inner furniture that the right
kind of investigation could catalogue has become increasingly difficulty to
reconcile with, for example, close studies of the use of personological language in specific occasions of use (Coulter, 1990; Edwards, 1994).

People are *simultaneously* constructing versions of the world and of their mental states and contents as they do a whole range of business. Objective, natural, bottom-line kinds of phenomena such as emotions suddenly become delicately organized constructions doing a range of subtle business, put together for the occasion but abandoned as if never existing when another job becomes relevant a few moments later (Buttny, 1993; Edwards, 1997; Gergen, 1994). And yet if nostalgia for something more solid and graspable and, well, plain psychological, is put aside, this approach can be seen to be getting at very deep and subtle issues about self, relationships and feelings in a way that traditional work has missed on its continued search for some solid inner stuff (Edwards, 1995; Gergen, 1991; Wetherell, 1994).

Relativism, Discourse Analysis and Transcription

Eh?! These topics do not seem to go together at all. Yet there *is* an interesting relation here. It sometimes seems like a self-evident consequence of relativism that research is not important – why do it if everything is social constructed? A systematic, reflexively applied constructionism accepts that everything has that status. Nothing is outside the net of theories, frameworks, descriptive assumptions, rhetorical commonplaces. But this is just as true of theorizing (big or small, grand or middle range, grounded or airy) and good old common sense. Empirical, analytic research can be a great way of disciplining argument. Relativism is not a reason for sloppiness or vagueness; nor is it a licence for doing research badly (although it is always aware that notions such as badly and vagueness can, at any moment, become the issue).

Take transcription, for example. It might easily be thought that a concern with good quality transcription is something that bothers realists, or at least those with a serious empiricist bent, but is far from relativist concern. However, the value of a representational practice such as transcription is what you can do with it, what stories you can sensibly warrant and what other stories you can undermine. A good transcription system – not the Jefferson Lite sometimes advocated in discourse analysis (Potter and Wetherell, 1987), but the full Jefferson Pilsner (e.g., Jefferson, 1985; Psathas and Anderson, 1990; ten Have and Psathas, 1995) – can throw up all kinds of reality construction business going on in talk, as well as highlighting some of the decontextualizing practices that have gone on in some discourse analysis using interviews (on this see Myers, forthcoming; Potter and Wetherell, 1995; Suchman and Jordan, 1990).

Realism as Rhetoric (1: Some Basic Rules of Production)

There are various kinds of rhetoric that can be used to construct realism and to produce the problematic status of relativism and/or constructionism. Here are some useful rules (developed from Potter, 1992) to sustain the plausibility of realism. Treat them as a rhetorical kitbag that can be drawn on as and where they are needed to debunk foolish relativists.

1   *Construct constructionism as something simple and unitary.* The weave of different approaches, levels of argument and quality can be sidelined.
2   *Avoid reflexivity at all costs.* It will soon eat away at any neat claims and foreground their rhetorical status.
3   *Avoid considering empirical studies of science.* They will only get in the way of the orderly progressive stories needed to buttress realism.
4   *Treat scientific practice as governed by logic.* Local practices of inference get awfully messy; keep to networks and deductive systems.
5   *Elide everyday and philosophical notions of realism.* The philosophical notion gives credibility, while the everyday notion builds up an air of self-evidence.
6   *Treat description as something obvious.* The rhetorical business needed to do description starts to make realism problematic.

Realism as Rhetoric (2: 'Death and Furniture' (a Story) and (a Tetchy) Defence)

'Death and furniture' came to be written as a response to experiences that Derek Edwards, Malcolm Ashmore and I had while giving seminars which dealt with discourse analytic, reflexive or constructionist material. At question time we were repeatedly faced with two kinds of criticism. The first involved the questioner hitting the table: 'you are not telling me that this (bang) is a social construction; what about the bruise I get if I walk into it'. This was so regular that we called it the furniture argument. The second was more oblique in face-to-face settings, although it is common enough in print, and that is that relativism promotes, or at least allows, a moral vacuousness which softens the reality of the massacres of fleeing Iraqis on the Basra Road, say, and is without the full resources for criticizing practices such as female genital mutilation. The aim was to be able to produce a paper which deconstructed the rhetoric of those arguments so that whenever someone produced one at a seminar we could say 'Ah, the furniture argument', say, and (metaphorically) slap the fully rebutting paper down on that same table in front of them, and perhaps be able to move the discussion on to more productive ground.

I am not going to repeat the arguments of the paper here. However, I do want to emphasize some features relevant to the recent attack on it by Ros Gill (1995).

Gill complains of a 'self-righteous and dismissive tone' (1995: 172), an 'epistemological correctness' even, but is perhaps forgetting that 'Death and furniture' is a *third turn*; it is a *response* (3rd) to an *accusation* (2nd) that a discourse analytic *talk* (1st) has propounded either something close to stupidity or something close to moral degeneracy. I suspect that whatever 'tone' there might be should be appropriately heard in that context. And it is interesting to note how Gill's blurring of relativism with political correctness repeats the right-wing Internet tropes which endlessly mix relativism, multiculturalism, feminism and political correctness as equivalent evils to be derided.

Gill attributes to 'Death and furniture' the view that the academy is 'a separate realm, divorced from the political and personal' (1995: 174) and claims 'disinterested inquiry is their regulative ideal' (1995: 175). I am not quite sure how Gill gets to this view; however, my own version of the implication of 'Death and furniture', in so far as it has one, is that the relationships between these kinds of philosophical/rhetorical arguments and specific and practical political issues are loose or, as I noted above, there to be constructed. Just as realism can give you Eysenck and Bhaskar, relativism can give you Mussolini (according to O'Neill, 1995, anyway) and Judith Butler (according to Gill). Such listings are themselves flexible and occasioned. This is not an argument for disinterest but a recognition of the complexity of political argument and the way realism and relativism may play different roles in different situations (cf. Kitzinger, 1995):

In a familiar move, Gill asserts that relativism is contradictory:

> contradictions there are. For whilst realists have a coherent and principled basis for their arguments, grounding them in ontological discourse, relativists do not. They offer no principled basis for choosing between any number of competing versions of events or phenomena, since they have neither ontological commitments nor explicit political commitments which inform their work. (1995: 174)

This seem to be the claim that realism is simply coherent *by definition*. Coherence is made equivalent to 'grounding' (such a wonderfully chosen word, reminiscent of Collins's rock) in . . . 'ontological discourse' (a beautiful oxymoron which cooks its broth and drinks it simultaneously). Given that one of the topics of relativist, constructionist analysis is *precisely* the rhetorical business that goes into making the choice between versions seem to be a matter of principle, or rule following, or something explicit and formal (e.g., Gilbert and Mulkay, 1984; Gill, 1993; Potter, 1996; Wetherell and Potter, 1992), it would be very odd to start pretending that principles do the job *on their own* (without commitment, interests, happenstance, authority, habit, the unconscious even). To this kind of idealism all a relativist can, surely, say is: get real!

Realism as Rhetoric (3: Everyday and Political Uses of Realism)

As I have already noted, one of the beauties of realist philosophical argument is the possibility of blurring together the abstract ontological arguments with the everyday tropes of realism talk. The patterning in these tropes can start to become clear if you look at a lot of them. For example, I took a year's worth of US broadcast news (including CNN, ABC, and Public Broadcasting System programmes) which are (conveniently, but poorly) transcribed on to compact disk and searched it for uses of 'realist', 'realism' and 'realistic'. The numbers come out like this:

Realist: 37
Realism: 85
Realistic: 648

Being realistic, then, is a recurrent trope in these materials. It is used in a range of senses, typically contrastive. Being realistic can be contrasted to being idealistic; it can emphasize an awareness of human limits, both physical and psychological; it can emphasize rationality and awareness of potential failure rather than ideology and hope. The following illustrate some of these features:

Hansen:	Do you think it is **realistic** for Mangosuthu Buthelezi to insist that the Zulu kingdom be autonomous, that it returns to the pre-1880s?
Prof. Guy:	I do not. How can we – How is it possible to turn back the clock in this fashion? How is it possible to ignore what has happened in the last hundred years? That's one problem. There are other problems, as well. (NPR, 17/04/94)
King:	Is it a foregone conclusion, Mary, that you will get full-blown AIDS? I mean, is that automatic in this story?
Ms Fisher:	Well, it's – it's automatic because that's what happened. That's the norm. That's what usually happens. I can hope that I won't, but – you know, we are optimistic, but we have to be **realistic**. (CNN, 15/04/94)
Student:	The kids have sex. And if you're gonna teach anything about it, then you should teach them to be safe. And abstinence is the only 100 percent way to be safe, but today that's not a – it's not **realistic** to only teach that kind of solution. (CNN, 18/03/94)
Wooten:	[voice-over] Dr Kunrad Hinkerts of Belgium, who led the first medical team in two weeks ago, takes a **realistic** view of his task.
Hinkerts:	It's physically impossible to help – to bring in help for one million people who arrived in three days' time. I think nobody can help at this moment. We do our best. You can bring in and you can help the people as much as you can, but I think the disaster was – you could not do anything. (ABC, 01/08/94)

Note the way that 'being realistic' is treated as the good or right alternative in these cases; this positive semiotic is almost invariable in the examples I have looked at. Indeed, realism in this discourse seems akin to 'community' as a notion with no negative pole (Potter and Reicher, 1987). Note also the way that being realistic is contrasted to being idealistic or optimistic. It might be nice for an HIV+ woman to hope not to get AIDS, but it is not *realistic*; nor should a doctor with a single team treating many refugees expect to do much.

There are a great many interesting features of this material, and the precise way that notions of realism are being used. However, I wish to make just one observation. Recent criticisms of relativism, and of the relativistic elements in discourse research, have claimed that relativism saps political practice by disallowing the commitment of true belief (Parker and Burman, 1993). Yet in this material it is not, I think, too far fetched to see the tropes of *realism* being used to eat away at ideals and ideology, reducing abstract political arguments to pragmatism and *realpolitik*.

Realism as Rhetoric (4: Constructing Reality as a General Topic of Study)

Although the deconstruction of realists' explicit argumentative tropes, whether in their philosophical form or their more everyday variety, is interesting and valuable, I think it is more important to look at realism more generally in the sense hinted at (but not followed through) by Berger and Luckmann in their *The Social Construction of Reality* (1966). The idea that reality is socially constructed has often remained something of a slogan; the idea that everything might be socially constructed, including the texts of the researcher, has even become something of an embarrassment at times.

However, recent research on fact construction in the very different traditions of ethnomethodology, sociology of science and postmodernism has opened the possibility of addressing the construction and stabilization of versions of the world rigorously and systematically. One way of thinking of this work is as an intensive analysis of the tropes and commonplaces of everyday realism and how they are deployed on particular occasions. For example, in *Representing Reality* (1996) I examine some of the procedures through which the potential discounting of versions through highlighting the (constructed) interests lying behind them is achieved and the way category entitlements to knowledge are built up. The book also explores a range of techniques through which accounts are made to seem objective and independent of their authors. Without going into detail here, this work is attempting to take seriously the ethnomethodological injunction to move from looking at realism as a resource to taking it as a topic.

So does this work have implications of a more general political and ethical kind? Perhaps. At least it highlights two points. First, it shows up the enormous subtlety and sophistication of people's everyday practices of fact construction. And this raises important questions about the sorts of status and authority that accrue to social scientists' own factual constructions. Are we so sure we know better? Secondly, it encourages us *again* (and I think more encouragement *is* needed despite the impetus given by Ashmore, 1989; Mulkay, 1985; Stringer, 1985; Woolgar, 1988 and others) to consider the reality-producing practices of social scientists and the tropes that they (we!) use to establish versions as solid.

Realism as Rhetoric (5: True Stories)

Realism can be a good story. There is no reason for a relativist to avoid realist narratives – indeed, it is pretty hard to do without them (as I have, no doubt, demonstrated again in the writing of this chapter). There may be all sorts of purposes for which a realist story is best. Donna Haraway (1989) provides one sophisticated example of working with realist narratives. She treats her massive study of primatology, and the way in which it promotes myths of human origins and reactionary stories about gender and race, as a form of science fiction.

It is telling a story about primatology, but that story draws on, yet resists the temptations of, four primary narratives: sociology of scientific knowledge; Marxism; the legitimating narrative of the scientists themselves; and finally histories of gender and race and their involvement with science. Why are these temptations? Because each risks taking over the account and turning it into The One True Story, a story that takes on the mantle of timeless and unimpeachable fact. The relativist use of realist stories involves living with, and even celebrating, the tensions between them rather than hiding them or forgetting them.

So this adoption of realist narrative does not elide relativism with realism. In relativism the realism never quite turns timeless, solid and true; there is always an edge of scepticism and self-doubt. Ros Gill (1995) approvingly quotes Judith Butler's (1992) suggestion that we should have permanent contestation at the heart of any radical political project; and this seems pretty close to what relativists are after.

Why the Realism/Relativism Debate Makes a Difference
(1: Members' Concerns)

One reason the realism/relativism debate makes a difference is that it is treated as making a difference. Every Web page, every article, every meeting at Manchester Metropolitan University builds another network of connections and stories linking (arcane?) philosophy to a range of political concerns. There comes a point where it is no longer possible to say that debate makes no difference to anything if it simply has got so big that it is making a difference.

Why the Realism/Relativism Debate Makes a Difference
(2: Some Virtues of Relativism)

Relativism is used most happily against authority, against the *status quo*, against established versions and taken-for-granted realities. As Edwards, Ashmore and I wrote:

> Relativism offers an ever available level of resistance. It is potentially liberating, dangerous, unsettling, with an appeal that is enduringly radical: nothing ever *has to be* taken as merely, obviously, objectively, unconstructedly, true. Reality can only ever be reality-as-known, and therefore, however counter-intuitive it may seem, produced by, not prior to, inquiry. For what *counts as* reality is, for any particular item, at least potentially a matter of consensus and disputation. (1995: 39; original emphasis)

Its political contribution, then, such as it is, supports freeing up from established systems, change and openness. To take over one of Michael Billig's (1992) tropes, relativism promotes a resistance to 'settlement'; it most easily supports critique, plurality, multiplicity of voices, a need for justification. Relativism does not simply do politics; but political implications can be built out of it.

Date: Wed, 29 Oct 11:10
To: Jonathan Potter
From: I.A.Parker@bolton.ac.uk
Subject: Social Constructionism, Discourse and Realism

Dear Jonathan

Sage want to cut the opening email bits from the beginning of your chapter.

I'm inclined to think this would be a good idea. Do you agree?

They wrote:

> Something I do need to raise with you is the opening of Jonathan Potter's chapter. Ziyad felt that it wasn't adding anything central to the work as a whole nor alto-gether appropriate for a wider international audience. Would you (and Jonathan) be happy to drop the opening? The copyeditor would pick up on any textual ref-erences which you would have the opportunity to check at proofs. Anyway let me know how wedded you both are to it.

Hope all is well.

Ian

Date: Wed, 29 Oct 1997 11:40
To: Ian Parker
From: J.A.Potter@lboro.ac.uk
Subject: Re: Social Constructionism, Discourse and Realism

Hi Ian

Hmn. I suppose I am slightly nervous about that stuff. It is slightly jokey and informal and alludes to tensions and issues that are not really addressed in the body of the chapter. However, that is part of the point.

It does have a clear rationale for inclusion, and that is that a relativist, anti-founda-tionalist approach treats knowledge as situated, contingent, accomplished for settings and institutional occasions. Realism/relativism is not a debate hanging in the air; it is made into one. And that informal exchange of letters and emails is (more) history of the debate in the making .

It also alludes to, and breaches, the standard form of academic writing – which is something that relativist writers, particularly those with a reflexive interest (Ashmore, Stringer), have been wont to do.

As I write this I think the ideal fix would not be to cut the introductory exchange, but actually to include this email exchange as an afterword. It shows, after all, the rela-tivism-realism-debate-as-accomplished-as-such rubbing up against international capitalism and cultural imperialism. And it spells out the point of the opening.

So that is my proposal. Any thoughts?

Jonathan

Date: Wed, 29 Oct 1997 12:08
To: Jonathan Potter
From: I.A.Parker@bolton.ac.uk
Subject: Re: Social Constructionism, Discourse and Realism

Hi Jonathan

Well, I must admit I don't think those opening bits do the subversive work you think they do. They just turn serious debate about language and reality into trivialized game-playing (exactly one of the problems with full-blown relativism). I'll forward your suggestion to Ziyad, but my feeling is that it compounds the problem rather than addressing it.

Ian

cc: Ziyad

Date: Wed, 5 Nov 1997 13:18
To: Ian Parker
From: J.A.Potter@lboro.ac.uk
Subject: Re: Social Constructionism, Discourse and Realism

Hi Ian

I am not claiming they are subversive. It is making public some of the contingent processes that lie behind knowledge production and are repressed in a lot of abstract discussion of epistemology.

It is not trivial. It relates to the very fundamental issue of how you understand epistemology, and whether you see it as abstract or situated (conceptual or sociological). This is a pretty important issue, and one which is near the heart of the realism/relativism debate.

For the same reason it is not game playing. It has a serious purpose and has a constitutive relation to the argument at hand. It is not merely play or gloss.

The international capitalism/cultural imperialism issues come from the point the publishers raise (quite appropriately from their perspective) about the way the book is marketed and the way the ideas are made to seem universal (not merely British?, not tied to a conference?, not developed at a 'new' university).

Now this exchange is even more interesting and would add excellently to the chapter.

Jonathan

cc: Ziyad

Date: Wed, 5 Nov 1997 13:25
To: Jonathan Potter
From: I.A.Parker@bolton.ac.uk
Subject: Re: Social Constructionism, Discourse and Realism

Jonathan

I'll forward this to Ziyad, I'd rather just cut those beginning bits. This seems a bit daft to me.

Ian

Note

I would like to acknowledge the helpful comments made on an earlier draft of this chapter by Charles Antaki, Mick Billig, Derek Edwards, Alexa Hepburn and Margaret Wetherell.

References

Ashmore, M. (1989) *The Reflexive Thesis: Wrighting Sociology of Scientific Knowledge.* Chicago: University of Chicago Press.

Berger, P.L. and Luckmann, T. (1966) *The Social Construction of Reality.* Garden City, NY: Doubleday.

Bhaskar, R. (1978) *A Realist Theory of Science* (2nd edn). Brighton: Harvester.

Billig, M. (1987) *Arguing and Thinking: A Rhetorical Approach to Social Psychology.* Cambridge: Cambridge University Press.

Billig, M. (1992) *Talking of the Royal Family.* London: Routledge.

Billig, M., Condor, S., Edwards, D., Gane, M., Middleton, D.J. and Radley, A.R. (1988) *Ideological Dilemmas: A Social Psychology of Everyday Thinking.* London: Sage.

Burr, V. (1995) *An Introduction to Social Constructionism.* London: Routledge.

Butler, J. (1992) 'Contingent foundation: feminism and the question of "postmodernism"', in J. Butler and J.W. Scott (eds), *Feminists Theorize the Political.* London: Routledge.

Buttny, R. (1993) *Social Accountability in Communication.* London: Sage.

Collins, H.M. (1990) *Artificial Experts: Social Knowledge and Intelligent Machines.* Cambridge, MA: MIT Press.

Coulter, J. (1990) *Mind in Action.* Cambridge: Polity Press.

Edwards, D. (1994) 'Script formulations: a study of event descriptions in conversation', *Journal of Language and Social Psychology*, 13: 211–47.

Edwards, D. (1995) 'Two to tango: script formulations, dispositions, and rhetorical symmetry in relationship troubles talk', *Research on Language and Social Interaction*, 28: 319–50.

Edwards, D. (1997) *Discourse and Cognition.* London and Beverly Hills, CA: Sage.

Edwards, D. and Potter, J. (1992) *Discursive Psychology.* London: Sage.

Edwards, D. and Potter, J. (1993) 'Language and causation: a discursive action model of description and attribution', *Psychological Review*, 100: 23–41.

Edwards, D., Ashmore, M. and Potter, J. (1995) 'Death and furniture: the rhetoric, politics, and theology of bottom line arguments against relativism', *History of the Human Sciences*, 8: 25–49.

Feyerabend, P.K. (1975) *Against Method.* London: New Left Books.

Gergen, K.J. (1991) *The Saturated Self: Dilemmas of Identity in Contemporary Life.* New York: Basic Books.

Gergen, K.J. (1994) *Realities and Relationships: Soundings in Social Construction.* Cambridge, MA: Harvard University Press.

Gilbert, G.N. and Mulkay, M. (1984) *Opening Pandora's Box: A Sociological Analysis of Scientists' Discourse.* Cambridge: Cambridge University Press.

Gill, R. (1993) 'Justifying injustice: broadcasters' accounts on inequality in radio', in E. Burman and I. Parker (eds), *Discourse Analytic Research: Repertoires and Readings of Texts in Action.* London: Routledge.

Gill, R. (1995) 'Relativism, reflexivity and politics: interrogating discourse analysis from a feminist perspective', in S. Wilkinson and C. Kitzinger (eds), *Feminism and Discourse: Psychological Perspectives.* London: Sage.

Greenwood, J.D. (1994) *Realism, Identity and Emotion: Reclaiming Social Psychology.* London: Sage.

Haraway, D. (1989) *Primate Visions: Gender, Race and Nature in the World of Modern Science.* London: Routledge.

Harré, R. and Secord, P.F. (1972) *The Explanation of Social Behaviour.* Oxford: Blackwell.

Jefferson, G. (1985) 'An exercise in the transcription and analysis of laughter', in T. Van Dijk (ed.), *Handbook of Discourse Analysis, Volume 3.* London: Academic Press.

Kitzinger, C. (1995) 'Social constructionism: implications for lesbian and gay psychology', in A.R. D'Angelli and C.J. Patterson (eds), *Lesbian, Gay and Bisexual Identities over the Lifespan: Psychological Perspectives.* New York: Oxford University Press.

Knorr Cetina, K. (1995) *Epistemic Cultures: How Scientists Make Sense.* Chicago: Indiana University Press.

Latour, B. and Woolgar, S. (1986) *Laboratory Life: The Construction of Scientific Facts* (2nd edn). Princeton, NJ: Princeton University Press.

Madill, A. and Doherty, K. (1994) '"So you did what you wanted then": discourse analysis, personal agency, and psychotherapy', *Journal of Community and Applied Social Psychology*, 4: 261–73.

Mulkay, M. (1985) *The Word and the World: Explorations in the Form of Sociological Analysis*. London: Allen and Unwin.

Myers, G. (forthcoming) 'Displaying opinions: disagreement and topic shifts in focus groups', *Language in Society*.

O'Neill, J. (1995) '"I gotta use words when I talk to you": a response to "Death and furniture"', *History of the Human Sciences*, 8: 99–106.

Parker, I. and Burman, E. (1993) 'Against discursive imperialism, empiricism, and constructionism: thirty-two problems with discourse analysis', in E. Burman and I. Parker (eds), *Discourse Analytic Research: Repertoires and Readings of Texts in Action*. London: Routledge.

Potter, J. (1992) 'Constructing realism: seven moves (plus or minus a couple)', *Theory and Psychology*, 2: 167–73.

Potter, J. (1996) *Representing Reality: Discourse, Rhetoric and Social Construction*. London: Sage.

Potter, J. and Reicher, S. (1987) 'Discourses of community and conflict: the organization of social categories in accounts of a "riot"', *British Journal of Social Psychology*, 26: 25–40.

Potter, J. and Wetherell, M. (1987) *Discourse and Social Psychology*. London: Sage.

Potter, J. and Wetherell, M. (1995) 'Discourse analysis', in J. Smith, R. Harré and L. van Langenhove (eds), *Rethinking Methods in Psychology*. London: Sage.

Psathas, G. and Anderson, T. (1990) 'The "practices" of transcription in conversation analysis', *Semiotica*, 78: 75–99.

Sacks, H. (1992) *Lectures on Conversation*. Vols I and II, edited by G. Jefferson. Oxford: Basil Blackwell.

Smith, B.H. (1988) *Contingencies of Value: Alternative Perspectives for Critical Theory*. Cambridge, MA: Harvard University Press.

Stringer, P. (1985) 'You decide what your title is to be and [read] write to that title', in D. Bannister (ed.), *Issues and Approaches in Personal Construct Theory*. London: Academic Press.

Suchman, L. and Jordan, B. (1990) 'Interactional troubles in face-to-face survey interviews', *Journal of the American Statistical Association*, 85: 232–41.

ten Have, P. and Psathas, G. (eds) (1995) *Situated Order: Studies in the Social Organization of Talk and Embodied Activities*. Washington, DC: International Institute for Ethnomethodology and Conversation Analysis and University Press of America.

Wetherell, M. (1994) 'Commentary: the knots of power and negotiation, blank and complex subjectivities', *Journal of Community and Applied Social Psychology*, 4 (4): 305–8.

Wetherell, M. and Potter, J. (1992) *Mapping the Language of Racism: Discourse and the Legitimation of Exploitation*. London: Harvester; New York: Columbia University Press.

Woolgar, S. (ed.) (1988) *Knowledge and Reflexivity: New Frontiers in the Sociology of Science*. London and Beverley Hills, CA: Sage.

4

Language, Practice and Realism

Andrew Collier

My main aim in this chapter is to suggest that the nature of language and practice is such as to support realism not idealism, including discursive and pragmatic idealism. In conclusion I shall say a little about the consequences for the study of the human world. In the earlier part I shall be arguing for realism in general; in the later part for the 'critical realist' movement that has arisen out of Roy Bhaskar's works *A Realist Theory of Science* (1977) and *The Possibility of Naturalism* (1979).

Modern philosophy – meaning the philosophy which started with Descartes and has not yet escaped his influence – tends to reject realism for the following reason. It sets up some privileged means by or through which what is known is said to be known – be that consciousness, experience, language or practice. It is then said that we cannot know reality in itself, only in so far as it is given in consciousness, experience, language, practice or whatever. What we can know in fact is said to be consciousness, experience, language or practice. It is then either concluded with Berkeley that reality has no existence outside this privileged means to its knowledge, or with Kant that though things in themselves exist, they are nothing to us – we cannot experience or talk about them or whatever, and so cannot know them. Both these positions are forms of idealism, which in this sense can be regarded as the peculiarly modern philosophy. Platonic idealism was something quite different, but recent pragmatic and discursive idealisms are identical in the structure of their arguments to Berkeleian or Kantian idealism, even though the nature of the ideas to which reality is reduced is different. Most modern non-realists reject the term 'idealism', and are even offended by it. But the basic feature of idealism – the denial that some cognitively crucial human activity essentially refers to some reality independent of it, and the claim that, on the contrary, human activity constitutes the supposed reality – is shared by modern non-realism. Indeed it can be argued, and I have argued it in chapter 3 of my book *Critical Realism* (1994), that twentieth-century non-realism is a more extreme form of idealism than those of Berkeley and Kant, and corresponds more closely to the caricature of idealism with which Marx and Engels open *The German Ideology* (1970).

Language and Reality

The first thing I want to do is to stand this argument on its head. I want to claim that each of these supposed privileged means – consciousness or experience or (what I shall concentrate on here) language or practice – is not an entity that can be understood in its own right. They can be understood only in so far as they open up reality to us. Consciousness is, as Brentano and the phenomenologists have taught, always consciousness of something. Without that something it is, as Sartre says, mere nothingness. Experience is always an encounter with what existed before the experience and is to a degree known to us as a result of the experience. Of course nothing is ever completely known by us, but the knowledge we have, so far as it goes, is of real properties of things, existing independently of us. We can make no sense of the concept of experience except as that in which reality is, in some degree, given to us. Grammatically, 'experience' can be a noun as well as a verb; but experience can never be a thing which we can inspect as it is in itself, independently of the reality that is given through it. And this 'aboutness' is characteristic too of practice and of language. Practice always works on something and with something. The learning of language would not only be miraculous in the absence of interaction with other people, it would be miraculous if that interaction were not *about* independently existing entities in a public world, which language too is necessarily partly about. (On this notion of aboutness, compare Ryle's suggestion that Heidegger's fundamental concept *besorgen*, which Macquarrie and Robinson translate as 'concern', should be translated as 'being-about' – see Murray, 1978: 58.)

Language can only be learnt by reference to reality. That indicates that there are other, prior means of access to reality. Not only is there no one privileged means of access to reality, language is not even the first runner. For linguistic interaction with reality presupposes practical interaction, in which the pre-linguistic child engages, through play and the satisfaction of its physical and emotional needs. Furthermore, language not only presupposes access to reality in order to be learnt, it gets its meaning from its relation to the world outside it. Language is a pointer, and to study it without reference to what it points to is like trying to understand what a signpost is by analysis of its metallic composition. That ought to be obvious – we know what the word 'goat' means when we know what goats are. But it is often denied for two reasons. First, people think that Saussure has shown that words get their meaning from their relation to other words, not by referring to reality. But what he has in fact shown is that words refer to reality by virtue of their relation with other words. The case is just like that of the relation of a map to the area mapped. The symbols on the map do not resemble what they symbolize – a blue line represents a river that appears in reality as a muddy brown expanse. But by virtue of their mutual relations, they represent real features of the landscape. If they did not, it would not be a map of anything.

The second reason is that language has features other than being about something. We use language to express emotions, to get people to do things, and so on. Of course, imperatives are about things too – 'shut the door' is about the door – but they do not on the surface of it have a truth value, and they appear to have a content independent of this aboutness as well. But it seems to me that if we are talking, not about grammar, but about the place of language in human life, we must recognize that language expresses emotions or guides actions by virtue of what it is about, and what it says about it. When Burns compares his beloved to a red, red rose he expresses an emotion no doubt. But he does it by saying something about the woman. (I am assuming that metaphorical language does say something about what it is about.) The poem tells us something about the woman, and only thereby, indirectly, does it tell us about Burns's emotion.

Perhaps a few more words would be useful here about this unfashionable idea of the primacy of the information-giving function of language. I doubt whether this primacy could be derived from a study of language in isolation from its place in society and in human life in general. However we need to understand the many-sidedness of language, and the relations between the many sides. One of the benefits which has come from the intervention of 'critical realism' (the type of realism to which I am committed) in the neighbourhood of the linguistic and social sciences is as follows. Many people working in this area want to reduce one discipline to another (for instance linguistics to sociology), or to isolate their own discipline from others, or to deny the boundaries between these disciplines. Critical realism avoids all these alternatives. It recognizes that each discipline may uncover real and distinct structures, mutually irreducible; yet that in explaining the open system of social life we will need to appeal to all these structures and so draw on all these disciplines. Linguistics is an autonomous science, not a branch of sociology. Yet it cannot tell us everything that there is to know about language. The other human sciences, and indeed ethics, aesthetics and logic all have something to tell us about it too.

It seems to be particularly common for some reason to make mistakes about language of the form 'language is A, so it cannot be B', when there is no reason to suppose that A and B are incompatible. Of entities other than language, this mistake is far less common – people don't say things like 'carrots are not salad vegetables that can be eaten, they are roots that grow in the ground'. But they do say 'language is not a means of conveying information, it is a means of communication between people', and 'linguistic signs do not refer to reality, they are defined in terms of other signs'. In each case, language is not just both these things, it is one by virtue of being the other. Language can communicate emotions or moral judgements. But apart from quasi-linguistic noises like 'oh' and 'wow' (and even these surely have an implicit cognitive content), language communicates these things by conveying information. If I say that the cabinet ministers are a load of liars, I am insulting them, but I am not just insulting them by saying 'yah boo sucks'. I am conveying information about them – information which may turn out to be true or false – and it is the nature of the information that makes the conveying of it an insult.

It is important to note that this is true of metaphorical language as well as literal language, for metaphor is far more central to language than has commonly been admitted. While the claim that all language is metaphorical trivializes the notion of metaphor by generalizing it, it is certainly true that we can only talk about abstract things by virtue of coining (and sometimes 'killing') metaphors drawn from the language of concrete things. As George Thomson put it

> such abstract ideas as rest, dependence, expectation, obedience, virtue, wicked, heavy, round, bear on the face of them the marks of their concrete origin: to rest is to resist movement, to depend is to hang on, to expect is to watch out for, to obey is to listen to, virtue is manliness, wicked is bewitched, heavy is hard to lift, round is wheel-like. (Thomson, 1955: 40)

The sciences, exact and otherwise, necessarily operate with dead metaphors: 'structure' in the linguistic and social sciences, 'wave' in physics, 'code' in genetics, 'market' in economics, 'follows' in logic. And live metaphors as used in more poetic speech convey information too. To return to the Burns example, C.S. Lewis points out somewhere that when Burns compares his lover to a rose and Wordsworth compares his to a violet, they are saying quite different things about two very different women – things which someone who knew the women might confirm or deny. They are not just saying 'cor, she aint half nice'.

Pragmatism and Practice

I shall return to the issue of prescriptive language when I have discussed practice. I will just mention here that the finest of all philosophical works on ethics – Spinoza's – is couched entirely in the indicative. He does not say 'do this' but that 'a free person' or 'a person who is guided by reason' will do this.

I have claimed priority for practice, but this is not going to lead me into pragmatism. Pragmatism is another form of idealism in that it reduces what is knowable to something anthropocentric. My claim is that if practice had been given the central place it deserves in epistemology, idealism would never have got off the ground. Modern philosophy starts from an essentially unpractical conception of consciousness and experience. In saying 'I think, therefore I am', Descartes sets up consciousness at its most unpractical and therefore its most alienated from reality as the starting point for knowledge. The Southampton students' Philosophy Society raises funds by selling drinking mugs inscribed 'I drink, therefore I am.' If that had been Descartes's starting point, he would never have concluded that he was an incorporeal substance. This is a serious point: the normal place of thought is as an aspect of practice. And such thought is never set alongside reality as something independent of it as Descartes's thought is. Of course Descartes had his reasons for starting from mere thinking rather than from the thinking which is an aspect of drinking, but they were bad reasons, connected with the search for an unobtainable kind of certainty.

We can see a similar divorce from practice in Hume's claim that we cannot experience causality. Experience is abstracted from practice and understood as a succession of distinct impressions. If Hume had, like Heidegger in *Being and Time* (1967), analysed the experience of hammering in a nail, he might surely have found causes in his analysis; or indeed in the experience of seeing Tanya close the door, since it is necessarily true that if Tanya closes the door, that door is shut immediately afterwards, and that Tanya's closing it is the cause of its being shut. Yet clearly Tanya closing the door is something that we can see.

There is a difference between the way reality is given in language and in practice. Language can be about reality, and could not exist if it were not sometimes about reality, but it can freewheel. Mistakes arise, said Wittgenstein, when language goes on holiday. But practice does not go on holiday in the same way. In practice, reality hits you in the face – at any rate, unless you take precautions to stop it doing so. Heidegger's account of language in *Being and Time* is interesting here. Language can always be hearsay, *Gerede*, idle talk. We can talk endlessly about things we don't know anything about. If we start acting upon things we don't know anything about, we soon learn a thing or two. It is no accident that idealism, including its pragmatist form, gains adherents only among us who, in our professional lives, engage only with words.

Marx clearly thought that modern philosophy had got off on the wrong foot by taking its cue from purely contemplative thought and experience, rather than from that which is an aspect of practice. But he did not indicate how a philosophy that did start from practice would have proceeded. He had other fish to fry. In the present century, Heidegger and John Macmurray have both started by analysing the knowledge that is inherent in practice. But both saw that this 'knowledge' was sometimes in error, and led the practice astray. Thought that is specifically designed to test reality – the practice of theory – then comes into its own. It is the growing point of practice, the aspect by virtue of which practice can be self-critical and self-transforming. Practice can only be self-critical and self-transforming to the extent that it is open to the buffets of reality, and draws theoretical, and thereby new practical, conclusions from them. And this makes clear the tendency and motivation of pragmatism, as a philosophy that relativizes reality to practice, allows practice to determine what reality is rather than transforming itself in the light of the reality that hits it in the face. The function of pragmatism is to conserve existing practices, to cut off their growing point, to incapacitate them for self-criticism and self-transformation. And that really is the role that pragmatist arguments play at the lay rather than the professional philosophical level. They are the means by which people defend the prejudices of their profession against the spirit of inquiry which might raise questions about them. And because people do sometimes cling to the ideas inherent in their existing practices, and turn a blind eye to reality, intervention into practices on behalf of 'realism' (in a non-technical sense) is often necessary. There are open practices which let reality hit them in the face, and transform themselves in the light of it; and there are closed practices which project their own conception of reality and won't see it questioned. Pragmatism is the philosophical normalization of closed practices; realism is the philosophical normalization of open practices. Let us look at an example.

In Laing and Esterson's book *Sanity, Madness and the Family* (1970), the following is said about the patient Maya Abbott and her parents:

> An idea of reference that she had was that something she could not fathom was going on between her parents, seemingly about her.
>
> Indeed there was. When they were all interviewed together, her mother and father kept exchanging with each other a constant series of nods, winks, gestures, knowing smiles, so obvious to the observer that he commented on them after twenty minutes of the first such interview. They continued, however, unabated and denied.
>
> The consequence, so it seems to us, of this failure of her parents to acknowledge the validity of similar comments by Maya, was that Maya could not know when she was perceiving or when she was imagining things to be going on between her parents. These open yet unavowed non-verbal exchanges between father and mother were in fact quite public and perfectly obvious. Much of what could be taken to be paranoid about Maya arose because she mistrusted her own mistrust. She could not really believe that what she thought she saw going on was going on. (Laing and Esterson, 1970: 40)

Here, the ongoing practice of the Abbotts' family life maintained certain prejudices by systematically turning away from the evidence; a closed practice with its own 'pragmatist truth' was maintained by the collusion of Mr and Mrs Abbott, and partly that of Maya herself. Their practice was closed to unwelcome realities. This is repression in a sense related to the Freudian, the difference being that the defence mechanism against reality is transpersonal instead of intrapersonal. It needs the intervention of someone (here the psychiatrist) open to the reality of the practice denied in the collusion, to reopen the possibility of the criticism and transformation of the practice. Note that it is not a matter of taking Maya's point of view against her parents' one. Maya herself is half colluding with her parents' point of view – she 'mistrusts her own mistrust' – and also she apparently suffered from a number of genuine delusions. The point is not to take sides with any of the contending positions within the family, but to take sides with the truth. Trevor Pateman says with regard to *Sanity, Madness and the Family* that what some patients need is not a psychiatrist but an epistemologist; since the point is to open a closed practice, one might add: a realist epistemologist (Pateman, 1972).

Pragmatism has sometimes appealed to political activists because they think it gives a licence to politicize knowledge. What is said to be true is determined by a pre-existing political commitment. My first question about this is: what determines the political commitment? My own political commitment is determined by a number of beliefs which I think are true about reality: that capitalism involves the exploitation of the workers, that it generates production without reference to human needs or environmental concerns, that the capitalist class has the power and motivation to prevent any merely parliamentary transition to socialism, and so on. These beliefs are not, unless I am deluding myself, determined by any prior political commitment. In general it is true that within any political standpoint, the factual beliefs will determine the practical aims; beliefs about the causes and possible cures of social ills generate political programmes. Bare 'value judgements' have a marginal role. Psychological questionnaires to people of various political persuasions have shown that there is a wide consensus about values between fascists, Tories, liberals, social democrats and communists in this country. But just try to get two politicians even slightly removed from one another on the spectrum to agree about the facts – about the causes and possible cures of unemployment for instance. And this grounding of prescriptions in descriptions and explanations is exactly what one would expect from everyday discourse. Bare prescriptions of the type that Kant and Hare place in the foreground of ethics have little place outside the armed forces. But if I tell you that this building is on fire, and you believe me, that factual belief will certainly be 'action guiding'.

This is a substantive question for ethics, and it cannot be resolved simply by looking at the 'language of morals'. The emptying of values and prescriptive implications from factual language by logical positivists, and the emptying of objective facts from evaluative language by postmodernists are just two consequences of modern metaphysics, which in itself is not a theory about language but about reality: the theory that reality is divided into two independent parts, brute matter and consciousness. Questions about what there is get assigned to the material side, questions about what to do get assigned to the side of consciousness. Hence it is supposed to make no sense to find grounds for action in the way things are, though in truth no one could make sense of even the simplest action – making a cup of tea or inviting a friend to the pub for a pint – unless they took for granted that the way things are does provide grounds for action.

Given that factual beliefs generate policies, someone who, on the basis of a factual belief, favours a particular policy, may want to persuade other people of the truth of other factual beliefs, which will generate the same policy, even though he or she may not share those beliefs. For instance someone may believe that full commitment of the UK to the European Union will increase capitalist profits, and may therefore try to get others to believe that such commitment will create full employment, whether this latter belief is true or not. In short, politicians may tell cynical lies. That is what no one will deny. But what is perhaps more contentious is that this is the most obvious sense that politicizing an intellectual discipline can have. Intellectual disciplines should seek the truth – and if the truth has political consequences, they should be followed. The legitimate project of 'politicizing' an intellectual discipline is simply spelling out the political conclusions that its well-evidenced results have, in the teeth of the positivist attempt to impose an alien neutrality upon the human sciences.

This is illustrated by a story about Marx. Annenkov recalls the following exchange of views between Marx and the utopian socialist Weitling (I omit parts of the passage for brevity):

Marx raised his head, turned to Weitling and said: 'Tell us, Weitling, you who have made such a noise in Germany with your preaching: on what grounds do you justify your activity and what do you intend to base it on in the future?'

... With a serious, somewhat worried face [Weitling] started to explain that his aim was not to create new economic theories but to adopt those that were most appropriate, as experience in France had shown, to open the eyes of the workers to the horrors of their condition and all the injustices which it had become the motto of the rulers and societies to inflict on them, and to teach them never more to believe any of the promises of the latter, but to rely on themselves, and to organize in democratic and communist associations. . . . Weitling would probably have gone on talking had not Marx checked him with an angry frown and started his reply.

Marx's sarcastic speech boiled down to this: to rouse the population without giving them any firm, well-thought-out reasons for their activity would be simply to deceive them. The raising of fantastic hopes just spoken of, Marx continued, led only to the final ruin and not to the saving of the sufferers. To call to the workers without any strictly scientific ideas or constructive doctrine . . . was equivalent to vain dishonest play at preaching which assumed on the one side an inspired prophet and on the other only gaping asses. . . . Weitling consoled himself for the evening's attacks by . . . the thought that his modest spadework was perhaps of greater weight for the common cause than criticism and armchair analysis of doctrines far from the world of suffering and afflicted people.

On hearing these last words Marx finally lost control of himself and thumped so hard with his fist on the table that the lamp on it rang and shook. He jumped up saying: 'Ignorance never yet helped anybody!' (quoted in McLellan, 1973: 156–7)

At the purely personal level, one can't help feeling that Marx was a bit unkind to poor Weitling, who after all was a decent enough fellow, as Marx himself must have believed, for he gave Weitling considerable financial help. But the issue at stake was clear: do we start from a political commitment ungrounded in knowledge of reality and select our theoretical beliefs pragmatically – one might say cynically – for their capacity to convince others of the same commitment; or do we take pains to discover how the world really is, and base our politics on that?

Critical Realism

So far, this chapter has been a general defence of realism, and I have said nothing directly about the form of realism which I favour – that which has recently come to be known as critical realism. As a result, three large question marks stand over what I have written. A few brief remarks on critical realism will point in the direction of some answers.

First, I have suggested that it is objective, factual discourse which generates practical – for instance, political – conclusions. Yet positivist social scientists equate objective science with neutral science, and many anti-positivists accept this equation and reject objectivity along with neutrality. Furthermore, most philosophers other than critical realists think that it is a straightforward logical fallacy to derive an 'ought' from an 'is'. Hence Marx is commonly accused of 'importing' value judgements into his theory when he is writing about exploitation. Yet a careful reading of Marx on exploitation (in *Capital* vol. 1 (1976)) shows that this concept is rigorously defined in terms of objectively specified economic relations. Indeed, Marx even appears to hold, perhaps oversanguinely, that the rate of exploitation could be measured. At the same time, any worker reading this account (I say nothing of a capitalist reading it) will, if convinced by it, conclude that he or she has a legitimate self-interest both in fighting for the maximum wages and minimum hours obtainable within capitalism, and in working towards the expropriation of capital by the workers. One reply to the positivist is simply to point to Marx's account of exploitation and say 'see how it's done? There's no trickery here. No evaluative cards hidden up Marx's sleeve.' But critical realism provides a more philosophical refutation of the 'is/ought' dichotomy. Roy Bhaskar points out that among the objects of social science are both beliefs and that which those beliefs are about. So it may show both that a given belief is false and that it is necessary to the society of which it is a part, in the senses both that it is necessarily generated by that society and that it is required for the functioning of that society. Given that we should believe what is true, that is a prima facie case against such a society. And that we should believe what is true is not an arbitrary value judgement, but follows from what belief is.

This theory of Roy Bhaskar's, spelt out in his *Scientific Realism and Human Emancipation* (1986) is known as the theory of *explanatory critiques*, that is, explanations which criticize an institution, not in addition to, but by virtue of, explaining it. Such critiques are characteristic of all the three 'masters of suspicion' – Marx, Nietzsche (where it is, however, in tension with his sporadically pragmatist account of truth) and Freud (for whom, in a sense, explanatory critique is the whole substance of his theory and practice). Marx's account of the wage form presents this as an inevitable and, from a capitalist point of view, functional feature of capitalist society. Yet it is a delusive one, which good social science can show to be false. It is just this capacity to contradict such appearances which makes social science emancipatory. And to contradict appearances, social science must assume that what is true is not the same thing as what is held to be true – that is, it must make realist assumptions about truth.

Of course, Marx does not only or even mainly denounce capitalism because it generates false beliefs, but because it exploits people and produces in a way indifferent to human needs. But in the first place, it can only get away with doing so because it hides its own nature from those it exploits and deprives by means of the sort of delusive appearance that explanatory critiques expose. And in the second place, once the supposed logical wall between facts and values has been broken down, the way is open for other sorts of explanatory critique. For instance, if it is shown that a given system necessarily frustrates satisfiable human needs, then that is also grounds (other things being equal) for abolishing that system. It does not entail this criticism with logical necessity, as do the first sort of explanatory critique. But unless one believes that there is a logical gulf between facts and values, it is very difficult to see any reason for resisting the inference from 'system S necessarily frustrates satisfiable human needs' to 'system S has to go (other things being equal)'. There is a full account of the varieties of explanatory critique in chapter 6 of my *Critical Realism* (1994).

The second question is that some of my language, and indeed my example of Maya Abbott, makes it look all too easy to practise realism in the human sciences. All Laing and Esterson had to do was to look at Mr and Mrs Abbott to see what they were doing, and denying to themselves that they were doing. It is rarely so easy. The point is rather that a practice, unless closed by the refusal to question its suppositions, will from time to time collide with reality and be forced to reconsider its position. Take social democratic politics for example. By this I mean the project of bringing about full employment and community provision of adequate health, housing and education, by means of parliamentary politics, and without incursions on private capital and the market economy. It has been tried again and again and has each time collided with reality in the form of market mechanisms and corporate power. For many, no doubt, social democracy is a closed practice. For them, each such collision appears to be a one-off accident. But anyone who takes the trouble to analyse the realities collided with will find themselves to be up against the necessary tendencies of real institutions, and will transform their own practice, either by projecting the transformation of those institutions or by giving up the welfarist aims. But this choice in the UK between Blairism and revolutionary socialism is itself not a arbitrary value judgement, but based on beliefs about what is really possible. If you think that capitalism can be given a social conscience and go on growing in perpetuity, you will opt for Blair. If you think that the developmental tendencies of capitalism are such that if they continue to operate, the days of civilized life and perhaps of any sort of life on earth are numbered in decades rather than centuries, you will not. But these are factual questions. The moral for realist social science is: analyse failures, your own or other people's, for they are collisions with previously uncomprehended realities.

Now this emphasis on failures as disclosing previously hidden structures is only possible on a realist account, and is particularly supported by a critical realist one. First, because if the non-realists are right about truth, then in a sense no one can be wrong about anything. To admit that one might be wrong is to recognize that there is a difference between what is held to be true and what is true. If there is no truth about reality independent of what anyone holds about reality, then everyone may be smugly certain that their own belief is irrefutable. Of course, one might find that ones own belief was a minority belief, a persecuted belief, or worst of all an unfashionable belief ('out of date', as if beliefs were pots of meat paste), and one might be cowardly enough to abandon it on that account. But one could not make mistakes. Non-realism thus licenses the dogmatist, and its prevalence has given rise to a frightening outbreak of dogmatism. Marking dissertations by postmodernist students, one is always coming across phrases like 'but Derrida says that . . .', used as if that clinched the issue and showed all who disagreed to be fools. Thomas Aquinas was never so uncritical of his sources.

Secondly, even if realism and therefore the critical and emancipatory possibilities of knowledge is admitted, one might hold a 'shallow realism' rather than the 'depth realism' that the critical realist movement espouses. By 'shallow realism' I mean what Roy Bhaskar calls 'actualism' – the belief that, while the flux of actual events is real, there are no relatively enduring structures underlying and generating that flux; any laws that there are will be seen as regular conjunctions of one kind of events in that flux with another. This view of things supports precisely the kind of social democratic politics that I have just criticized: one which assumes that we can improve states of affairs without changing the structures that produce those states of affairs; that we can achieve equality, for instance, without expropriating private capital. The repeated and progressively worsening failures of social democratic politics suggest that there are such underlying structures. What they are, it is the task of social science and not realist philosophy to find out. But at least critical realism can make the distinction between 'transforming structures' and 'ameliorating states of affairs', and so make it possible to show why a politics aimed at doing the latter without doing the former may be doomed to failure. (Compare Roy Bhaskar's paper 'Critical realism, social relations and arguing for socialism' in Bhaskar, 1989.) While critical realism does not entail any particular political position, it is no accident that it tends to go with standpoints further left than social democracy.

The third question is how, apart from non-neutrality and concentration on the analysis of failures, would realist social science differ from positivist social science. The first point to make about this is that whereas idealism might prescribe a common method for all social scientific disciplines based on the nature of the privileged means of access to knowledge, realism cannot. For a realist, the method in each discipline must be dictated by the peculiar nature of the reality which that discipline studies. Negatively though, critical realism can give a few warnings. Its analysis of the nature of experiments shows that their relevant features which make them so fruitful in some natural sciences —namely mainly their ability to isolate single mechanisms which normally operate alongside others – are necessarily absent in the human sciences, for the latter study open systems, that is systems co-determined by a number of mechanisms. So-called experiments in the human sciences generally imitate only certain accidental or secondary features of experiments, such as their artificiality or capacity for mathematicization. And since it is only in experimental conditions that accurate predictions are possible, the human sciences cannot be predictive, or at least no more confidently so than meteorology, which likewise makes its forecasts in open systems, with notorious results. In place of predictions of what event B will follow what event A, of which the human sciences have never managed to find plausible examples, they should specify what *tendencies* given institutions will have: capitalism will tend to lead to larger and larger firms (Marx), a liquid capital market will tend to lead to the dominance of speculation over enterprise (Keynes) and so on.

Finally, since it is experiment which, by isolating abstract mechanisms, makes the measured and accurate use of abstract concepts possible, non-experimental sciences should be much less confident about their abstractions, and should keep their eyes firmly fixed on concrete particulars, the detailed analysis of which is the sole source of their abstract concepts. Freud's analysis of dreams on the assumption that symbols have meaning only in terms of the individual dreamer's unconscious is to be preferred to statistical analyses of large samples of dreams, which necessarily turn a blind eye to individual meanings. I have discussed this at some length in my paper 'Scientific realism in the human world: the case of psychoanalysis' (1981), and in the final chapter of my *Critical Realism* (1994). It coincides with Lenin's prescription for Marxist social science: the concrete analysis of the concrete conjuncture.

In short, my opinion is that orientation towards practice and particularly towards its failures, and orientation towards the depth analysis of concrete particulars, are the nearest things to methodological prescriptions from realism for the human sciences. And the non-neutrality of the objective findings of the human sciences, their capacity to contradict appearances and entail revolutionary conclusions, is the chief political relevance of realism in the human sciences. I have expounded these practical implications at greater length in the conclusion to my book *Scientific Realism and Socialist Thought* (1989), and in chapters 4 and 5 of my *Socialist Reasoning* (1990).

References

Bhaskar, R. (1977) *A Realist Theory of Science*. Hemel Hempstead: Harvester.
Bhaskar, R. (1979) *The Possibility of Naturalism*. Hemel Hempstead: Harvester.
Bhaskar, R. (1986) *Scientific Realism and Human Emancipation*. London: Verso.
Bhaskar, R. (1989) *Reclaiming Reality*. London: Verso.
Collier, A. (1981) 'Scientific realism in the human world: the case of psychoanalysis', *Radical Philosophy*, 29: 8–18.
Collier, A. (1989) *Scientific Realism and Socialist Thought*. Hemel Hempstead: Harvester.
Collier, A. (1990) *Socialist Reasoning*. London: Pluto.
Collier, A. (1994) *Critical Realism*. London: Verso.
Heidegger, M. (1967) *Being and Time*. Oxford: Blackwell.
Laing, R.D. and Esterson, A. (1970) *Sanity, Madness and the Family*. Harmondsworth: Penguin.
Marx, K. (1976) *Capital*. Harmondsworth: Penguin.
Marx, K. and Engels, F. (1970) *The German Ideology*, Part One. London: Lawrence and Wishart.
McLellan, D. (1973) *Karl Marx*. London: Macmillan.
Murray, M. (ed.) (1978) *Heidegger and Modern Philosophy*. New Haven and London: Yale University Press.
Pateman, T. (1972) 'Sanity, madness and the problem of knowledge', *Radical Philosophy*, 1: 22–3.
Thomson, G. (1955) *The First Philosophers*. London: Lawrence and Wishart.

5

What is to be done?
(With Apologies to Lenin!)

Ruth Merttens

> Words and language are not wrappings in which things are packed for the com-
> merce of those who write and speak. It is in words and language that things first
> come into being and are. (Steiner, 1978: 41)

This chapter explores the relation between theory and practice, with particular reference to education. It is based upon my experiences as the director of
an educational intervention project called IMPACT. Started in 1985,
IMPACT is currently operating in over 40 LEAs and thousands of schools. It
provides a means by which parents become involved in their children's learning of maths, or of English, through the use of teacher-selected take-home
tasks which are completed in collaboration with an adult/older sibling. The
project also incorporates many hundreds of schools in the USA, Canada,
Europe, Africa and Australia. The difficulty for those involved both in a project which overtly attempts to change practice, and also in the struggle to
reflect such work within the context of current thinking in the social sciences in the wake of writers such as Foucault, Derrida, Bourdieu and Lacan,
is plain. The effort to relate what one is doing to what one is thinking or reading is often too schizophrenic for comfort. There are those who would argue
that this discomfort is precisely the point; that the two activities are *in principle* not interconnected, but anyone of average sensibility, as Kate Soper puts
it, will be unable 'to espouse the post-modernist position and practise the
modes of . . . dissociation that are the logical implication of some of their critiques' (1990: 13).

When it comes to the point, many of us find ourselves persuaded only
momentarily by the view that there is nothing which is experienced which is
not constructed through discourse, and hence agree that, 'by severing the
reference to a non-linguistic determining reality . . . discourse theory plunges
us into an uncontrolled – and arbitrary – relativism for which the aspiration
to truth ceases to be even a regulative idea' (ibid.). For people working during
the day-time on an intervention initiative and during the night time on an
attempt to theorize this work, the 'aspiration to truth' becomes the source of
much 'angst', if they are not to feel themselves similar, in a lesser degree, to
George Steiner's (1972: 36) SS guard practising Bach's fugues by night and
performing his duties in Auschwitz during the day.

Three related aspects of current theory underpin these anxieties. The first two have their origins in literary theory or semiotics – Eco, Derrida, Paul de Man. The third arises out of the post-Foucauldian debates surrounding the role of expert discourses in the construction of subjectivity.

Language and Reality: Meaning Destabilized

The first strand concerns the unhinging of the connection between language and reality, and the insistence upon the instability of all meaning. There can no longer be said to be any unproblematic theoretical conception of language as 'representing' some non-linguistic reality. The assumption that signs reflect real things, events or experiences has been replaced by a formative and rhetorical notion of language as constructing 'reality' rather than 'representing' it. To paraphrase Lacan (1966), the world of words creates the world of things. This disturbs the belief in the transparency of what we say or write, the idea that our words can have a final or 'grounded' meaning. In this sense, then, it is not that lies and half-truths, professional or otherwise, are possible or even probable but that the aspiration to truth itself becomes unattainable. By disconnecting the connection between sign and reality, truth becomes relegated to its position as merely a style effect of discourse.

The abandonment of an uncritical belief that language reflects reality, either truthfully or not as the case may be, has been seen by many as tantamount to a refusal of the very category of a knowable external and physical reality, and eventually leads to a state where ontology and epistemology are one and the same. Derrida (1967) characterizes the claim that a text can be 'totalized' (that is, the extent to which a 'final meaning' may be produced by reference to an origin, end, centre or ground) as *theological* – 'God is the beginning and the end of all things' (quoted in Levinas, 1982). Steiner, too, emphasizes the extent to which the meaning of meaning is a transcendent postulate, and is one which the deconstructionists refute. To assume a ground to meaning is to wager on transcendence, he argues: 'Deconstruction rules that the very concept of "meaning-fulness", of a congruence, even problematic, between signifier and signified, is theological . . .' (Steiner, 1989: 119).

It would be difficult to exaggerate the theoretical weight – and I use the term with all its emotive connotations advisedly – of this decoupling of word and world. What Mallarme saw as the 'covenant of reference' is broken; words refer not to experience or being but to other words. The consequence of this shift is, philosophically speaking, an ontological nihilism. Thus, any claim to truth or falsity is always 'dissolved by the textuality in which it adheres' (Steiner, 1989: 123). The effects of this sea-change in our approach to truth is evinced in almost all aspects of modern life. The seeker after truth becomes a stylist or a politician rather than a disciple; one who is interested in rhetoric rather than accuracy. And in our professional lives, we cope with the multiplicity of 'truths'; the only difference between one account and another is one of rhetorical modes – this account is 'professional', that one is 'anecdotal', this one is 'objective' and that one is 'subjective'. The question of truth cannot arise.

The Birth of the Reader in the Death of the Author

The idea that meanings are not purely a function of authorial intention and are instead produced by the reader(s) has had profound effects upon work in literary criticism, in cultural and media studies, and is currently producing a series of ripples in the already troubled waters of research in the social sciences, including education. Following Barthes's assertion that meaning can no longer be thought of as originating in the mind of the author, and emerges only in the act of reading (Barthes, 1977), writers in these areas disputed the degree to which the text could be said to produce the reader or indeed, *the* reading. Stephen Heath (1981), wrestling with this issue, stated that texts are neither closed, in the sense of containing a 'final grounded meaning', nor absolutely open, in the sense of being able to mean anything at all.

But as Barthes reminds us, the death of the author is the birth of the reader. Readers *read* texts; they 'elicit the strategies which the author has employed, consciously or unconsciously; they make visible the cunning, the ruses, the displacements between signs and emptiness inherent in the author's game . . .' (see Steiner, 1989: 126). But this 'game' has no possible winner. There is no longer any privileged judge, interpreter or explicator. There is no way of privileging any one reading over any other. Certainly, there is no decided or decidable meaning. No longer, as professionals, can we refer with confidence to 'the truth of the matter'.

In the social sciences in general and in education in particular, the acceptance of a plurality of interpretations of any text accompanied by a refusal to ascribe validity on the basis of an 'accurate' representation of reality, appears to have successfully pulled the rug out from under any partnership between theory and practice in terms of advice or prescription. To what extent can it be said to be possible to generate a reading of a particular set of practices, on the basis of which advice as to their subsequent modification will be offered, while simultaneously maintaining that no one reading can be said to describe 'what is really going on'? While remaining sympathetic to a cautious avoidance of definitive accounts, it is, I believe, essential that we make some attempt to bridge the widening rift between those who act 'at the chalk face' and those who theorize those practices. That one account is more faithful than another, that not all readings of a text or a context are equal with regard to truth, that it matters which reading, which account, we believe; these are the maxims of those committed to changing practice for the better. Without a faith that one way of working may be fairer, more democratic, less cruel, more egalitarian than another, *and* that it may faithfully be so described, we are unable to commit ourselves to any course of action or, indeed, to offer any assistance to others.

Related to the above arguments surrounding the multiple possible readings of any text and the demise of an overriding authorial intention, is the scepticism with which any notion of generalization has gradually come to be regarded. General statements appear suspect in one of two ways: either they involve a type of essentialism, usually predicated upon some notion, implicit or explicit, of how 'human nature' is, or they attempt to unify the subject, to create what is termed 'a totalizing discourse'. In both cases the appeal to a universal object, such as 'parents', masks the plurality of concrete differences between parents and evades the diversity of actual parents and parenting practices.

Putting this in a slightly different way, it is fair to say that post-structuralism has been associated with a refusal of essentialism and a celebration of difference. That is to say, the unifying idea of a common 'us' or 'we' which underlies such groupings as 'parents', 'children' or even 'teachers', has been rejected in favour of an emphasis on the plurality of practice and of experience which characterize actual teachers, parents or children. Rather than a focus on those common features which may be said to unite us, post-structuralism, at the level of theory, draws our attention repeatedly to the particular rather than the general, to the contingently specific rather than the necessary or essential, in short, to the inevitable differences.

However, once again we find the rug being pulled out from under any symbiotic relation between theory and practice, since to reform practice is essentially a matter of 'making common cause' and of drawing general inferences from specific instances. Without this commonality, this 'common cause', it becomes impossible to suggest general remedies for 'common' problems. As theorists, if not as practitioners, we flounder in a welter of particularities – specificity is all there is, and advice transferable from the specific is quite literally theoretically non-existent. While wanting to eschew the construction of stereotypical 'subjectivities' possessed of a unity all their own, such as the 'parents' mentioned above, we may nevertheless wish to allow for statements which, in that they discriminate between world and text, enable us to suggest qualities or constraints endemic to certain types of context.

Legitimating Practices

The third aspect of theory with which we, as practitioners in education, have to engage as problematizing both our experience and our activities, concerns Foucault's insistence upon the effectivity of expert discourses, in relation specifically to their normalizing and disciplining functions. Education may be viewed as one such discourse, an 'expert system' through which certain practices (such as 'teaching' and 'learning') come to be described and categorized. As we go about our daily lives in schools, classrooms and families we create institutions, rituals and routines where what it is to teach and learn comes to be defined and reproduced, and, indeed, our very identities, as pupils, as teachers, as learners, as managers and so on, come to be constructed and sustained.

Of course, we now take it as read that education as a professional discourse, together with that of child psychology, has provided the rhetorics, the codes, the behavioural strategies and the forms of knowledge by means of which the intimate practices of families and classrooms and the most personal and private experiences of adults and children come to be described, evaluated and monitored. Nikolas Rose (1989) has provided an account of how this normalizing function of the human sciences is instantiated through the detail of our everyday lives.

So the forms of language we use, the polarities we adopt when discussing each other, events, life, the universe and everything – clever/stupid, teacher/pupil, mad/sane – are chronically embedded in discursive structures through which particular institutions and forms of authority are sustained. In this way, teachers and pupils at all stages in education *routinely and unconsciously* reproduce the conditions under which these expert systems are maintained. This process, which Foucault calls '*disciplining*', reinforces the cultural assumptions and ideologies through which the social order is preserved. Of course, these practices, these ways of acting and speaking, are conceived as 'natural', as 'the way things are' by those involved in education.

This is to remind ourselves that education is an important site of social regulation. We should, as Foucault (1972: 49) warned us, treat discourses 'as practices that systematically form the objects of which they speak'. However, not all discourses are equal with respect to each other, and neither are they insulated, one from the other. Power relations are inscribed in discursive practices, but discourse, as Foucault also reminds us, does suggest a subversion as well as a sustaining of these forms of authority and canonical texts. Human subjectivity is not unproblematically produced via discursive practices. And discourses are not water-tight or discreet. Indeed they may be said to 'leak', to be *in*discreet.

The effect of Foucault's inspired analysis here is to reinforce a warning. The very judgements and advice provided by the educational 'experts' must be read both as legitimating practices and as of necessity produced from within the very discourse through which the 'problem' itself is constituted. To make this point concrete, if we take a situation where a child is failing to learn to read and the parents have come to us for advice, we are aware simultaneously of two things:

1 Any advice is produced within the expert discourse of education which has itself constructed the problem qua problem. The 'learning difficulty' is only a learning difficulty at all because of the norms and expectations, the identities of reader/non-reader, which are defined through these educational practices.

2 It is impossible to see how, *at the level of theory*, we can, as practitioners, privilege one set of practices over another. What gives us the right, other than an act of faith, to say 'you should do this . . .' or 'doing this is better than doing that'? Upon what theoretical basis do we advise at all?

Stories

On IMPACT, we have been exploring one way out of this dilemma. This has involved both a method of implementing the intervention itself and also a means of theorizing its implantation into the schooling system. I want to suggest that the move from experience to theory can best be accomplished by means of stories. Stories, I shall argue, are *useful*, a cardinal notion in this argument. Their usefulness can take many forms: as cultural representations, as rhetorical devices, as therapeutic tools. But here we are concerned with the story as a means of generating both prescriptions and generalizations.

The approach I shall develop rests, as I said, on the notion of story. The exploration of 'everyday life' beliefs and scenarios through the idea of narrative is, of course, not new, and more than one writer has argued that social existence itself is structured by controlling narratives which organize and focalize our ways of acting, seeing and feeling. As de Certeau writes, 'the listener walks all day long through the forest of narratives, . . . these have a providential and predestinating function: they organize in advance our work, our celebrations and even our dreams' (1984: 84). This perspective is reinforced by Jeremy Tambling when he argues that 'Narrative seems not only to affect all our thinking, but to be a mode of thinking, the only way it is possible to think . . .' (1992: 109). Here he is clearly following Barthes's (1977) idea that narrative 'is simply there, like life itself'. However, I want to retreat a little from this broader notion of narrative as a constitutive and articulating function in the practices of everyday life, and to focus attention upon a rather less ambitious, almost 'naïve' idea of a story.

Stories have been the single most important ingredient in the intervention side of our work – persuading and enabling teachers to use IMPACT. The in-service training programme relies heavily upon the use of stories, and this may be one reason why it has proved unusually popular and effective, in terms of the actual numbers of teachers, parents and schools who go off and actually follow the suggestions. The stories we tell are oral verbalizations of our experiences, amusing, touching, puzzling, even contradictory, gained while doing IMPACT. They are 'real' stories, and in the words of Walter Benjamin, 'An orientation toward practical interests is characteristic of many born storytellers. . . . Gotthelf gave his peasants agricultural advice, Nodier concerned himself with the perils of gas light and Hebel slipped bits of scientific instruction for his readers into his *Schatzkastlein*. . . . All this points to the nature of every real story. It contains, openly or covertly, something *useful*' (1970: 86). The stories we tell on IMPACT share this quality; they take our personal experiences, and the reported experiences of others, and turn them into the experience of the listeners. They are 'useful' in Benjamin's terms, although at the same time they are primarily neither explanatory or informative.

'Stories are the means by which values are made coherent in particular situations' (de Certaux, 1984). Hence, I believe, they may provide us not only with a proven and excellent means of motivating changes in practice, that is, of providing prescriptions, but also a valuable probe by means of which a way of theorizing those practices, involving the production of more generalized statements, may be constructed. Stories allow us to describe '*what is going on*' in such a way as to enable a dialogue between our own values and those implicit within it, and hence the generation of prescriptive readings.

As Bettelheim (1975: 89) points out, it is the crucial amalgam of elements of commonality with highly specific readings which enables the power of the story. Although Bettelheim is speaking particularly of fairy tales and fables in the context of psychoanalytic or psychological events or experiences, the analogy to a more general story and a wider audience holds good for this aspect of his thesis. There is an important sense in which a story speaks uniquely to each listener – 'The fairy tale is therapeutic because the patient *finds his own solutions*' (Bettelheim, 1975: 89; added emphasis). Stories afford a much greater degree of individual interpretation and extrapolation to other specific contexts than do explanatory or informative texts which, while inevitably furnishing a range of readings, *rhetorically* constrain probable (even possible) *sensible* interpretations and thereby delimit the possibilities for discursive hegemonic variation. Again, to quote Benjamin, 'The most extraordinary things, marvellous things, are related with the greatest accuracy, but the psychological connection of the event is not forced on the reader. It is left up to him to interpret things the way he understands them, and thus the narrative achieves an amplitude that information lacks' (1970: 89).

In an effort to demonstrate the ways in which stories allow us to encompass the move from the particular to the general, from the construction of what 'is' to the suggestion of what 'might be', from description to prescription, I shall draw upon two of the stories we have used previously. Neither of these should be seen as case studies. They are not representations of extensive transcriptions of taped data (although their genesis can be traced to data recorded as a part of the research carried out on IMPACT). These *are* stories, and I have attempted to keep them 'explanation-free'. Walter Benjamin attributes the almost 'universal' quality of stories, that they can be told and heard in times and places far from the original setting, that they will make the teller's experience the experience of the listener, precisely to the lack of explanation; 'No event any longer comes to us without being shot through with explanation. In other words, by now almost nothing that happens benefits storytelling; almost everything benefits information. Actually, it is half the art of storytelling to keep a story free from explanation as one reproduces it' (ibid.).

Story 1

A quiet IMPACT classroom. The teacher is sitting on her chair surrounded by children on the rug. They are discussing the maths task the children have done at home. One small boy, A, is insistent that he had done his. 'We drew a map!', he says loudly. 'It was wicked fun!' The teacher soothes him and turns to the maps drawn by other children. 'Here's a nice map.' She points to a careful map drawn by one of the children. 'And this one is interesting.' She holds up a much messier map drawn on the back of the IMPACT sheet which outlined the task. 'You have drawn the post boxes, Gail. That was very observant of you. You must have looked very hard to notice where those were.' Gail is pink with pleasure at having hers singled out. 'My Nan showed me them', she explains. The discussion continues and the teacher manages to compliment all the children on some detail of their work. Then it is story time, and she allows A to choose the story. Although at seven years old he is one of the older children in the class, he cannot yet read and when he brings her the book he has chosen, the teacher allows him to sit beside her so that he can see the text as she reads. This is a favoured position and A is happy as the class ends and he goes to get his things to go home. 'I *did* do that map, Miss!', he says, as he pulls on his coat and runs out into the playground.

A is a child who has had quite a few difficulties settling in class and in the past had been given to violent and uncontrolled outbursts of rage. His background of a violent father, from whom he and his sister and mum were now separated, was believed by the teachers to account for many of his problems. Gradually, they felt, he had begun to trust the teachers and his fellow pupils in the school, and he was now calmer and less easily enraged and appeared to have more friends in the playground. However, he was one of only two children in the class who never brought back his IMPACT. Some of the others were a little haphazard, but they all did some of the tasks set, and the general opinion of both children and parents was extremely positive. The teacher kept a record of all their comments, written into their weekly IMPACT diaries, and she only rarely got a remark which suggested that the task had not been suitable or enjoyable. Indeed, on one occasion when she had been away, and the children had not been given an IMPACT activity on Friday as usual, the voices raised in complaint the following Monday, not only by the parents but also the children, surprised her by the genuine regret they expressed in not having had an activity to share that weekend.

Each week, the teacher discussed the task they had done at home and commented on their work. She would then pin up their IMPACT on a 'Homework' board which was right in the entrance to the room so that any parents who came in could see it. Since most children brought back most weeks' IMPACT, she would make sure that those who had not had a chance to do it at home, got a chance to perform something very similar in class. However, A was always reluctant to do this, asserting with great certainty that he had done his IMPACT at home. Since he was collected by a child-minder, the teacher did not see his mother on a daily basis as she did some of the other children's parents, and so she had not been able to ask her where A's IMPACT diary, not seen since the first IMPACT activity went home, had got to. She intended to mention this at the end-of-term parent interviews, when each parent was given the opportunity to discuss their child's progress on an individual basis with the teacher.

It was not until this occasion that A's protestations about IMPACT took on a new light. The teacher was sitting waiting for the next parent. It was the last one of the evening and since she had already seen eight parents and discussed each of their children with them, she felt tired and relieved that she would soon be 'shutting up shop' as she put it to herself. A's mother staggered in carrying two large plastic bags. Never the world's most organized or tidy parent, she looked about as tired as a person could get. 'I'm sorry I'm late!', she said, sitting heavily down on a child-sized chair at the low table. 'I couldn't get A to go to bed, and I can't leave him with the lady downstairs if he's still running around. She'll only mind him if he's in bed!' Then, before the teacher's astonished eyes she tipped the contents of both plastic bags on to the table. About ten IMPACT sheets and their associated work spilt out – maps, a small animal made of play dough (recipe given courtesy of IMPACT), a number-line with objects carefully stuck on to it – all the paraphernalia of a term's maths at home. 'I thought you might want this', A's mum said. 'A is always telling me to bring it in so I thought now was probably as good a time as any.' There, amidst all the evidence of A and his mother's shared maths, lay the IMPACT diary. It was crumpled, it had a smear of what looked suspiciously like jam on the cover, but it was quite definitely filled in.

Story 2

This parent was rung on the last day of term by the secondary school attended by her son. She was informed over the 'phone that he had been involved in an 'incident' in which he was extremely rude and that the school needed to talk to her immediately. Since her son was coming up to his final examinations year, this alarmed her not a little. With visions of his being expelled from school for some unmentionable and outrageous behaviour (what sort of an 'incident'?), she rushed up to the school. After a short wait in the school office, she was shown into a room containing the history teacher, the head of year, the head of history and a deputy head. As it so happened, three out of the four were men. The year tutor opened the conversation, 'I do hope you'll forgive the fact that it's four against one!' A somewhat shocked response, 'I hope we don't have to see it that way.' Not an auspicious start. The son-in-question was not invited in, but out of the corner of her eye as she was ushered in she could see his miserable and awkward form hovering uncertainly on the corner of the stairs across the corridor.

The interview proceeded. The year tutor explained that F (her son) had been asked by the history teacher to remove some chewing gum from his mouth, it being a contravention of the school rules for the children to chew gum. F had retorted that he was not chewing gum. Further investigation of the matter proved him to be correct, he was in fact chewing his pen lid. The teacher, by now extremely irritated, insisted that he throw the pen lid into the bin. After a short pause, F had complied with this request, albeit in what the teacher described as 'an insolent fashion'. The teacher had then insisted that, as a punishment for his rudeness, F should finish the lesson working outside the door in the corridor. Again, after some hesitation, F had complied, in the same 'insolent fashion'. At the end of the lesson, the teacher had prevented F from leaving with the others. She had demanded an apology for his behaviour.

F, outraged, had refused to offer this, claiming that he had complied with every request the teacher had made. To the charge of insolence he had no comment to make, reiterating several times, 'But I did do what you said.' The teacher had then said that, since F refused to apologize for his insolent and rude behaviour, she had no alternative but to call his parents. Whereupon, F had agreed that was what she should do.

This was all explained in the measured and eminently reasonable tones of the year head. The parent had an immediate and intuitive vision of the whole incident. She could see how the teacher had been caught in the situation of having put herself on the line, 'Spit out whatever you're chewing!' She knew F to be headstrong, wayward and, like many windswept teenagers today, full of totally unwarranted and ephemeral certainties. Both the major participants in the drama had, for the sake of their credibility with their audience, to be seen to triumph. A recipe for disaster. She felt tired; it was, for them all, the end of a long hard year. She also felt an immense sympathy – almost a tenderness – for both the teacher and her son. It was as if they were both engaged in playing the leading parts in a play they neither of them much liked.

She began on a conciliatory note. Obviously there was no excuse for rudeness, and she would personally make it plain to F that in future there was to be no insolence, dumb or otherwise. The teacher concerned interrupted her attempt at a rough apology. 'F was very rude. And I have to tell you, Mrs X that this is not the first time I have had to speak to him about his general attitude. He is often insolent and he seems to lead the others astray.' The parent was quick to respond, 'Does F work? Is he behind on any of his assignments? If you set work in class, does he do it, or is he disruptive?' These seemed to her to be important questions. If F was disruptive or behind with his work, this 'incident' started to assume a quite different significance. The head of history replied quietly that F was a diligent student; that, as far as he knew, F was up to date with his academic work and that there was no cause for concern in this area. The problem, the history teacher reiterated, was one of attitude. 'I don't like his attitude', she explained for the third or fourth time. The parent began to feel less conciliatory, and more protective. It seemed almost as if F was being condemned for being F. At this point, the head of year seemed to feel that his colleague needed support. 'Yes; you see Mrs X, F does seem to have a real problem with his attitude. I've spoken to him about it before. He seems to be getting more and more insolent – nothing too extreme, just a sort of rudeness and a desire to be a smart alec in front of his mates. I've had complaints from several staff . . .'

As the discussion – and the complaints – escalated, the parent felt herself to be increasingly the subject of an implicit set of almost indefinable criticisms. F was rude – not disruptive, not lazy or inattentive, nothing you could put your finger on precisely, but rude. And hence she was, by implication, failing as his mother. But as her sense of isolation within the group increased, so her irritation also mounted. 'I think it might help if we had F in on this conversation', she said, with hesitation. The year tutor leapt on her suggestion with evident relief. 'Certainly, certainly', he said, 'I'll just call him in.'

F entered the room, and immediately the parent felt the shock of his presence. He looked guilty and defiant. She had known him before like this; when he had, aged four, cut his sister's hair, when he had, aged 5, truanted from his infant school to go fishing for tadpoles with a friend, and on innumerable occasions since. There was only one chair left in the room and that happened to be the only high hard seat. F perched on it, looking like a bedraggled and unhappy captive bird. The year tutor asked F if he had anything to say about this incident. F, somewhat hesitantly at first and then with increasing assurance as he recalled what had happened, described the whole event as he saw it. He had not been chewing gum. He had been wrongly accused, in front of the whole class. Nevertheless, he had complied with the teacher's request to put his pen lid in the waste bin, again 'in front of the whole class'. He had then been asked to work outside . . . and so on through the whole sorry story again. The history teacher interrupted, her irritation and impatience showing through, 'Surely F, you are not denying that you are frequently rude and difficult. This is not the first time I have had to speak to you about your attitude.' F, whose gaze had never left the floor, looked up. 'You're always getting at me', he said. 'The others do the same things and you never tell them off. Lots of people were sucking their pen lids but you always pick on me!' 'Well, that's because your attitude is affecting the whole class, F', retorted the teacher. F started to argue, but was interrupted by the head of year. 'I don't think, F, that arguing like this is getting us anywhere. Surely you must see that we cannot have rude behaviour in this school. We have to preserve our standards. I appreciate that in your previous school, standards may have been a little different, but here you will have to learn that we do expect you to stick to the rules and behave according to them. You have been here long enough now to know what we expect.'

The debate wound round in decreasing and depressed circles for a while, with F saying little and each teacher contributing their perception. Finally the parent thought that perhaps they had all said enough. 'Well, hopefully we can move on from here in a more positive way. I shall certainly make sure that F understands the importance of being polite and of working hard during lessons. I am sure he has appreciated the gravity of the situation, and hopefully next year we can all start off on a new note.' She could see the head of year and the head of history looking relieved and preparing to stand up to shake her by the hand and, with a few polite pleasantries, call the incident closed.

But the history teacher was having none of it. Perhaps she felt that there had been altogether too much equivocation, or perhaps she remained so irritated with F that she had to press for further punishment. 'Well, I do not consider the incident finished and done with', she said, 'and I certainly cannot think of having F back in my class until he has offered me a full apology for the way he has behaved.' This stunned the rest into silence. After a pause, the head of year rallied himself. Perhaps he felt that the time had come to show which 'side' he was really on, or perhaps he was aware of her implicit criticism that he had been too lenient, that he had not taken the 'incident' seriously enough. 'Certainly,' he said, 'F cannot continue to attend his history class if he cannot apologize for what is, after all, rude and unmannerly behaviour.' The parent sat still and quiet. She felt strangely detached from the situation. It was as if it had suddenly ceased to be personal at all and had instead become a matter of politics. 'I will wait,' she thought, 'and see if they are actually prepared to throw him out of his examination class for this. Then I shall ask them to help me get all the facts straight so that I can be clear about it when I write to complain.' But she said nothing aloud, staring hard at the patch of floor in front of her.

There was a long silence. Perhaps the head of history was wondering how to get out of this corner into which they all seemed to have painted themselves. Then F spoke. 'I am very sorry for the way I behaved', he said, fixing the history teacher with a serious and unwavering stare. 'I apologize for my attitude. I will attempt to behave better in future.' This took everyone by surprise. The parent was amazed and impressed. She felt a sense of admiration for F who had so effectively called their bluff. The head of year rallied first. 'Well, thank you F. That was very nicely said', he replied, with a hasty glance at the history teacher to make sure that she was not intending to throw any more spokes in the wheel, now that he had, so to speak, got the apples safely back in the cart, and the whole thing on its way again. The head of history, too, was inclined to be conciliatory. 'Good, well let's hope that we can all get off to a good start next year. After all, you have your exams to think about F. You're a bright boy and you will want to work hard . . .' The history teacher, having only limited options now available to her, decided to accept the situation gracefully. 'I would like to say that I'm sure, F, that you will do very well in your history if you continue to work hard.' With a few polite remarks, the head of year got to his feet and, with an almost audible relief, ushered them all out of the door.

Walking home together, the parent and her son were silent, each thinking their own thoughts. He was the first to break the silence, 'You know, Mum,' he said wryly, 'there were six people in that room and one of them had no power at all. You didn't have much power, but I had none at all.'

Conclusion

It may be complained that the story is being used here where, in more orthodox educational writing, a transcript or case study would have had its place. However, there are two differences to be noted. First, a difference of *function*. In other, seemingly similar, analyses of school or home situations in which sections of transcript are analysed to *reveal* the shifting power relations, the pivotal notion is that of 'subject positions' or 'positioning in discourse' (see Walkerdine, 1988, 1989; Walkerdine and Lucey, 1989). We are invited to witness the ways in which subjects come to be differentially constituted through social practices (discourses), themselves predicated upon hegemonic forces necessarily invisible to those embedded, or, perhaps we should say, *inscribed*, in the particular discursive practices under analysis. As Jeff Vass (1992) has pointed out elsewhere, the use of transcriptions of 'everyday conversation' to persuade it to *reveal* the regulative aspects of an institutional surveillance which produces 'self-policing' subjects fails to allow for a crucial factor. This may be summarized as the *dislocated nature of the operations of power* through discursive practices; 'persons are not the at the centre, fully aware and self-present masters, but have been decentred by these relations to the symbolic order' (Vass, 1992).

What is important in the context of our initial dilemma is the ability of the story, unlike the transcript or case study, to afford a series of *enabling potentials* for action, prescription and interpretation. In the case of the transcripts described above, it is the inevitably deterministic nature of such accounts which fail to animate a vision of 'what might be' rather than of what is, or to provide a means of comparing possible (imagined) alternatives. Transcripts totalize, stories diversify, to paraphrase de Certeau (1984: 107). And we may recall the image of the story as a spring, a source of potential and creative energy. The story enables us to '*recast our own experience as the experience of others*' (Benjamin, 1970: 87; original emphasis). It is the immediacy of the *story as such* which de Certeau emphasizes; 'stories are already practices. They say exactly what they do. They constitute an act which they intend to mean. There is no need to add a gloss that knows what they express without knowing it, nor to wonder what they are the metaphor of' (1984: 80). If we wish to probe deeper, to elucidate their value, de Certeau advocates simple repetition, 'You ask what they "mean". I'll tell them to you again. When someone asked him the meaning of a sonata, it is said, Beethoven merely played it over' (ibid.: 81). We may, if we choose, produce explanations, observations, perspectives – whole sets of constituting or articulating narratives – on the back of the story. But simultaneously the story will suggest new possibilities in terms of our structuring and re-structuring of the social spaces in which we are inscribed.

Stories enable those who are embedded in professional practices to 'go on from here', not only in the sense of being able to continue with their professional activity but, importantly, in terms of being able to generalize and subsequently prescribe or advise, to theorize and then transform the practice. Used as parables, as utilitarian devices, stories have moved and animated teachers, parents and advisers, providing both a rich source of experience and an intoxicating glimpse of future potentialities. *The story starts us on a process of more than interpretation.* We may extrapolate; our own circumstances and experiences may be re-read in the light of the story. Its experiences may, in a real sense, become our own so that we may learn from them. By attending to the story, to its text as text, we can read with a degree of 'tact' (note the etymology of touch), and then follow on.

Stories allow for contingencies – not only in the experiences shared, but in their telling or 'recital' (calling again). A story is never the same twice. Unlike the transcript, which remains the same across the different situations in which it is used, the relationship of the story to the context of its telling, to its audience, is unashamedly confessed. It is this contingent character of the story which enables truth to 'leak', and Lacan reminds us that the 'truth is bound to emerge in some contingent detail' (1966: 801). This is neither the Rortyan relativism of a plurality of factual truths, nor the post-structuralist reduction of the truth dimension to a 'textual truth effect'. It is the recognition that once truth becomes factual accuracy it loses its character of an encounter and becomes 'part of the universal ruling lie' (Žižek, 1991: 54). It is through the contingencies, the lack of objectifying third-person distance, that, as 'encounter', unwarranted, by some felicitous accident, truth, the repressed, emerges. And the story imparts a given text, which demands our attention. All that is left is to manage the encounter and move on.

John Shotter (1989: 134–9) complains that in our researches we have focused attention upon 'external' events, upon third-person actions – what he/she/they did – upon what is supposed to occur 'inside' isolated individuals 'studied "externally" from the point of view of third-person observers, socially uninvolved with them'. But he also reminds us that 'we' need the 'you' to whom we speak, the audience we address, as 'someone to whom it makes sense to address my remarks . . . and whom I can reasonably expect to be moved by them'. Stories, I submit, can assist us in breaking with third-person, passive voice, 'scientific' talk and, acknowledging our positions as 'Is' and 'yous', as moral as well as social agents, enable us to re-cast our own experiences as those of others. In this story-telling, the 'truth' of my experience becomes the truth of your experience. In this recitation, experience is 'passed from mouth to mouth', and in that passage we find a celebration of contingency and specificity at the same time as we can construct the general and the prescriptive. As teachers, as educators and as researchers, all we need is a 'way to go on from here'. Perhaps it is in the ancient art of telling stories that the modern dilemma is to be resolved.

References

Barthes, R. (1977) *Image, Music, Text*. London: Fontana.
Benjamin, W. (1970) 'The Storyteller', in W. Benjamin, *Illuminations*. London: Fontana/Collins.
Bettelheim, B. (1975) *The Uses of Enchantment*. Harmondsworth: Penguin.
Collini, S. (1992) *Introduction to Interpretation and Overinterpretation*. Cambridge: Cambridge University Press
de Certeau, M. (1984) *The Practice of Everyday Life*. Berkeley, CA: University of California Press.
Derrida, J. (1967) 'Violence and metaphysics', in *Writing and Difference* (trans. Alan Bass, 1978). London: Routledge and Kegan Paul.
Eco, U. (1990) 'Interpretation and Overinterpretation'. The Tanner Lectures, Clare Hall, Cambridge.
Foucault, M. (1972) *The Archaeology of Knowledge*. London: Tavistock.
Foucault, M. (1988) 'Technologies of the self', in L. Martin, H. Gutman and P. Hutton (eds), *Technologies of the Self*. London: Tavistock.
Heath, S. (1981) 'Contexts', in S. Heath (ed.), *Questions of Cinema*. London: Macmillan.
Lacan, J. (1966) *Ecrits*. Paris: Editions du Seuil.
Levinas, E. (1982) *De Dieu qui vient a l'idee*. Paris: Vrin.

Rose, N. (1989) *Governing the Soul: The Shaping of the Private Self.* London: Routledge.

Shotter, J. (1989) 'Social accountability and the social construction of "you"', in J. Shotter and K.J. Gergen (eds), *Texts of Identity.* London: Sage.

Soper, K. (1990) *Troubled Pleasures.* London: Verso.

Steiner, G. (1972) *Extraterritorial.* London: Faber and Faber.

Steiner, G. (1978) *Heidegger.* London: Fontana.

Steiner, G. (1989) *Real Presences.* London: Faber and Faber.

Tambling, J. (1992) *Narrative and Ideology.* Milton Keynes: Open University Press.

Vass, J. (1992) 'Apprenticeships in the absence of masters', in R. Merttens and J. Vass (eds), *Ruling the Margins: Problematizing Parental Involvement.* London: University of North London Press.

Vass, J. and Merttens, R. (1990) 'Sensuous cognition: the micro-ethnography of adult–child instructional speech'. Paper delivered at the OMEP conference, Goteborg University, Sweden.

Walkerdine, V. (1988) *The Mastery of Reason.* London: Routledge.

Walkerdine, V. (1989) *Counting Girls Out.* London: Virago Press.

Walkerdine, V. and Lucey, H. (1989) *Democracy in the Kitchen.* London: Virago Press.

Žižek, S. (1991) *For They Know Not What They Do: Enjoyment as a Political Factor.* London: Verso.

6

As One in a Web? Discourse, Materiality and the Place of Ethics

Steven D. Brown and Joan Pujol with Beryl C. Curt

The relationship between psychology and philosophy is, to put it at best, a little strained. As with any long-term commitment, there are numerous histories in circulation, from the romance with logical positivism to the acrimonious parting words spat by William James at 'that nasty little subject' (see Robinson, 1995). The temptation is to draw upon these selectively to produce an account of, say, the 'divorce' of the psychological from the philosophical. The strong current of anti-intellectualism that marks much contemporary cognitive psychology could then be understood as an identity project of the recently estranged.

Perhaps the metaphor of divorce is too strong. A more apposite image might be of a couple where the partners have long since ceased to talk to one another, and have organized their respective everyday business so as to minimize the possibility of any contact. In either case, the point to be emphasized is that it seems often to be a matter of making a choice between either doing psychology or doing philosophy. It is as though one must identify with the one or the other or else chance becoming the recipient of their mutual suspicion and enmity, risk getting 'stuck in the middle'.

There seems little option but to repeat the process. From the outset, then, (if) it needs to be stated: this chapter is not an attempt to present a comprehensive argument concerning ontology: it is not intended as a piece of philosophy. But in making this assertion it does not hold that the discussion cannot participate of the philosophical, in the same manner that statements regarding motivation or belief are not immediately disallowed to a philosopher. Although realism and relativism are at issue, it is plausible to speak to these themes from psychology. It follows that the effects intended are solely confined to the one discipline and are not formulated as a general intervention on what can be known, what can be said to exist and so on. To grasp another nettle, it can also readily be recognized that there are practical mechanisms of exclusion that locate this text 'within the true' of psychology rather than anywhere else (see Foucault, 1972).

This should not be taken as an extended apology. Quite the contrary, there are advantages in speaking from psychology. Some of these are summarized by Deleuze and Guattari's (1986) conception of 'minotorian writing'. The process involves writing into a 'major' language concerns which are alien to it. Deleuze and Guattari's extended example displays how Kafka composed his narratives in German rather than his native Czech; the coruscating results of working in a different major language involved features such as the contraction of textual space, forcing new relations between elements, and the adoption of collective values in the absence of a direct tradition. Rabinow (1995) extends the concept to include writing across different disciplines, notably attempts at inscribing socio-political concerns into science. Utilizing the notion of 'minotorian writing' it is possible to read recent debates in critical or discursive psychology around the merits of realism versus relativism (e.g., Curt, 1994; Greenwood, 1994; Parker, 1990; Potter et al., 1990) not as instances of psychologists trying their hand at philosophy, but instead as strategic attempts at writing limited political and methodological concerns into a major language.

Thus for Parker (1996), the issue is that of establishing a grounding for praxis:

> Insofar as social constructionism helps to develop a historically materialist account of the development of particular forms of social structure, action and experience in a society at a given point in time, it represents a positive addition to the range of conceptual debate in psychology. Insofar as relativism corrodes each and every critical vantage-point on the theories and practices of the discipline of psychology at the very same moment as it bathes psychology in its sceptical light, it represents a danger to radicals who participate in that conceptual debate. (Parker, 1996: 369)

Note that this is not a philosophical plea, based on extensive argument about the state of current epistemology, nor is it an attempt to lay out the sufficient causes of action (as with Harré and Madden, 1975). It is an attempt to clarify the relationship between psychological discourse and those who seek to utilize it.

Similarly with Potter (1996) it is a strategic decision to adopt a stance of methodological relativism (following Collins, 1983) that acts to ground research practice. It is not a formal philosophical position, rather the setting out of 'rules of engagement':

> Methodological relativism means that the analyst is not starting with a set of assumptions about what is true and false in any particular setting and then trying to work out what led some people to get it wrong. Instead, the analyst will be indifferent to whether some set of claims is widely treated by participants as 'true' or 'false'. Truth and falsity can be studied as moves in a rhetorical game, and will be treated as such rather than as prior resources governing analysis, to avoid subordinating the analyst to a current scientific orthodoxy. (Potter, 1996: 40–1)

With both Parker and Potter what results is best characterized as the work of ethics, involving the investing and divesting of responsibilities and the specification of future projects through the adoption of imperatives. In the one case this takes the form of a commitment to a particular way of speaking about and for the subjects of psychology; with the other it is with a refusal to stand in judgement over talk and text and hence a rejection of the task of adjudication.

Our intention is to treat the realism/relativism debate in critical psychology as a series of ethical problematics that bear upon local concerns with the possibilities for research viewed against the contentious history of the discipline, with its many and varied moral and governmental projects (see Cohen, 1987; Rose, 1989; Stainton Rogers et al., 1995). To what and whom does critical psychology owe responsibility? In short, outwith the satisfaction of local performance indicators, 'what is to be done?' (see also Merttens, this volume). The partial answers that will be supplied to this overly broad question take several forms, bearing on the nature of discourse, the production of 'visibility', theorizing the self and the issue of justice.

Discourse Analysis and Limitation

The case for the study of discourse in psychology is by now well established (e.g., Edwards and Potter, 1992; Gergen 1985; Shotter, 1984) and does not require full repetition here. What instead warrants attention is the form of the argument by which cognitive operations are dismissed and discursive processes installed as objects of study. Typically, the structure of the argument is that the kinds of human activity purportedly explained by reference to cognitive mechanisms can equally well be understood by analysing joint productions of meaning in conversational exchanges and other speech settings. Memory, for example, can readily be viewed as a construction achieved in discourse that is contingent on the kinds of action and forms of accountability at issue in a given sequence of social interaction (see Middleton and Edwards, 1990).

A further layer of the argument is the revelation of the means by which cognitive psychology produces knowledge – principally the controlled experiment – as themselves the site of a dialogical performance where the cognitive phenomenon under study, such as implicit learning, is negotiated into being a posteriori through interpretation of utterances and actions dislocated from the actual conditions in which they were occasioned. The upshot is that:

> [T]he word discourse is to be understood very broadly. Its usual implications of verbal presentation of thought and argument are broadened, to provide a handy word for all sorts of cognitive activities, that is, activities which make use of devices that point beyond themselves, and which are normatively constrained, that is, are subject to standards of correctness and incorrectness. Language use is just one among the many discursive activities of which we are capable, if we broaden the use of the term in this way. The second cognitive revolution is nothing other than the advent of discursive psychology! (Harré, 1995: 144)

The effect of the discursive critique is the substitution of one term (discourse) where previously there were two (thought and language; cognition and behaviour). False tensions are collapsed on to a single analytic plane, albeit one with its own particular forms of complexity. It is tempting to assert that monism of the kind offered in the bolder versions of discourse analysis is always greeted by suspicion, if not outright hostility, as the ill fate of radical behaviourism displays. The irony here is that a putative discursive psychology is forced to go 'one better' than the cognitive paradigm. In order to display its analytic credentials it is led not only to account for practically all 'cognitive' phenomena in discursive terms, but to locate further such activity in conditions amenable to social theory. Hence discursive psychology falls into the lure of attempting to explicate that which cognitive researchers only ever promised that they would 'one day' explain (e.g., motivation, judgement, the link between attitude and behaviour); it inherits the formulations and limitations of a failed project.

The implied relationship to philosophy is complex. In giving priority to discourse, ontological as well as epistemological, the basis from which judgements regarding appropriate 'levels of explanation' (see Willig, this volume) can be made is eroded. Philosophical discourse is set in play alongside the myriad other rootstocks of authority (on the resulting paradoxes, see Derrida, 1978). If there is something ineluctable about the discursive turn – and it is our wager here that there is – then we cannot expect philosophy to delimit which forms of complexity we may question and which we may not. We have instead to work psychological concern into different configurations through a process of translation involving whatever is to hand, engage in a minor writing which begins to hollow out its own space within the major language. In other words, what is needed is an elucidation of how practical, concerned psychology can emerge by neither avoiding nor simply reiterating but instead passing through philosophical discourse.

Reality and Manifestation

Positivism, that most despised of the '-isms' against which discursive psychology is defined, assumes an isomorphism between reality and those manifestations by which humans come to know it. To be 'against' positivism is commonly understood to involve making an incision between manifestation and reality, such that the latter can be jettisoned as the mere rhetorical double of the former. Manifestations will suffice as the stuff of the world, without the metaphysical trickery of claims to 'the real'. Here the strong formulation of social constructionism is often interpreted as issuing in an absolute relativism where 'anything goes'; pure possibility abounds without foundational criteria to specify the options that should be pursued. Only in its crudest formulations does social constructionist work come to resemble such linguistic neo-Platonism. Foucault, for example, quite apart from his explicit writings on power, places organized, stabilized force at the heart of his archaeological system when he defines a discursive 'statement' in terms of its 'repeatable materiality' (1972). Regarding the other route to discursive psychology, ethnomethodology, Garfinkel (1967) and his subsequent interpreters rely heavily upon the 'Agnes' case to describe the actual workings of the 'documentary method' and the practice of making out a gendered identity. It bears reiteration that it is the very material intransigence of Agnes's transgendered body that locates such discursive labour.

There is no question that much of the work now appropriated as social constructionist considers language – or more properly discourse – and materiality to be inextricably entangled. In this respect we find nothing to the immediate contrary in Bhaskar's statement that: 'Social practices are concept-dependent; but . . . they are not exhausted by their conceptual aspect. They always have a material dimension' (Bhaskar, 1989: 4).

For Bhaskar, this material dimension gains its proper standing, though, when viewed as the object of a critical reflection which seeks to gain purchase on the real processes which undergird the manifest world. The project of 'critical realism' (Bhaskar, 1975, 1989) distinguishes between the epistemological and ontological dimensions of the realist/relativist debate, contra discursive psychology. It allows that knowledge of the real cannot escape the limitations of our particular social context, but nevertheless holds it a mistake to abandon the task of searching for traces of the real in the manifestations which compose the actual world as we conceive it. Given that there is no necessary correspondence between reality and actuality, and moreover that some real processes may never come to be manifest, sustained rational reflection provides the surest means by which possible realities may be proposed and evaluated. Epistemological relativism is then anchored by a reasoned and enlightened quest for the real.

The political appeal of the critical-realist position lies precisely with its potential to provide a foundational criteria for emancipatory action (see Collier, this volume). It is not this promise of foundations that we find problematic, but rather the ethical formulation by which it is secured – the appeal to shared 'rationality'. This seems to us to rely upon three contestable moves. First, the legitimacy of 'rational' dialogue (whose definition we leave here undetermined) must be accepted. Secondly, rationality must be accepted as the common ground of consensus (rather than as a site which may be claimed, to the exclusion of others, by a line of argumentation). Thirdly, action must be seen as plausibly to follow the appeal to rationality (instead of the inverse strategy, where rationality is used to legitimate action – oppression may, for example, be 'very reasonable').

Rationality is not immune to rhetorical challenge. Even if the necessary consensus was secured at every step, there is no guarantee that the 'reality behind' would in fact be taken as the shared object of study. This is not a fundamental objection, Bhaskar is not after all attempting to naturalize completely the political so that it flows from pure metaphysics – a 'leap of faith' is still required. But given that (a particular version of) the rational must be affirmed at every step of the process, and the instability of such a thread to rhetorical attack, thereby making it possible for either closure of debate or a programme of action to be overturned at any point, the question has to be raised as to whether it would not instead be better to recognize rationality in terms of, say, a 'rhetoric of truth' (Ibáñez, 1991), or as having its conditions in a 'local interpretive tradition' (Barnes et al., 1996). This would begin with inevitable dissension rather than illusory consent.

Questioning the appeal to rationality does not of itself challenge Bhaskar's realist ontology. We are indeed loath to do so directly, which would necessarily lead us away from our own strategic concerns – with a practicable critical social psychology – towards a major language that is not, and could not be our own. We prefer instead to see in Bhaskar's scheme an opportunity for analytic experimentation. What happens, for example, if a switch is made from epistemological relativism to realism? Manifestation becomes 'real', it is affirmed in some way. What then follows if a further modification is made to ontology, if it is now posed in relativist terms? One would make a commitment to something other than manifestation, but fail to specify or limit what that is. As a philosophical argument this is clearly insufficient, yet it is not in that major language that we seek to work. The reversed critical realism does something to how psychology is articulated; it is as a piece of minor writing that it has effects, particularly with regard to the issues of responsibility. It is to these that we now attend.

A Psychology of the Visible

In their reworking of organization theory, Cooper and Law (1995) describe how the human sciences typically concentrate analysis on static results or 'distal' effects, rather than the processes or 'proximal' relationships wherein these effects come about. Numerous points flow from this assertion: that it is possible to study 'organizing' as well as 'organizations', that effects will be perpetually unstable in the face of ongoing process and that what we take to be the stable, orderly world of individuals, organizations and formal interaction is but the residue of a perpetual 'labour of division' (Cooper, 1997).

In mistaking epiphenomenal order for the very stuff of the world, the error of what Chia (1995), following Whitehead, calls 'the fallacy of misplaced concreteness' is made. It might then seem that adopting a realist epistemology is but to compound this error. This is clearly not our intention. The adoption of realism is but another way of acknowledging that ordered familiarity is how the world is generally regarded, it is the default mode of social existence – doors, for example, seem to have a timeless existence as such and not as relatively durable solutions to the wall-hole problem (see Latour, 1992). Epistemology is composed to a high degree of 'formal representations' (see Star, 1989) – models, maps, equations, theories and so on – all of which act to stabilize what would be otherwise liminal or disorderly, indeed such is their very power. Formal representations may be accorded the status of truth, like logical proofs that $2 + 2 = 4$ or computer tomograph images of dysfunctions in the cerebral cortex. Nevertheless, they can only achieve this status of truth through a process of deletion, where the manifold things that a formal representation could be about, could make visible, are excluded. The logical proof of $2 + 2 = 4$ needs, for example, to ensure that only 'ordinary' and not some other system of arithmetic is followed, whereas a computer tomograph requires interpretation by a technician trained in the current norms and practices of medical imaging.

This is one way of re-presenting Foucauldian archaeology, as the study of the innumerable deletions, exclusions and transformations, all the 'work' (Star, 1989) that must of necessity be done to produce knowledge that can be said to lie 'within the true' of a given discipline and so appear to have arrived 'ready formed' (Foucault, 1972). What is affirmed of formal epistemology can scarce be denied of the everyday – all knowing engages in a work of exclusion that is 'forgotten' as part of its very operation (Chia, 1995). It is in this respect that Curt (1994) has previously made so much of the 'taken-for-granted' character of social knowing in the constitution of 'practical reality'. To put it another way, the 'reality' of what is articulated in everyday discourse is given by a successful, perhaps unmindful act of reduction and location which cuts out the world to some effect while locating what is said with relation to matters of accountability (see also Munro and Mouritsen, 1996). In suggesting epistemological realism we are both respecting and taking seriously the full implications of a socially constructed world. Where, for example, could we find a criterion of 'real-ness' with which to dispute the general epistemological status of a piece of discourse other than by reference to some equally textual resource? It is, of course, entirely possible that someone is mistaken, lying, otherwise 'incorrect' or else referring maybe to entirely imaginary entities, but these are matters necessarily internal to discourse and their settling does not bear upon the wider question. Once the real is recognized as entirely co-extensive with the force of exclusion, then a practical or 'weak' epistemological realism becomes adequate for analytic purposes.

What then of 'ontological relativism'? Is this not the point when epistemological realism is revealed as pure somnambulism, the waking dream of human will impressed upon an illusive world? One reply to this charge is to reiterate the prior comments about materiality; the textual and the material are in every way inextricable. If this seems at odds with social constructionist concerns with textuality, discourse and speaking, then this is evidence merely of the sway of critical linguistics and neo-deconstruction on current formulations of discursive psychology. There is nothing here which prevents analysis from proceeding to the study of what Dreyfus and Rabinow, with regard to Foucault, describe as the 'thick tissue of non-discursive relations' that compose the 'background of intelligibility for those actually speaking' (1982: 58). This is to recognize the role of those non-discursive elements that intervene in everyday discursive interaction. If actors use and recognize specific formulations and devices during talk-in-interaction, they also recognize and act upon the objects that form part of that interaction. Compare the following:

1 A: *CAREFUL!*
   B: ((Breath)) ↑*Thank* ↓you!

2 Traffic Light in Pedestrian Crossing: Red
   A: *CAREFUL!*
   B: ((Breath)) ↑*Thank* ↓you!

With the second example the context of the action taking place at a pedestrian crossing is made clear. The traffic light in effect constitutes another actor in the interaction. Different speeds of talk could be expected, for example, from people waiting for the traffic light to change to green and people crossing when the traffic light has just changed to red. The traffic-light needs to be considered as entering into the interaction as a fully blown actor (or 'actant', see Callon, 1986). This can be seen more clearly in the following extract from Rae (1994: 826–7):

1   Human: (puts money in slot)
2   Machine: (coin exited to reject slot)
3   →Human: (re-inserts coin)
4   Machine: (dispenses ticket)

Rae is attempting to show how the conversation analytic principle of 'repair' during talk-in-interaction (Schegloff et al., 1977), where speakers utterances attend to restoring a breakdown in meaning, can be applied to human–machine interactions. Here the human 'repairs' the interaction (at 3) by re-inserting the coin previously rejected, thereby successfully completing the transaction. Rae (1994: 827) goes on to display how this could hold for purely machine–machine interactions, such as between fax units:

1   Machine 1: (transmits chunk of data)
2   Machine 2: (indicates a problem with receiving the data)
3   Machine 1: (re-transmits the data)

While there are grounds to question these specific examples, particularly the way the machines are near anthropomorphized, the general point is cogent: the speaking subject is only one of many actants in any sequence of action, their powers depending for the most part on a series of relations to machines, materials and a whole cast of non-humans (for a more critical evaluation of this Actor Network symmetry, see Lee and Brown, 1994).

From this flows a further reply, that human speakers themselves should not be supposed the main object of analysis. It is not to them entirely that we owe responsibility. They are but effects of the wider processes of organizing in which their talk is embedded. As Cooper and Law put it with regard to the manager of a successful research laboratory, 'Andrew . . . is a particular location in the self ordering cycle of organizing' (1995: 263). He is effectively 'the *creature* of a set of other materials and the way these interact together: the telephones and the fax machine; the electronic mail; the postal system with its constant flow of papers and reports' (Cooper and Law, 1995: 263). The fragility of the entity 'Andrew the Manager' could be rapidly shown were any of these elements to be removed (see also Callon and Law, 1995).

In advancing a 'relativist ontology' we are placing the assemblages of relations at the centre of the analysis, with the implication that the real owes its certain, ordered nature to the unfinished, unstable 'hybrid' patterns-in-production of materials and texts which labour within it. It is here that the notion of 'presencing practices' (Curt, 1994) deserves emphasis. Unfinished organizings take on the character of stable entities via the mediation of practices which order, stabilize and moreover ensure the repetition of the appearance of certain meaningful patterns – think of the ritual of the haruspex (divination of the future through animal sacrifice) as being fundamentally no different in kind to the immunological assay (Brown, 1996). Presencing practices are ways of making the world 'visible' in stable, orderly fashion, thereby providing the conditions for 'articulability', for speaking about the world in particular ways. All forms of technology contribute to the production of visibility (see Cooper, 1993), thereby underpinning textuality. Hence, to say that the textual and the material are intertwined is also to underscore the mutual relations between 'saying' and 'seeing'.

We would like to suggest something like a 'psychology of visibility' corresponding to that of discursive psychology, which would examine the relationship between the production of visibilities in technologies, formal representations and presencing practices with that of textuality, discourse and rhetoric. An example of the general way such analysis might proceed, the kinds of material it would grasp, can be illustrated with Deleuze's reading of Foucault's (1977) work on penal institutions:

> The content has both a form and a substance: for example, the form is prison and the substance those who are locked up, the prisoners (who? why? how?). The expression also has a form and a substance: for example the form is penal law and the substance is 'delinquency' in so far as it is the object of statements. Just as penal law as a form of expression defines a field of sayability (the statements of delinquency), so prison as a form of content defines a place of visibility ('panopticism', that is a place where at any moment one can see everything without being seen). (Deleuze, 1988: 47)

Here the technologies ('panopticism') on which the prison is constructed are brought into question alongside those of the discourses (penal law and delinquency) which comprise its textuality. The prison is recognized as an assemblage of materials, technologies, prisoners and documents (Brown and Stenner, 1995). The visible and articulable elements of the prison assemblage support, further and reinforce one another.

For Deleuze and Guattari (1988) an assemblage is two-sided: the one face concrete, finished, actual, to which we would add 'distal' and 'real'; the other unformed, incomplete, virtual – here 'proximal' and 'relative'. It is therefore a mistake to assume that in actual emergence the potential of organizing is exhausted, to imagine that any specific prison, for example, contains within it the full story of 'anatomo-politics' (see Foucault, 1977). The process of organizing is endless, unbounded, perpetually on the way to becoming something other to any given actual (Nietzsche's 'dice roll'). There is an ethical thread: with ontological relativism this quality of continual variation or becoming is affirmed as within and ultimately carrying off the real. Hence there is affirmation that things can and will always be different from how they are grasped in their current actuality. We recognize here the outlines of a politics of visibility, through the systematic consideration of how a presencing practice or technology give us *this* real rather than any other.

Taking Issue with 'the Self'

A 'minor writing' has enabled us to make a series of (partial) connections between critical psychology and the study of technology and materialities. We might allow though for at least two major objections to these moves. First, that it spreads psychology too thin, away from its 'proper' subject matter. As a defence we should reiterate that it is part of the logic of ontological relativism that psychology be seen as incomplete, unfinished and as in a process of becoming something other. The second objection is that previously levelled at discursive psychology: the absence of 'selves', understood as the logical guarantees of personal experience and durable identity, with the endorsement of 'anti-humanism' (see Burr, this volume). The counter claim for selfhood deserves serious consideration since it is presented as the revelation of an ethical aporia. It can be roughly apportioned to three related affirmations: the necessity of an 'operator' that selects discursive utterances; the self as a 'point of organization' underpinning identity; and the defence of the moral-political subject. These are addressed in turn.

For Madill and Doherty (1994), the relativist empiricism of Edwards and Potter (1992) provides a cogent account of how selfhood is attributed and worked up in conversation. What it fails to do, however, is to provide an explanation of precisely what it is that is doing the work of selecting between plausible utterances. A self alone – the entity that expresses itself in communicable acts – is sufficient to ground discourse as a human achievement. To 'bracket out' or to otherwise elide the reality of selfhood is to produce an a-causal, ethereal model of interaction that is excised from the common-sense experience of speaking and acting. Taking this latter point first, while it is undoubtedly the case that reality-effects are such that one may experience being a 'self' that 'gropes for what to say', 'chooses his or her words carefully' or is 'stunned into silence', it does not follow that there is a literal entity which can be posited as the causal origin of these acts. Harré (1993), for example, while stressing the importance of personhood, is at pains to emphasize that powers to act do not 'cause' discursive utterances in any straightforward manner: discourse and physical actions, although interlinked in act-action structures, belong to entirely different realms of explication.

The second assertion is presented succinctly by Bruner:

> Self . . . is the centre of gravity of all systems of meaning-making. . . . She is an origin point in intersubjective space; she is an invariant protagonist in accounts of the world; she is the beneficiary and the victim of norms; and she is the logical operator and unmarked case in the conceptual-logical domain. (1995: 26)

Again, there is nothing here that requires the prior existence of self as actual entity. Working through Bruner's statement, the 'origin point' is taken as such through either the use of personal pronouns and deixis (intrinsically cultural) or by reference to the physical presence of the body. With the latter there are innumerable examples of bodies, such as those of children, the severely disabled, 'mentally ill' or comatose, that are often not treated as *de facto* intersubjective presences. The 'invariant protagonist' might be considered a product of certain narrative conventions, such as the realist novel, whose ensemble of coherent motives and identity is elsewhere fragmented (see Potter, 1996). As a 'beneficiary or victim of norms', the self would seem to resemble more the product of the application to the person of disciplinary power in the Foucauldian sense (e.g., Foucault, 1977), than a coherent object brought before the law. Finally, self certainly acts as an important grammatical operator, to the degree that it seems implied (the 'unmarked case') in much of what is taken to be meaningful discourse regarding persons, but once more there is no reason to make the leap that grammar recapitulates ontology: to do so is to miss the work of exclusion and selection that language achieves.

Regarding the last assertion, the self as moral-political subject, here it seems is the strongest moral imperative. A social psychology that refuses to consider the practical means by which the citizen, the child or the delinquent are hailed as such should return in shame to its testing room. But is there a need to concatenate these strong reality effects of different organizing regimes with the infra-worldly self? If it is taken for granted that analysis of legal and civic subjects is intended in some way as a contribution or an intervention in the culture that sustains them, then to double such subjects with an ontic self seems almost an irrelevance. If the issue is, say, the injustice of refusing to grant legal status to a particular group of persons, the response can be to question what it is about the formulation of that legal status that enables it to be withheld, which may entail its systematic deconstruction and replacement with other conceptions of judicial subjectivity. This has long been the route taken by critical legal studies (see Goodrich et al., 1994). The self is, in effect, masking a more far-reaching critical concern: that of justice.

Ethics, Justice and the Self

To reach towards a conclusion, the elements of this chapter can be brought together around the figure of justice. Although the notion of a stable, complete self has been denied as a matter of ontology, it is clearly an epistemological reality – a durable effect. As such it can be treated, for research purposes, as an empty 'organizing concept'. This is a way of stating that 'selfhood' will not be considered as one of the critical concepts (such as assemblage, discourse or technology) through which analysis can progress; what it does instead is to orient analytic concern to issues of personhood and their constitution.

To make a further assertion, if the gridlock of the realist/relativist debate as we read it condenses around theorizing selfhood and anti-humanism, this latter is itself being moved by a questioning of justice. In what sense? What does a psychological concern with justice involve? The first point to dismiss is that it concerns the ontogenesis of morals. In as much as this is a feasible topic of study, and the many critiques of a Kohlberg-influenced individualist theory of morals suggest it is not (e.g., Gilligan, 1982; MacIntyre, 1981), it could surely only take the form of a situated ethnography or other study at the communitarian level examining the structuring of local moral universes. The second possibility is of analysing how the moral is worked up and played out in sequences of activity, as with Davies and Harré (1990), or in the court room interactions that attract conversation analysts (e.g., Atkinson and Drew, 1979). This features the moral as topic rather than as immanent to the concerns of the research. What is meant by justice as a critical concept is this latter formulation: that ethical commitments are a part of opening up the space where research happens, they are not, in this sense, 'topic' or 'censor', but in some way made interior to the unravelling of inquiry.

What does this mean in practice? It is possible to return again to the discussion of ethos at the beginning of the chapter. Ethos is worked out in many ways, from the impulse to reveal what is hidden to the refusal of judgement (which is no less an act involving a version of justice). Van Dijk, for example, formulates the act of research in terms of an urge to 'do something' (1994: 5) about, in this case, the abuses of the Bosnian conflict. This is achieved through positioning academic research as a social resource which may (or may not) then be 'effectively applied in scholarly or practical forms of resistance against various forms of social, political and cultural domination' (Van Dijk, 1995: 564). Implicit here is the notion that research may be able to reveal some facet of the social backdrop that is not already available to those who dwell there. Curt (1994) suggests something along these lines in the project of 'possibilizing alternative understandings' of some issue by means of a thorough description of its discursive ecology.

There are problems with this assumption. The notion of a 'possibility' existing silently in the 'hurly burly', which although responsible for the extant reality we experience might also, through the intervention of the researcher, be 'realized' in a different state of affairs, involves a subtle contradiction. In a socially-constructed world everything is given at once, albeit subject to an unequal distribution of knowledge across the social – nothing is lacking. The possibility of 'possibility' belongs to a different order, to the relativist potentials of the assemblage in its capacity to become manifest in many different, as-yet-unthought orderings of the real.

Everything is given already in the real, to paraphrase Foucault. There may be secrets, deliberate mystifications or lies, but these themselves are part of the ordering of the real and the possibility of their decipherment or violent overthrow is itself a given. Intervention cannot then take revelation as a critical concept, depending as it does on a simple doubling of extant ordering or the hubris of defining a hidden 'really real'. Respect, not suspicion must be given to the real. Where does that leave the notion of justice? The problem is well defined in the following exchange:

Foucault: [T]he proletariat doesn't wage war against the ruling class because it considers such a war just. The proletariat makes war with the ruling class because . . . it wants to take power. And because it will overthrow the ruling class it considers the war to be just.

Chomsky: Yeah, I don't agree.

Foucault: One makes war to win, not because it is just.

Chomsky: But it is in terms of justice; its because the end that will be achieved is claimed as a just one.

Foucault: It seems to me that the idea of justice in itself is an idea which in effect has been invented and put to work in different types of societies as an instrument of a certain political and economic power or as a weapon against that power . . . in a classless society I am not sure that we would still use this notion of justice.

Chomsky: Well here I really disagree. I think there is some sort of an absolute basis . . . ultimately residing in fundamental human qualities, in terms of which a 'real' notion of justice is grounded. . . . And I think that in any future society . . . we'll have . . . concepts . . . which we hope will come closer to incorporating a defence of fundamental human needs. (Chomsky and Foucault, 1974: 182–5)

The choice offered here is to see justice as either a warrant to action, subservient to the actual determinations of power or as grounded in a conception of 'fundamental human needs'. While it is difficult (and probably undesirable) to imagine a synthesis of these positions, there are elements from both that are recoverable. 'Justice' can be taken as entirely constructed, with Foucault, but also as implying a commitment to matters of ontology, with Chomsky, without formalizing the substantive to which this commitment refers. To break this into several steps: a relativist ontology offers the prospect of always becoming other to what it currently consists. The ethical commitment is to this *process of becoming*, to contribute to the perpetual re-invention of the ontological, wherein lies the possibility of different, as-yet-unthought orders of the real. Justice proceeds from such a commitment, it pertains to the contingency of judgements in a perpetual shifting of the basic categories of existence (human, animal, machine, spirit). It may be said that it is this recognition of an indeterminacy or otherness before judgement that gives justice its potency:

> [W]e may say that language and ethics precede the law in the precise sense that justice, the right to a hearing, to a day in court, to judgement, is the precondition of law. . . . As against the moralism of maxims and codes, as against the complacency of established institutional ethics or more properly institutional ethos, the critical concern with the ethical is a return to the political and an embrace of responsibility: for the other, for the stranger, the outsider, the alien or under-privileged who need the law, who needs, in the oldest sense of the term, to have a hearing, to be heard. It is the responsibility of all law to heed the appearance of she who comes before the law. (Goodrich et al., 1994: 22)

A two-fold commitment then. To hear what is spoken (but also to see what becomes visible) while refusing to 'name' or otherwise en-frame what speaks in terms beyond those afforded by local contingency, by concrete specificities. What should psychological research do? It should participate in the becoming of the real, in its precipitation as well as its mapping.

Note

We'd like to thank Bob Cooper, Rolland Munro and Martin Parker for comments and helpful readings, and Ian Parker for prudent editing.

References

Atkinson, J.M. and Drew, P. (1979) *Order in Court: The Organization of Verbal Interaction in Judicial Settings*. London: Macmillan.

Barnes, B., Bloor, D. and Henry, J. (1996) *Scientific Knowledge: A Sociological Analysis*. London: The Athlone Press.

Bhaskar, R. (1975) *A Realist Theory of Science*. Brighton: Harvester.

Bhaskar, R. (1989) *Reclaiming Reality: A Critical Introduction to Contemporary Philosophy*. London: Verso.

Brown, S.D. (1996) 'The textuality of stress: drawing between scientific and everyday accounting', *Journal of Health Psychology*, 1 (2): 173–93.

Brown, S.D. and Stenner, P. (1995) 'Implicating bodies: Spinoza and the psychology of emotion'. Paper presented at BPS History and Philosophy of Psychology Section Annual Conference, Aberdeen.

Bruner, S. (1995) 'Meaning and self in a cultural perspective', in D. Bakhurst and C. Sypnowich (eds), *The Social Self*. London: Sage.

Callon, M. (1986) 'Some elements of a sociology of translation: domestification of the scallops and fishermen of St Brieuc Bay', in J. Law (ed.), *Power, Action, Belief: A New Sociology of Knowledge?* London: Routledge and Kegan Paul.

Callon, M. and Law, J. (1995) 'Agency and the hybrid collectif', *The South Atlantic Quarterly*, 94 (2): 481–507.

Chia, R. (1995) 'From modern to postmodern organizational analysis', *Organization Studies*, 16 (4): 579–604.

Chomsky, N. and Foucault, M. (1974) 'Human nature: justice versus power', in F. Elders (ed.), *Reflexive Water: The Basic Concerns of Human Kind*. London: Souvenir Press.

Cohen, D. (ed.) (1987) *The Power of Psychology*. London: Croom Helm.

Collins, H. (1983) 'An empirical relativist programme in the sociology of scientific knowledge', in K.D. Knorr Cetina and M. Mulkay (eds), *Science Observed: Perspectives on the Social Study of Science*. London: Sage.

Cooper, R. (1993) 'Technologies of representation', in P. Ahonen (ed.), *Tracing the Semiotic Boundaries of Politics*. Berlin: Mouton de Gruyter.

Cooper, R. (1997) 'Systems of visibility', in K. Hetherington and R. Munro (eds), *Ideas of Difference: Social Spaces and the Labour of Division*. Oxford: Blackwell.

Cooper, R. and Law, J. (1995) 'Organization: distal and proximal views', *Research in the Sociology of Organizations*, 13: 237–74.

Curt, B.C. (1994) *Textuality and Tectonics: Troubling Social and Psychological Science*. Buckingham: Open University Press.

Davies, B. and Harré, R. (1990) 'Positioning: the discursive production of selves', *Journal for the Theory of Social Behaviour*, 20: 43–63.

Deleuze, G. (1988) *Foucault*. Minneapolis: Minnesota University Press.

Deleuze, G. and Guattari, F. (1986) *Kafka: Towards a Minor Literature*. Minneapolis: Minnesota University Press.

Deleuze G. and Guattari, F. (1988) *A Thousand Plateaus: Capitalism and Schizophrenia*. London: The Athlone Press.

Derrida, J. (1978) *Writing and Difference*. London: Routledge.

Dreyfus, H.L. and Rabinow, P. (1982) *Michel Foucault: Beyond Structuralism and Hermeneutics*. Brighton: Harvester.

Edwards, D. and Potter, J. (1992) *Discursive Psychology*. London: Sage.

Foucault, M. (1972) *The Archaeology of Knowledge*. New York: Pantheon.

Foucault, M. (1977) *Discipline and Punish: The Birth of the Prison*. Harmondsworth: Penguin.

Garfinkel, H. (1967) *Studies in Ethnomethodology*. Cambridge: Polity Press.

Gergen, K.J. (1985) 'The social constructionist movement in modern psychology', *American Psychologist*, 40 (3): 266–75.

Gilligan, C. (1982) *In a Different Voice*. Cambridge, MA: Harvard University Press.

Goodrich, P., Douzinas, C. and Hachamovitch, Y. (1994) 'Introduction: politics, ethics and the legality of the contingent', in C. Douzinas, P. Goodrich and Y. Hachamovitch (eds), *Politics, Postmodernity and Critical Legal Studies: The Legality of the Contingent*. London: Routledge.

Greenwood, J.D. (1994) *Realism, Identity and Emotion*. London: Sage.

Harré, R. (1993) *Social Being* (2nd edn). Oxford: Blackwell.

Harré, R. (1995) 'Discursive psychology', in J.A. Smith, R. Harré and L. Van Langenhove (eds), *Rethinking Psychology*. London: Sage.

Harré, R. and Madden, E.H. (1975) *Causal Powers*. Oxford: Basil Blackwell.

Ibáñez, T. (1991) 'Social psychology and the rhetoric of truth', *Theory and Psychology*, 1 (2): 187–201.

Latour, B. (1992) 'Where are the missing masses? A sociology of a few mundane artifacts', in W.E. Bijker and J. Law (eds), *Shaping Technology/Building Society*. Cambridge, MA: The MIT Press.

Lee, N. and Brown, S. (1994) 'Otherness and the actor-network: the undiscovered continent', *American Behavioral Scientist*, 37 (6): 772–90.

MacIntyre, A. (1981) *After Virtue: A Study in Moral Theory*. London: Duckworth.

Madill, A. and Doherty, K. (1994) '"So you did what you wanted then": discourse analysis, personal agency, and psychotherapy', *Journal of Community and Applied Psychology*, 4: 261–73.

Middleton, D. and Edwards, D. (eds) (1990) *Collective Remembering*. London: Sage.

Munro, R. and Mouritsen, J. (eds) (1996) *Accountability: Power, Ethos and the Technologies of Managing*. London: Thomson Business Press.

Parker, I. (1990) 'Discourse: definitions and contradictions', *Philosophical Psychology*, 3: 189–204.

Parker, I. (1996) 'Against Wittgenstein: materialist reflections on language in psychology', *Theory and Psychology*, 6 (3): 363–84.

Potter, J. (1996) *Representing Reality: Discourse, Rhetoric and Social Construction*. London: Sage.

Potter, J., Wetherell, M., Gill, R. and Edwards, D. (1990) 'Discourse: noun, verb or social practice?', *Philosophical Psychology*, 3: 205–17.

Rabinow, P. (1995) 'Through the genetic matrix'. Paper presented at the Labour of Division, Centre for Social Theory and Technology First Annual Conference, Keele.

Rae, J. (1994) 'Social fax: repair mechanisms and intersubjectivity', *American Behavioral Scientist*, 37 (6): 824–38.

Robinson, D.N. (1995) *An Intellectual History of Psychology* (3rd edn). London: Edward Arnold.

Rose, N. (1989) *Governing the Soul: The Shaping of the Private Self*. London: Routledge.

Schegloff, E.A., Sacks, H. and Jefferson, G. (1977) 'The preference for self-correction in the organization of repair in conversation', *Language*, 53 (2): 361–82.

Shotter, J. (1984) *Social Accountability and Selfhood*. Oxford: Blackwell.

Stainton Rogers, R., Stenner, P., Gleeson, K. and Stainton Rogers, W. (1995) *Social Psychology: A Critical Agenda*. Cambridge: Polity Press.

Star, S.L. (1989) 'Layered space, formal representations and long-distance control: the politics of information', *Fundamenta Scientiae*, 10 (2): 125–54.

Van Dijk, T. (1994) 'The discourses of "Bosnia"', *Discourse and Society*, 5 (1): 5–6.

Van Dijk, T. (1995) 'A rejoinder', *Discourse and Society*, 6 (4): 563–6.

7

Social Constructionism and Revolutionary Socialism: A Contradiction in Terms?

Carla Willig

My starting point has to be an acknowledgement of my problematic positioning as social constructionist academic and committed international
socialist. The basic tension in my positioning is this: as a socialist, my understanding of capitalist society and my political actions which are informed by
this understanding, appear to presuppose or require a realist epistemology. As
a discourse analyst in psychology who explores the constructed and constructive nature of language and its role in the constitution of subjectivity, I
appear to accept epistemological, or even ontological, relativism. How do I
deal with this apparent contradiction?

I would like to start this discussion with two observations which constitute
my starting point in this debate. First of all, I recognize that (critical) realists,
unlike empiricists, accept the inevitability of ultimate epistemological relativism by acknowledging 'the linguistic and historical constitution of all
knowledge' (Isaac, 1990: 9). Bhaskar himself points out that, 'Epistemological relativism . . . is the handmaid of ontological realism and must be
accepted. . . . Epistemological relativism insists only upon the impossibility of
knowing objects except under particular descriptions. And it entails the rejection of any correspondence theory of truth' (1978: 249). It could be argued
that Marxism's recognition that the ruling ideas in a particular historical
epoch are the ideas of the ruling class also undermines any simple epistemological realism (see Young, 1996: 35). Therefore, this discussion is *not* about
whether or not ultimate epistemological relativism is indeed the case, but
how we are going to deal with it.

Secondly, we need to reject the presentation of the notion of false consciousness as the linchpin of the realism/relativism debate (see Burr, 1995:
81–2). Here, it is suggested that a Marxist realist position leads one to diag-
nose people as objectively oppressed on the basis of their location in the
socio-economic structure of society, even when people deny a subjective experience of oppression. However, the issue for Marxists in practice is not to
make a diagnosis of false consciousness on the part of unsuspecting, con-
tented individuals. Rather, the issue is one of *taking sides*. In other words,

Marxist realism informs one's decision of *whose* reality to relate to and act upon, within the context of competing versions of social reality.

To summarize, I take for granted the unavoidability of ultimate epistemological relativism as well as the permanent ontological contestation among individuals and groups in society. As a result, I am concerned with finding a method of analysis which is historically and linguistically reflexive, and which is also capable of guiding active intervention in ideological and material struggles.

Epistemology and Political Action

It has been argued that relativism's greatest weakness is its paralysing effect (e.g., Burman, 1990; Gill, 1995), resulting from an inability to commit to a definitive political position. Consequently, my concern with political intervention may be seen logically to require a rejection of a relativist position. However, I think it is important to acknowledge the possibility of a paralysing effect of realist arguments. Isaac (1990: 24), for example, in his discussion of the relationship between theory and practice, uses critical realism's combination of historicity and pragmatism, together with its commitment to a scientific method, in order to recommend 'caution on the part of any theory with practical intent'. Starting off with a reminder that all knowledge is ultimately provisional and that actors cannot know all consequences of their actions, Isaac goes on to reject the adoption of a 'particular substantive conclusion or political programme' in favour of the adoption of 'a particular attitude – a chastened rationalism' (ibid.). This is followed by an explicit call for 'political compromise' and 'authentic pluralism' (ibid.). In other words, Isaac's cautious realism can be used to justify the *status quo*, that is bourgeois democracy, but not revolutionary change. Isaac's argument illustrates how a realist approach can actually be *more* of an obstacle to political action than the current scapegoat, postmodernist relativism (see also Edwards et al., 1995: 16–17, who demonstrate the use of realist rhetoric in advocating inaction via tropes such as 'you can't walk through rocks' or 'face the facts'). At least, the latter can be taken to be entirely forward-looking so that political action is seen to create or construct what we want. Nothing is to stop us from acting here, once moral-political choices have been made. In this context Gergen (1985) talks about how 'descriptions of the world are themselves a form of social action and have consequences' (quoted in Tiefer, 1995: 22–3). Here, we are urged to look forward and focus upon the consequences of our actions, rather than look backward and worry about how we can be sure that we are right in what we are saying or doing. Isaac's cautious realism can always be used to stop us in the flow of action by reminding us that our actions *may* be informed by a false understanding; therefore, it may be safer not to act in order to avoid having to take responsibility for making mistakes or to wait in order to do some more thinking so that we can be more confident about the validity of our premises for action.

The crucial point seems to be the suitability of one's approach to the context within which one is working. Isaac's circumspect realism may be fine for academic purposes but is unworkable for revolutionary practice which does require the (admittedly ultimately unwarrantable) 'metaphysical confidence' (Isaac, 1990: 23) which Isaac rejects. Thus, realism does not necessarily equip us with a basis for political action.

Furthermore, the consequentialist criterion, that is the requirement that a philosophical position has to be able to allow for and possibly even give direction to political action, is itself problematic. This is because it lacks philosophical or theoretical grounding. Rather, what seems to happen is that people adopt a political position as a result of experience (personal, political, collective, etc.) which is then made sense of by using philosophical arguments. These can be used to sustain one's position in the absence of or during the fading of the memory of the experience itself. In addition, consequentialism, or defining truth by its implications, can encourage an uncritically idealistic attitude. It is reminiscent of the argument that we must believe in God because if God doesn't exist there is no afterlife. . . .

The next question that arises is: why do we feel the need to formulate a philosophical justification for our political actions? Who expects this from us, and what do we gain from providing it? For example, Terry Eagleton (1990) seems to suggest that such a demand is really a way of avoiding specific political arguments. He has this to say to relativists:

> We [i.e., political radicals] do not mind in the least being informed that what we are doing is merely carrying on the conversation that is Western civilisation, a set of moves within an existing language game, as long as we can be allowed to get on and do it. If we in Britain are permitted to pull out of NATO, scrap our so-called independent nuclear deterrent, socialise industrial production under workers' self-management, dismantle the structures of patriarchy, return the Malvinas to the Argentinians and recall the troops from Northern Ireland, then it is really neither here nor there in our view whether what we are doing remains dismally imprisoned within a metaphysical problematic. Our theoretical opponents must either tell us that this means we cannot really do it, a case which has a somewhat implausible ring to it, or that we *should* not really do it, in which case they are going to have to engage in a little more detailed political argument than they customarily do. They will have to come out from behind the cover of general theories of belief or anti-foundationalism or anti-logocentrism or the ontological ineluctability of micropolitics, and let us know a little more clearly why they would like us to remain in NATO. (Eagleton, 1990: 92–3)

In other words, Eagleton accepts epistemological relativism, but does not feel that it can be used convincingly to argue against particular political positions because it cannot be used to argue convincingly *for* any position either. Thus, political arguments require a political, not a philosophical, level of debate. Eagleton does not, in fact, provide an argument against relativism. Instead, he highlights its limitations as a substitute for political analysis.

Having accepted that ultimate epistemological relativism is 'the case', but that ontological relativism is not capable of informing political interventions and that such intervention can, in fact, not be avoided, since all human

activity transforms or reproduces the world (Spears and Parker, 1996: 14), we
need to develop a reflexive, historically sensitive method of analysis of the
social. This is in part required by revolutionary practice which has specific but
(in contemporary Britain) ultimately long-term objectives. Therefore, political interventions must be coherent and mutually reinforcing and cannot be
left to individual, context-dependent moral-political choices.

Implications for Discourse Analytic Research

What does this position have to offer to discourse analytic research in psychology? In my view, it fulfils two functions. First, it can help us choose our
objects. Discourse analytic theory on its own cannot tell us which discursive
objects to deconstruct. This is a political choice which requires grounding, in
just the same way that any research question we might ask requires social and
moral justification. The choice of what to study, how and for what purposes
cannot be separated from the knowledge that is being created in the process.
It could be argued that any contribution to a body of knowledge is always
also a recommendation about how things should or should not be done (see
Howitt, 1991: 146–7). For example, it is no coincidence that Marxist psychologists have been interested in exploring reasons for workers' reluctance to
overthrow capitalism whereas mainstream psychologists ask questions about
the personality profile of criminals. Secondly, it can inform the ways in which
the researcher wishes to apply his/her work. This has been a problematic
issue for discourse analysts. Discourse analysts in psychology have used their
method in order to deconstruct and thus question and challenge dominant
constructions of psychologically relevant concepts and associated practices.
Such concepts include the psychological subject (Hollway, 1989), emotions
(Stenner, 1993), psychopathology (Parker et al., 1995), prejudice (Potter and
Wetherell, 1987), schizophrenia (Harper, 1994) and many others. These studies explore the ways in which particular categories are constructed and used,
and with what consequences. In addition, discourse analysis also allows the
researcher to identify subject positions which may constrain or facilitate particular actions.

   Thus, discourse analysis is an attractive research tool for critical psychologists because it allows us to question and challenge that which is taken for
granted in psychology. Many discourse analysts are motivated in their work
by the belief that such deconstructions have a liberatory effect: they serve to
demonstrate that things could be different, that our customary ways of cate-
gorizing and ordering phenomena are reified and interest-driven rather than
reflections of reality. By revealing the constructed nature of psychological
phenomena, we create a space for making available alternatives to what 'is'.
Thus, it could be expected that discourse analysts have something to say
about how things could be done differently. For example, if discourses of psychopathology and their associated practices and institutions disempower
users of mental health services, then how can this be changed? Are there

ways of talking about emotional distress which are preferable? And how can such alternative constructions and practices be promoted? On the whole, discourse analysts have been reluctant to move beyond deconstruction and make recommendations for improved (social, political, and/or psychological) practice (but see Parker et al., 1995 for an exception).

Reasons for and Problems with Abstentionism

The two major reasons for such reluctance are (i) fear of becoming guilty of reification, together with a strong commitment to contextualized analysis, as well as (ii) an acute awareness of the possibility of political abuse of research findings. Widdicombe (1995) discusses the dangers of reification. Having drawn attention to the ways in which social scientists' accounts can be intended to liberate oppressed groups but end up by simply locking the latter within different but equally restrictive discourses, Widdicombe advises critical psychologists against ever committing themselves to particular recommendations based on research. Instead, she argues that the best way to avoid imposing categories upon others is to stick entirely to contextualized analysis and never to generalize from one's research findings. This, she argues, allows respondents to redefine themselves and their situations each time they are studied by researchers. According to Widdicombe, giving respondents this space is more empowering for respondents than any progressive policy recommendation could ever be.

Cromby and Standen (1996) draw attention to the ways in which research findings can be abused by powerful bodies and institutions. For example, psychological research has been used to justify early discharge from hospital as well as care-in-the-community policies, both of which are primarily motivated by economic considerations, and both of which have detrimental consequences for carers, especially those who are economically disadvantaged. Also, Cromby and Standen (1996) remind us that those who provide research funding are in a position to define what 'the problem' is. For example, psychological research can be used by those interested in maintaining the socio-political *status quo*, in order to privilege a focus upon individual behaviour change and thus neglect the role of socio-economic factors such as poverty and unemployment.

As a result of these concerns about the dangers of application, discourse analysts remain observers and commentators while others formulate policies and design interventions. While it is crucial to maintain a critical attitude and a large measure of scepticism with regard to the intentions and/or actions of policy-makers and politicians, I believe that discourse analytic studies have an important contribution to make to some form of applied psychology. For example, where discursive constructions have been identified which facilitate limiting or oppressive positionings and practices (e.g., in AIDS education materials, Willig, 1995; or police-suspect interviews, Auburn et al., 1995), discourse analysts have a responsibility to call for alternative formulations.

These may have their own limitations and are certainly always open to abuse; however, discourse analysts' continued abstentionism is unhelpful at best and dangerous at worst. The political danger lies in its applied relativism: if it is the case that all possible constructions are equally limiting once reified, and as open to abuse as one another, it follows that we may as well stick with our current dominant constructions after all. The best we can do is constantly to remind ourselves of the occasioned nature of discourses and practices. However, certain discourses and practices are privileged and thus dominant in certain historical periods, and they serve to legitimate power. It is highly unlikely that regular reminders in academic journals about the occasioned nature of discourse are going to challenge effectively such dominance. In order to ground his/her recommendations for (improved) social and psycho-logical practice, the discourse analyst must adopt a political position. Thus, it appears that, after all, my dual role as committed international socialist and as academic discourse analyst is not as contradictory as it may seem. Both activities require grounding, and for that they require a reflexive, historically sensitive method of analysis of the social which acknowledges ultimate epis-temological relativism. The main difference is that the former requires a high level of coherence and consistency in thought and action, whereas the latter is more open to contradictions and absences.

To summarize, my identification of the need to adopt a critical realist type of analysis of the social is *not* the result of a rejection of ultimate epistemo-logical relativism. Rather, it is a result of the recognition that we as human agents find ourselves within a context in which things are always already going on or being done. Within this context it is impossible to abstain from involvement since inaction is always a form of action. Thus, we can only ever argue for or against, support or subvert particular practices or causes but we can never disengage ourselves from them. An attempt to disengage neces-sarily serves to consolidate the *status quo*. This is why the postmodernist position so easily slides into political conservatism (see Callinicos, 1989). The fact that we can never be absolutely sure about our understanding of social reality does not make our actions any less transformative of this social reality. Thus, instead of engaging in futile attempts to disengage, we need to find a way of improving our understanding of the social world and our role within it.

Overcoming the Limitations of Relativism

Those concerned with social transformation have attempted to develop approaches to knowledge which overcome the limitations of both empiricist realism and postmodernist relativism. For example, critical psychologists (e.g., Parker, 1992) have attempted to draw on J.J. Gibson's theory of affordances in order to transcend a subject (the knower)/object (the known) dualism. The theory of affordances constitutes a challenge to epistemological relativism, in that it rejects the idea that all perceptions of (social and material) reality are based upon representations, since all stimuli must pass through a medium such as a bodily organ or language, and ultimately always the nervous system, before they can be interpreted by the subject. Gibsonian direct realism holds that the human being's relationship with the environment generates knowledge (about the environment) directly; that is, that perception *is* knowledge (rather than giving rise to knowledge). The theory was developed as an alternative to representational theories of visual perception, and it was designed to account for the remarkable ease with which successful visual perception takes place in daily life. It can be attractive to critical psychologists because it conceptualizes the human subject as directly, almost organically connected with its environment, thus being part of a system, an ecology, as opposed to the Cartesian subject of cognitive psychology, a homunculus, cut off from the 'outside world', trapped in the human skull and thus condemned to eternal solipsist isolation. However, in my view, there are a number of serious problems with a critical reading of the ecological approach. First, in its application to social perception, the theory of affordances encounters both conceptual as well as political difficulties: social categories are human creations and can therefore not be directly perceived. As Noble (1993: 389) points out, the meanings of words do not 'spring from' their objects' being; rather, 'they are (metaphoric) inhabitants of the discursive ecology, and may be applied (and self-applied) as identities from time to time for different practical purposes' (ibid.: 390). For example, the same individual can be described as 'a man', 'a person', 'a citizen', or 'an animal' but 'none of these words springs from anyone's being' (ibid.). Rather, they have different social functions, and it is these which inform their strategic deployment.

Niemann and Secord (1995: 2) provide an ecological account of stereotyping in which they argue that 'stereotypes often represent accurate perceptions or judgements of the behaviour of person categories in societal settings', and that 'features of the social environment shape, facilitate or afford stereotyping' (ibid.: 5). Thus, they suggest that stereotypes are a reflection of real attributes of real people, but that their veridicality is limited because such attributes are generalized to all members of a group and because they are treated as permanent traits rather than situated behaviours. The problem with this account is that it uses two, in my view incompatible, definitions of 'person category'. On the one hand, there is an almost positivistic reading of the term 'person category' as an unproblematic, descriptive term referring to a collection of self-evident, inherent attributes. On the other hand, the authors acknowledge that 'person categories' are social constructions in that they are created through language and social practices (e.g., slave, immigrant, grandmother, politician). If the latter is the case, it makes no sense to talk about the 'veridicality of stereotypes' (Nieman and Secord, 1995: 2), except in a self-referential, circular way, by saying that once social categories are in use, the very act of applying them to people generates further evidence which can be used to consolidate them. However, this is quite different from suggesting that 'most stereotyping has some veridicality in the sense that attributes assigned to the person category fit the situated actions that they repeatedly exhibit' (ibid.: 2). This is because the reading of what kind of action is 'exhibited' is itself dependent upon the stereotype used: for example, the behaviour of an individual who challenges authority may be described as 'disruptive', 'assertive', 'challenging', 'irrational', etc., depending upon the 'person category' allocated to the individual.

Furthermore, the application of direct realism to social perception raises the question of who is to be the arbiter of what is veridical perception. For example, Rantzen's proposal for a psychological research programme informed by direct realism includes '. . . specification of the conditions of information presentation . . . which prevent the subject from cognizing certain facts; organismic variables which render particular subjects unable to cognize certain facts; and the motivational constraints imposed on subjects in experimental situations that serve to inhibit subjects' cognition of certain facts' (1993: 169). This type of research programme moves us away from an exploration of different ways of understanding the world and its origins, and towards an assessment of shortcomings and limitations of certain (groups of) people's ability to perceive reality, that is to say, their willingness to agree with the researcher's interpretation of reality. Finally, direct realism depends upon the assumption that particular species share a particular perceptual apparatus as well as options for actions. For example, for an object to look portable, the perceiver must have or know of the option of carrying objects. The relationship between affordances and organisms, which is the focus of study in direct realism, presupposes homogeneity among members of the species. In my view, this assumption becomes particularly problematic when direct realism is applied to social perception where options for action are sociohistorically and culturally specific. However, it is important to acknowledge that a neat conceptual distinction between physical and social perception is not justified, since all perception takes place within the context of a 'social reality' where 'objects have been shaped, even deliberately designed, through the intentional activity of others; they have a "place" in relation to definite cultural practices and "represent" various human purposes; their reliable and safe functioning depends on a social system of mutual responsibilities and obligations' (Costall, 1995: 477). It follows that direct realism cannot simply be retained as a satisfactory theory of, say, visual perception but rejected as an account of social perception.

Other attempts at developing alternatives to relativist epistemology have been made. Gill (1991, 1995) recommends a form of 'passionately interested inquiry' (1995: 175), a politically informed relativism which rejects the search for truth and argues instead for an acknowledgement of the values which guide our (and others') knowledge production: 'In the absence of ontological guarantees, then, values, commitments, politics must be at the heart of analyses' (ibid.: 177). Here, reflexivity requires both an acknowledgement as well as a critical analysis of the knower's perspective. This position is close to feminist standpoint theory (e.g., Harding, 1991). Harding develops the notion of 'strong objectivity' which 'requires a commitment to cultural, sociological, historical relativism' as well as a rejection of 'judgmental or epistemological relativism' (1991: 142). Strong objectivity involves moving beyond a mere acknowledgement of the 'historical character of every belief or set of beliefs' (ibid.: 156) by incorporating a systematic exploration of the historical (and social and cultural and economic, etc.) conditions which gave rise to and made possible these beliefs. Such a reflexive dimension is missing from traditional scientific practice and it is, according to Harding, what makes strong objectivity *more* scientific and *more* likely to generate (maximally) objective knowledge. In other words, it 'transforms the reflexivity of research from a problem into a scientific resource' (ibid.: 164). Thus, it is suggested that rather than abandoning notions of science and objectivity, critical researchers should appropriate, re-define and improve them. In other words, we may reject the (dominant, contemporary) *practice* of science but not its aspirations. In my view, Harding convincingly demonstrates the importance of something like reflexive underlabouring; however, she does not discuss the criteria which would allow us to evaluate the results of this activity. For example, how are we to decide which of a number of conflicting accounts, all of which claim to come from 'the perspective of women's lives' (e.g., socialist feminism versus radical feminism versus bourgeois feminism) is, in fact, more objective or 'less false'? Having argued in favour of the theoretical possibility of judgemental realism, we now need a methodology as well as criteria for evaluating theories and beliefs.

A focus upon methodology and criteria also allows us to clarify the relationship between ethics and politics. An acceptance of epistemological relativism frequently leads people to conclude that political positions must be a result of moral choice. It is argued that since we cannot *know* what constitutes a superior form of social organization, our views on what kind of society we would like to live in must be informed by our moral values of what constitutes the good life. It is assumed that one's political position cannot be derived from one's analysis of the social. Burkitt (1996) invokes the example of the conservative and the left-winger, both of whom can agree that inequality exists but disagree about whether or not it should continue to exist. Burkitt suggests that the latter is a question of ethics. I disagree. First, the recognition that inequality exists is not based upon social analysis, and that is why it does not in and of itself give rise to a particular political position with regard to the desirability of inequality. However, it is precisely the conservative's and the left-winger's different explanations of why inequality arises (e.g., individual effort and ability versus a social structural explanation), which leads them to adopt different political positions. These explanations are not moral choices, but the result of their respective analyses of the social. Such analyses involve the development of arguments which are capable of accounting for events and phenomena. Differences of opinion exist when more than one theory can explain the phenomenon under investigation, and discussions about the validity of these theories must revolve around the extent of their explanatory power, that is, their ability to account for a wide range of diverse phenomena. It is, of course, true that in day-to-day political discourse such discussions are shaped by the immediate concerns and interests of the participants rather than the requirements of scientific analysis. Thus, in such situations, moral arguments can be used rhetorically in order to position one's opponent as morally inferior or irresponsible or whatever. However, this does not mean that political positions are themselves simply a matter of moral choice. Also, it is interesting to note that the qualifier 'just' frequently accompanies the term 'choice' in these arguments. People say that political positions are 'just' a matter of (moral/political) choice. This suggests that political positions are adopted easily and almost unthinkingly, once-and-for-all, on the spur of a particular emotional moment. This conjures up the image of a shopper in a supermarket, who passes through the aisle, selecting, say, the Marxism package off a shelf, and who, having made the choice, uses the Marxism package as a matter of routine thereafter. This, however, is not how political positions are developed and maintained. Rather, each new event, both personal and political, constitutes a potential challenge to a person's politics. Political positions have to be constantly justified and defended, and are thus being tested, both in arguments with others as well as in practice. Consequently, political positions are not, and certainly not 'just', moral choices, but rather the product of an ongoing engagement with the (social and material) environment. This process, of course, by no means guarantees that the best positions are always eventually arrived at. It does mean, however, that a discussion of the criteria which enable us to judge whether or not something is 'a good story', or a convincing account, is badly needed. In other words, instead of allowing epistemological relativism to reduce politics to moral choices which require no justification, we should acknowledge that political positions emerge out of material and ideological struggles, and that they are constantly being evaluated as a result.

Not all criteria for evaluation, however, are satisfactory. For example, Rorty (1987, 1991; in Billig, 1995) argues that because all knowledge is necessarily socially, historically and culturally specific, we may as well embrace our own specific socio-cultural set of norms and values and judge the rest of humanity by them. He argues that morality and politics should start from specific communities or societies, rather than aim to represent a shared common humanity. Thus, criteria for evaluating political positions and arguments must necessarily be ethnocentric and ungeneralizable: 'There is nothing to be said about either truth or rationality apart from descriptions of the familiar procedures of justification, which a given society – ours – uses in one or another area of inquiry' (Rorty, 1987: 42, cited in Billig, 1995: 162). Rorty's argument may appear liberal in that he advocates the co-existence of diverse, culturally specific moralities and value systems. However, in a world characterized by an unequal distribution of power both within and between communities and nations, ethnocentrism must necessarily entail cultural imperialism and further oppression of the powerless. This becomes clear when Rorty describes the 'history of humanity . . . as the gradual spread of certain virtues typical of the democratic West' (1991: 216, cited in Billig, 1995: 172). In addition, as a result of the emergence of multicultural societies as well as the increasing ease with which ideas can be communicated across the world, different socio-cultural sets of norms and values necessarily engage with one another. They are argued over, and they are used to defend a range of interests; sometimes alliances are formed around particular issues (e.g., when Christian fundamentalists, Muslims and radical feminists can campaign together against pornography). As a result, sets of norms and values cannot remain sealed off from one another, and any discussion about their respective merits will involve appeals to shared criteria of evaluation – without which no discussion would be possible in the first place.

Critical Realism

Critical realism (e.g., Bhaskar, 1978, 1986) offers a set of criteria for evaluating claims about reality as well as a methodology for investigating the social world. Critical realism proposes that events (observable or experienceable phenomena) are generated by underlying, relatively enduring (intransitive) structures. These can never be directly accessed; rather, they can be known through their effects. Deep (intransitive) structures and the generative mechanisms through which they operate possess tendencies or potentialities which may or may not be exercised. Furthermore, events are generally co-determined by multiple mechanisms. Thus, the objective of critical realist science is not to predict outcomes but to explain events and processes. Criteria for evaluating attempts at explanation include: explanatory power, that is the extent to which a proposed mechanism is capable of accounting for a wide range of diverse as well as newly emerging phenomena; the extent to which proposed structures and mechanisms can account for absences (non-entities, non-events, non-beings) as well as for possibilities for change; and underlabouring, which can identify the extent to which closure in scientific analysis has taken place. Closure refers to a state of affairs where moral and political agendas dictate the ways in which concepts may be defined and consequently the ways in which theoretical as well as empirical research may (or may not) progress. Finally, critical realism's understanding of the world as stratified, so that there are layers of reality which cannot be reduced to one another, provides a further criterion for evaluating claims about reality. For example, people are animals, humans as well as physical objects. Explanations of human behaviour and animal behaviour and of physical movement cannot be reduced to one another; however, they need to be compatible in order to be capable of making sense of people's lives.

A critical realist approach can also help us address a number of challenging psychological questions. First, critical realism allows us to differentiate between theories which attempt to explain how ideas are formed and maintained (e.g., neuropsychology; connectionism) and those which explore their content and dynamic change (e.g., discursive psychology; psychoanalysis). A critical realist psychology would hold that the 'how' and the 'what' of consciousness constitute different layers of reality. These are incommensurable, they require different levels of explanation, and consequently, they cannot be accounted for by one and the same theory. It could even be argued that those psychological theories which attempt to collapse the 'how' and the 'what', the form and content of ideas, such as Gibsonian ecological psychology or radical behaviourism, cannot provide adequate accounts of either.

Secondly, critical realism can help clarify the concept of reality by differentiating between the 'real' and the 'actual'. Here, the reality of the experience of a particular content or quality of consciousness is acknowledged, without having to deny that such phenomena themselves require further explanations in terms of (real) structures and mechanisms. In other words, 'real' phenomena still need to be accounted for, but the provision of an explanation does not make the phenomenon any less 'real'. Furthermore, we need to differentiate between 'reality' and 'truth'. For example, an individual's strong belief that the outgroup eats babies for breakfast and the accompanying emotions of fear and hostility are very real, but at the same time the belief itself can be quite false.

Finally, critical realism's dialectical approach to science, in my view, makes its (always ultimately provisional) truth claims less open to abuse and misrepresentation. This is largely due to its emphasis upon the need to understand objects and events in relation to their history and relationships with other objects and events. Thus, an organism (or a society) can only be understood within the context of its own history, and the present can only be understood with reference to the past. Therefore, while positivistic psychology is able to take snapshots of a particular socio-historical moment and build theories of human functioning on the basis of it, a critical realist psychology would have to engage in a critical examination of concepts and their meanings through historical, cross-cultural and political analyses in order to be able to generate satisfactory explanations of contemporary human behaviour.

So far I have presented some of the arguments that lead me to take seriously a critical realist philosophy. I have not, however, addressed the merits (or otherwise) of critical realism as developed by Bhaskar and others. Within this context, the relationship between critical realism and historical materialism deserves particular attention. The following questions need to be addressed. To what extent does critical realism prohibit the identification of only one underlying social structure, and to what extent are 'deep structures' identified by critical realist research genuinely independent from one another? To what extent can reflexive underlabouring be applied to the relatively enduring structures identified by critical realists? Does a conceptual differentiation between structures, mechanisms and events lead us to identify a proliferation of structures which are really mechanisms of yet deeper structures? And finally, how often is critical realism used as a way of warding off accusations of 'Marxist dogma' by triumphantly pointing to the saving grace of 'more than one structure'?

Note

I would like to thank Pete Green for making helpful comments on an earlier draft of this chapter.

References

Auburn, T., Willig, C. and Drake, S. (1995) '"You punched him, didn't you?" Versions of violence in accusatory interviews', *Discourse and Society*, 6 (3): 353–86.

Bhaskar, R. (1978) *A Realist Theory of Science* (2nd edn). Brighton: Harvester.

Bhaskar, R. (1986) *Scientific Realism and Human Emancipation*. London: Verso.

Billig, M. (1995) *Banal Nationalism*. London: Sage.

Burkitt, I. (1996) 'Relations, communication and power: selves and material contexts in constructionism'. Paper presented at Social Constructionism, Discourse and Realism (day conference), 20 April 1996, Manchester Metropolitan University.

Burman, E. (1990) 'Differing with deconstruction: a feminist critique', in I. Parker and J. Shotter (eds), *Deconstructing Social Psychology*. London: Routledge.

Burr, V. (1995) *An Introduction to Social Constructionism*. London: Routledge.

Callinicos, A. (1989) *Against Post-Modernism*. Cambridge: Polity Press.

Costall, A. (1995) 'Socializing affordances', *Theory and Psychology*, 5 (4): 467–81.

Cromby, J. and Standen, P. (1996) 'Psychology in the service of the state', *Psychology Politics Resistance Newsletter*, 3: 6–7.

Eagleton, T. (1990) 'Defending the free world', in R. Miliband and L. Panitch (eds), *The Retreat of the Intellectuals*, Socialist Register. London: Merlin Press.

Edwards, D., Ashmore, M. and Potter, J. (1995) 'Death and furniture: the rhetoric, politics and theology of bottom line arguments against relativism', *History of the Human Sciences*, 8 (2): 25–49.

Gergen, K. (1985) 'The social constructionist movement in social psychology', *American Psychologist*, 40: 266–75.

Gill, R. (1991) 'Ideology and popular radio: a discourse analytic examination of disc jockeys' talk'. Unpublished PhD Dissertation, Loughborough University, UK.

Gill, R. (1995) 'Relativism, reflexivity and politics: interrogating discourse analysis from a feminist perspective', in S. Wilkinson and C. Kitzinger (eds), *Feminism and Discourse*. London: Sage.

Harding, S. (1991) *Whose Science? Whose Knowledge? Thinking from Women's Lives*. Milton Keynes: Open University Press.

Harper, D.J. (1994) 'The professional construction of "paranoia" and the discursive use of diagnostic criteria', *British Journal of Medical Psychology*, 67: 131–43.

Hollway, W. (1989) *Subjectivity and Method in Psychology: Gender, Meaning and Science*. London: Sage.

Howitt, D. (1991) *Concerning Psychology. Psychology Applied to Social Issues*. Milton Keynes: Open University Press.

Isaac, J.C. (1990) 'Realism and reality: some realistic reconsiderations', *Journal for the Theory of Social Behaviour*, 20 (1): 1–31.

Niemann, Y.F. and Secord, P.F. (1995) 'Social ecology of stereotyping', *Journal for the Theory of Social Behaviour*, 25 (1): 1–14.

Noble, W. (1993) 'Meaning and the "discursive ecology": further to the debate on ecological perceptual theory', *Journal for the Theory of Social Behaviour*, 23 (4): 375–98.

Parker, I. (1992) *Discourse Dynamics. Critical Analysis for Social and Individual Psychology*. London: Routledge.

Parker, I., Georgaca, E., Harper, D., McLaughlin, T. and Stowell-Smith, M. (1995) *Deconstructing Psychopathology*. London: Sage.

Potter, J. and Wetherell, M. (1987) *Discourse and Social Psychology: Beyond Attitudes and Behaviour*. London: Sage.

Rantzen, A.J. (1993) 'Constructivism, direct realism and the nature of error', *Theory and Psychology*, 3 (2): 147–71.

Rorty, R. (1987) 'Science as solidarity', in J.S. Nelson, A. Megill and D.N. McCloskey (eds), *The Rhetoric of the Human Sciences*. Madison: University of Wisconsin Press.

Rorty, R. (1991) *Objectivity, Relativism and Truth*. Cambridge: Cambridge University Press.

Spears, R. and Parker, I. (1996) 'Marxist theses and psychological themes', in I. Parker and R. Spears (eds), *Psychology and Society: Radical Theory and Practice*. London: Pluto Press.

Stenner, P. (1993) 'Discoursing jealousy', in E. Burman and I. Parker (eds), *Discourse Analytic Research. Repertoires and Readings of Texts in Action*. London: Routledge.

Tiefer, L. (1995) *Sex Is Not a Natural Act and Other Essays*. Boulder, CO: Westview Press.

Widdicombe, S. (1995) 'Identity, politics and talk: a case for the mundane and the everyday', in S. Wilkinson and C. Kitzinger (eds), *Feminism and Discourse*. London: Sage.

Willig, C. (1995) '"I wouldn't have married the guy if I'd have to do that": heterosexual adults' accounts of condom use and their implications for sexual practice', *Journal of Community and Applied Social Psychology*, 5: 75–87.

Young, R.M. (1996) 'Evolution, biology and psychology from a Marxist point of view', in I. Parker and R. Spears (eds), *Psychology and Society: Radical Theory and Practice*. London: Pluto Press.

PART II: COMMENTARIES

8

Across the S–S Divide

Don Foster

Along with others I am sorely tempted to fall in with the weary remark of Walkerdine (1997: 169) regarding 'sterile debates about realism and relativism' or the more politically exasperated stance of feminists against the extremes of postmodernists and their 'self-referentiality, their intellectual gloss over power relations, and their refusal to recognize the material effects of repression' (Wilkinson, 1997: 182). Nevertheless I am persuaded by the charming rhetorical turns of Potter, by the increased sound and fury of the debate (a literary construction, in one view) and by my own contradictory positioning (as for Willig), that there may be uneven merits in participation, not least in self-referentially (how wearisome) grappling with my own confusion. The debate is important not merely because it spills over into, but rather is central to questions of method (or theory-method, as Potter rightly has it), ethics, politics, criteria for evaluating research (Willig) and 'good-stories', and not least as 'guides for action' (Harré, 1990: 303) in our everyday dilemmatic circumstances (backwards or forwards? side to side? yo-yoing up or down? zig-zag, weave, reconnoitre or purposefully straight ahead?).

Peering out of a much longer set of struggles, the recent debate has been around for some time with roots into the early 1970s crisis in social psychology (Ibáñez and Íñiguez, 1997; Parker, 1989), skirmishes in the philosophy of science and social sciences (Bhaskar, 1979, 1989; Gergen, 1982, 1994; Greenwood, 1989, 1991; Harré, 1986, 1992), debates in the sociology of knowledge tradition and in the history of psychology (Danziger, 1990, 1997). The debate is sprinkled about in the pages of various journals such as *Philosophical Psychology* (1990), *Theory and Psychology* (1992), *Feminism and Psychology*, *History of the Human Sciences* and in the numerous edited volumes and monographs appearing over the past decade on social constructionism, rhetoric, postmodernism, discursive psychology, discourse analysis, post-Marxism and the like. Almost unheard and unspoken in psychology just over a decade back, these new and bewildering concepts have swept over (some of) us like a small tidal wave, have shaken the portals of the mainstream but have also been summarily dismissed in certain quarters. Most prominent in – but erroneously restricted to – social psychology, the issues here are part of a very much wider movement in feminism, cultural and media studies, post-colonialism, literary studies, sociology and Marxism. Within social psychology the contours of the debate have been pulled together in the splendidly sane summary by Spears (1997), matters have been 'troubled' by Beryl Curt and the unusual recent critical textbook (Stainton Rogers et al., 1995), different voices of prominent (mainly male) social psychologists have appeared within one set of covers (McGarty and Haslam, 1997), some have tried to note the voices of missing 'others' (Billig, 1996; Sampson, 1993; Wilkinson and Kitzinger, 1996), while the neglected and now beleaguered Marxist tradition – evident even in the title of the work *Psychology and Society* – has been given an airing (Parker and Spears, 1996). The currents of constructionism have even touched the far-distant shores of newly democratic South Africa in the form of some fragments of research, two special editions of the *South African Journal of Psychology* 1996 and 1997, and the recent edited collection by Levett, Kottler, Burman and Parker (1997). If Billig is halfway right in suggesting that intellectual argument and debate is worthy of celebration, not misery, we are indeed in heady times.

But just before we cheer our heads off, some sombre notes are in order. This small wave remains a distinct minority; the mainstream marches blithely on, relatively undisturbed. The fringe encampment is riven even in the pages of this book. The lines of debate are confusing with criss-crossing alliances and numerous border-crossings, some counter raids. The collective, so central in struggle, is shaky. And lest we forget, matters of power are never far away. The clutch of busy hands remains still largely Anglo-American with the odd Spanish outpost. The spatial positionings of North–South divides are markers of power (Burman, 1997). Poverty, starvation and draconian rule constitute the governance of the majority of subjectivities across the globe; globalization might signify the spread of misery and exploitation rather than the celebration of equalized pluralities of difference. There is not too much, in the preceding pages, of this sort of world, despite some good intentions. If this sort of missing world, riven by terror, inequalities, hunger and power blocs were to be our 'starting point' (Parker, 1996), then the sound and fury over relativism versus realism, while certainly not inconsequential, might nevertheless be held by some of those 'other' than ourselves to be of less pressing significance.

Some Themes

What do we have in the debate in this book? First, we have some anxieties and worries; a picture of premature celebration of the discursive followed by hesitation and hobblings (Burr; Merttens) or of pullings hither and thither in contrary ways (Willig). The worries appear to emanate more from the would-be realists than the relativists, though I puzzle about Merttens. If Potter has some anxieties about a competition for the most politically acceptable, then I too have worries, positioned in part as an anti-apartheid activist, and positioned also by 'death and furniture' (Edwards et al., 1995). My worries: to be pinned by the Mandy Rice-D trap: 'well he would say that, wouldn't he'; in a realist reminder of death, torture, oppression and gross violations of human rights under apartheid South Africa. Just another good story (Potter, 1992).

Worries and anxieties have certain consequences. They could lead some into laagers and others into a search for other route maps. So we should be concerned. Some alternative terrains sought out in recent years in partial retreat from relativist fringes include a turn to 'bodies' (Harré, 1991; Radley, 1991; Ussher, 1989) and to spatial explorations (Dixon et al., 1994), territories already and earlier mapped out by Foucault, so they need not necessarily be seen as retreats. Empiricists of course continue to *skuil* behind the encircled ox-wagons of the laager.

Secondly, we have some celebrations; particularly of the critical spirit of relativism. Relativism is championed as being in service of 'offering resistance', maintaining contestation and raising scepticism (Potter) and in service of a vision of be-coming other than our present selves (Brown and Pujol with Curt). In this tenor there is resonance with Billig's (1996) celebration of dilemmatic arguing and debate, in particular a cheer for 'Aspasian rhetoric'. I doubt whether any of us (another rhetorical strategy) would be hesitant about celebrating the critical spirit, but some of us may be more than hesitant about limiting it to the province of relativism. There is also *critical* realism (Collier; Willig). The realists for some odd reason seem wary of celebration. Perhaps there is something after all in the stereotype of grim-faced realists in the recognition of 'death', exploitation and poverty. Not much to celebrate. But perhaps also we can be-come both: sombre-faced recognizers of realities and nimble celebrators of critical 'witcraft'. In South Africa at last we are able, in part, to celebrate the spirit of resistance. But not for too long for the realists: there is work yet to be done.

Thirdly, there are stories; and stories about stories. Well there would be, in an age when 'narrative' is back in fashion. For Potter, at various times (1992, 1996, 1997 and here) realism is one good story. Over this period he has shown with considerable skill the rhetorical devices and strategies of building up a successful story of 'facts', and has also turned his scalpel-like analytical gaze upon realism itself. We should be grateful: in this constructionist age nothing should be above or beyond unpicking. In Potter's words, we should not 'insulate our own practices from scrutiny' (1997: 64). Nevertheless, while Potter does well to unpick the story-telling of realism, and does in the present chapter recognize a range of realisms, rather naughtily bunging in empiricists and equating Eysenck and Brand with Bhaskar and Parker (I thought we were way beyond that kind of rhetorical skirmishing and slurring), he fails entirely to turn his analytical gaze on the nuanced, layered and more serious varieties such as Harré's (1986) modest realism or Bhaskar's critical realism. In each side of the debate, akin to in- and outgroup stereotyping, there are tendencies to oversimplify and selectively construct the target outgroup.

With stories, Merttens tries something else. For her, rooted in struggle education (if that term makes sense) and faced with paralysing tensions between relativist theorizing and requirements to do something concrete, stories, based in her own experience, constitute a practical solution. We should be sympathetic: the political question of 'what is to be done' is a far more difficult problem than most of us are prepared to square with. The matter of becoming something other (Brown and Pujol with Curt) does not deal with what kind of other. But I worry about her solution of stories grounded in her immediate experiences. 'Experience' is too tepid and unreliable a theoretical position (Gergen, 1994) to pass muster. Others, rooted in their experience may also tell good stories: of racism, sexism, or of the goodness of authoritarian rule. We appreciate with both Potter and Merttens that stories are powerful devices in creating subjectivities and realities. That is why there is the necessity for ideology critique as a means of resistance.

Fourthly, we have a good deal of agreement. Most notably there is agreement that social constructionism, or a discursive-rhetorical psychology (labels vary among key players), constitutes a radical break from the vacillating polarities of rationalism and empiricism as hegemonic foundations for truth-seeking claims. Pragmatism also gets a bad press here. There is a shared attack on empiricist assumptions of value neutrality. There is a shared rejection of both cognitivism and individualism. As Gergen (1994) puts it, individual mind loses not only its ontological grounding, but also its constituents: memory, emotion, beliefs, traits, attitudes. All become 'contingent constructions of culture' (1994: 70). Individualism is replaced with appeals to reflexively social, communal, relational or dialogical (joint action) ontological forms. Appeals to the linguistic turn, albeit in terms of somewhat differing traditions and emphases – ethnomethodological, speech-act theory, rhetoric, Wittgensteinian, Foucauldian, Bakhtinian – are held in common. There is indeed much common territory. But within this shared framework, cracks and divergences appear. Although there are varieties of both anti-foundationalism and realism, and as Potter suggests the targets and constructions differ within specific debates, can we discern core elements of disagreement?

Divergences

One way of depicting differences is to locate positionings within sets of well-worn distinctions such as those of agency–structure, micro–macro levels of analysis, synchronic–diachronic emphasis or in Harré's distinction between practical and expressive orders. If agency does present problems for both sides, differences do appear to be discernible with relativists on the side of active constructions ('presencing practices' or rhetorical strategies) and with emphasis on the expressive, synchronic and micro-levels of analysis. Realists, it could be argued, frequently appear to favour the structural, diachronic, macro and practical dimensions. Where does that leave us? If, on the one hand, there were to be substance in such patternings, it would merely entrench the stalemate (Burr), reproduce the dualisms and exacerbate polarization, something which Gergen (1994: 92) for one is apparently not keen to encourage. If, on the other hand, it were possible to locate sufficient border crossings, invariances, and context-bound disavowals of such simple positionings, one could be left with the swirls, fluidities, fragments and kaleidoscopes which anti-foundationalists seem to celebrate and which render realists queasy.

Another possibility exists for the location of difference. Let us return to the Saussurean signifier–signified (S–S) relation – both a useful earlier advance, and itself part of the problem – and Eagleton's (1991) treatment of this in respect of ideology. I suggest that the core difference between realists and relativists is (i) their location in and across this divide, and (ii) the conflation of two separate meanings of discourse.

Eagleton suggests that relativists are in danger of merely inverting the empiricist model: the representationist position where the signifier follows spontaneously from the signified. In the inverted position it is now a question of the signified 'following obediently from the signifier' (1991: 208). Now all is linguistic construction. Moreover for Eagleton, the S–S linguistic relation is inadequate for understanding relations between material conditions and ideological discourses.

The relationship in the case of the linguistic S–S is arbitrary; meaning takes place in terms of local communal conventions. Constructionists take this position; realists would not (yet) demur. But there is a second meaning of discourse which suggests that the purely linguistic S–S version is inadequate for grasping social structural-ideological relations. Eagleton suggests that ideological views have an internal (not merely arbitrary or contingent) relationship to social structures 'not in the sense that the condition is the automatic cause of them, but in the sense that it is the reason for them' (1991: 208). Ideological discourse fashions reasons about those structures/material conditions, including among others, legitimating functions. For anti-foundationalists, two meanings of discourse – 'those which are said to constitute our practices, and those in which we talk about our practices' (ibid.: 209) – are falsely conflated. The relationship between an object and its means of representation is, for Eagleton: 'crucially not the same as that between a material practice and ideological legitimation or mystification' (ibid.). Conflation of the two indicates a 'fatal semiotic confusion between *signified* and *referent*' (ibid., original emphasis).

The gap or divide between discourses and material practices/structures provides an enabling distance which requires transformative labour (ideology goes to work on the 'real' situation); ways of talking (legitimating, dissimulating, distracting, justifying) about our practices. The notion of transformative labour suggests that 'something preexists this process, something referent, something worked upon, which cannot be the case if the signifier conjures the "real" situation into being' (ibid.).

Taking the example of members of an oppressed ethnic minority and their discursive involvement in anti-racist politics, Eagleton claims that the relation is not purely contingent. While for both realists and relativists the relation is 'not necessary in the sense of natural, automatic or ineluctable', it *does* bear a relation in terms of reasons about something; it is a 'motivated' rather than a purely arbitrary relation.

Differences between anti-foundationalists and critical realists may be located in positionings across this relational divide or gap. Whereas relativists, like empiricists, breach this divide, but from an inverted position, realists, making appeals to a referential theory of meaning (Harré, 1986), wish to maintain the divide. Relativists, in privileging the signifier as well as operating with a limited discursive frame, elide the tensioned gap which enables ideology critique: a capacity to contradict appearances. The tensioned divide is, for Collier, the 'aboutness' of language, for Bhaskar, the distinction between transitive and intransitive realms, and for Parker (1992), located in distinctions between three forms of object status: when something is in a text, it does not necessarily mean that it loses other forms of object status.

From this perspective of maintaining space; neither privileging nor foreclosing the relation between discourse and practice, it is possible to propose a 'both and' rather than an 'either or' resolution of the apparent impasse. This inclusionary approach may be seen in the fashion in which Parker (1996) wishes both to unpick critically Wittgensteinian views as well as to argue for a combination of such views with those of Marxist and Foucauldian traditions.

An inclusive approach has a central place for fine-grained studies of the creative procedures for managing and producing rhetorical versions of facts and realities. Billig's (1995) recent study of the everyday story-telling of nations and nationalism, ubiquitous and banal, and Shotter's (1993) work on creative management of joint action are splendid examples. It clearly involves recognition and analysis of the 'skids' and 'slips', themes and counter-themes (Billig, 1996), of the shifts, fluidities and 'swirling patterns' (Potter, 1997) as well as the complex 'presencing practices' and 'assemblages' (Brown and Pujol with Curt) that assist in the becoming of the real. Nor is there any quibble with Potter's request for reflexivity to 'address critically our own constructions' (1997: 63). Indeed, Bhaskar, as a realist, provides the identical advice: 'since the social sciences are part of their own field of inquiry' (1986: 101). Examination of the rhetoric on both sides of the debate will find little difference on this score.

Across the divide are the 'referents': economic and social relations, social interests and positionings, spatial structurings and bodily orderings that 'do not (simply) lie around the place like slabs of concrete waiting to be stumbled over' (Eagleton, 1991: 206), but nor are purely contingent relations waiting to be constructed into becoming real by the omnipresent signifier. That there may not be purely contingent relations across the divide remains a task that always provisionally – open to revision as language and material-political circumstances change – awaits the communal labour of realist social scientists.

A Case Example

One of the disappointments of the debate chapters above, was the lack of examples of actual studies: realism put to work on psychological topics. An illustration is provided here, drawing on a set of recent South African studies by colleague and former student Kevin Durrheim (1995) on the matter of under-lying explanations for racism and prejudice. According to a lengthy literature, one core construct apparently underlying bigotry is the notion of 'intolerance of ambiguity': a rigid and dogmatic cognitive style. It lies at the core of the thesis of 'authoritarian personality', at the heart of understanding conser-vatism as a trait reflecting a need for certainty and order, and at the centre of Allport's (1954) classic account of prejudice. It reappears with regularity in sub-sequent literature. It is a beguiling thesis since it hopes to link a particular style of mind (cognition) with a particular ideological content and worldview, thus potentially affording a royal road to ideology critique. Let us tell a story.

Durrheim opens with a reminder that the Nazi psychologist Jaensch invented the S-type to explain those predisposed to adopt a liberal ideology. The S-type mind was irrational in having no firm tie to reality. On the American side, Frenkel-Brunswik argued that it was the authoritarian J-type, not the S-type, who was irrational, clinging to the familiar while employing a rigid and firmly bounded categorization style termed 'intolerance of ambi-guity'. For both protagonists a political orientation could be ascribed scientifically to a state of mind: irrationality – also offering a 'scientific' basis for critique. It was an empiricist encounter; the morality and political cor-rectness of liberalism against fascism could be settled by science in terms of Humean criteria – the observation of 'constant conjunctions'. It is a long and meandering tale since then, affording a range of heroes and villains (few women in this saga, apart from Billig's Aspasia; anything but rigid) with names such as Shils, Eysenck, Rokeach, Allport, Mischel and more recently Sidanius, Tetlock, even Furnham, with a host of supporting actors: measur-ing, theorizing, sampling, observing and debating.

Enter Durrheim, placing his labour on the treadmill of scientific enterprise. His earlier studies, based on standard empiricist theory-methods, showed roughly: (i) that groups of differing position and political orientation (liberal to conservative) varied in terms of 'relative deprivation' and stated readiness to employ violent means of resistance within a changing South African socio-political context (Durrheim et al., 1995), and (ii) that socio-political attitudes in South Africa, measured in quite standard ways (scales of conservatism, authoritarianism, racial prejudice), were structured in particular clusters, dif-ferentially for white, black and coloured participants (the usual disclaimers for use of this terminology). For example, for white and coloured, political and economic conservatism were associated with punitiveness, authoritari-anism and racism, whereas for blacks, political-economic conservatism was not linked with any other dimensions of conservatism. Various aspects of the study led us to question 'whether personality dynamics are sufficient to account for the structure of ideological attitudes' (Durrheim and Foster, 1995: 399). We asked 'if ideological beliefs are structured by a basic person-ality dimension, such as need for certainty, why is it not reflected in different samples?' We suggested further that: 'It may be precisely the alienation from the state that underlies the different ideological structure of the black sample'; a social structural argument, if you like.

Note that in these studies, the methods, measures and terminology remain strictly within conventional empiricist frames, using terms such as 'attitudes', 'personality', and the like. But at work here, despite its mainstream frame, was the depiction of patterned structures: relations between structural positions and different political beliefs; doubts about individualistic dynamics. Further studies may be regarded as steps in an argument towards critical realism.

At the next step Durrheim plunged more directly into investigation of rigidity of mind: intolerance of ambiguity. Again he went to work with empiricist tools, in this case however with a notable exception: use of a new scale which specifically allowed for variability in assessment of ambiguity (see Durrheim and Foster, 1997 for details). This procedure allowed respondents to express both likes (respect) and dislikes (disrespect) towards particular authorities ranging from God, doctors, parents and the family to the Afrikaner Weerstands Beweging, the South African government (prior to 1994 democratic elections) and the African National Congress (ANC). Details of complex results are not given here, but the contours of argument are provided, a sequence which could be described as steps to refuse empiricist ontology. In step form, for simplicity, these are as follows: (i) the new scale allowed for variability beyond a single score – quite unusual in empiricist methods; (ii) results using standard forms of analysis (correlations, factor analysis) showed variability, but some regularities – not all was flux. Measures distinguished clearly between domains of authority (political, familial, religious) – in other words were *context*-dependent. Further results showed particular forms of relation between ambiguity tolerance, ideological content and social structural positioning; (iii) types of regularities in these studies are not consistent with an empiricist ontology on the following grounds: (a) there is not a constant conjunction of events, and (b) dimensions are not ontological, rather they are partially *produced by* investigative practice – factor analysis, sampling procedure. Similar patterns could not necessarily be produced in other contexts, or with other items. However, that does not preclude the possibilities of 'generative structures' assisting in producing these regularities; and (iv) results suggest a meaning- and praxis-based, rather than a substance-like ontology. Different dimensions of ambiguity tolerance arise due to variable structural positioning (black or white) and different meanings that various authorities (apartheid or ANC authorities) have due to being embedded in different discursive practices. A published version, about which a whole tale of woes and difficulties could be told, concluded that there were 'strong grounds for rejecting the personality-based understanding of ambiguity tolerance' (Durrheim and Foster, 1997: 748). This work, still within the shapes of conventional psychology, allowed nevertheless for a critique of empiricist models with the claim that cognitive style was not a property of individual 'mind'. But what about the generative mechanisms?

The next study employed a shift to textual analysis, drawing on a range of theory-methods, including rhetoric and joint action, Bakhtinian speech genres, and embedded in critical realism with a search for generative structures. The text involves analysis of the talk of one Koos Vermeulen, leader of the World Apartheid Movement, a small but vocal South African neo-fascist organization. The interview, which took an argumentative form, was broadcast on public television soon after the assassination (at the hands of two white right-wingers) of Chris Hani, a leading member of the ANC and South African Communist Party, in April 1993. Scrutiny of the text showed a high degree of variability; contrary to the rigidity thesis, Vermeulen evidenced flexible, shifting rhetorical skills in attempting to justify his organization's support for Hani's assassins (see Durrheim, 1997).

Vermeulen argues for contrary themes, peace and violence. In backing the assassin Vermeulen takes a stance supporting violence. Indeed, the organization is renowned for support of right-wing violence. He also argues for peace, reiterating his 'heartfelt desire for peace', preferring talking to violence. As the rhetorical perspective would have it, the values of peace and violence were debated and reconstructed through the interview. No rigidity here. Vermeulen engages in particularization, lifting out the assassin from the categorization of 'violent' by psychologizing his motives and portraying him as the victim. As further markers of his rhetorical dexterity, ambiguity tolerance itself is referred to as a topic of debate/discussion, particularly in blaming Hani for 'double talking', that is talking war and peace, or supporting war in practice but talking of peace, or supporting killings in the past but peace in the present – flexible depictions of 'double-talk'. Accusations of Hani's 'double talk' denoting ambiguity and inconsistency, construct a rhetorical case for insincerity and a warrant for the assassination. More could be said but this is sufficient to show rhetorical flexibility, dexterity, fluid variability, deft counter-themes: a poor case for rigidity of mind.

Along with variability, there is also rhetorical organization. Accusations of 'double-talk', a pervasive feature of Vermeulen's utterances, is read through Bakhtinian notions as an ordered form: a speech genre. Durrheim argues that the speech genre which is associated with accusations of 'double-talk' among the far right is conspiracy ideology. While clearly not limited only to the right, in terms of the relational juxtapositioning with other groups, conspiracy theory is usefully suited to the rhetorical purposes of the right. In South Africa conspiracy themes of a communist plot – the 'double-talk' of black leaders – have been ubiquitous in the rhetoric of the right wing (Foster, 1991). Rhetorically active and flexible, but not simply free-floating, Vermeulen's talk, relationally positioned in dialogical argumentative forms of joint action, contains sedimented forms of organization, styles and commonplaces which require explanation. In the perspective of critical realism which shifts from a substance-like ontology to a relational, praxis- and concept-dependent ontology, 'reference to generative mechanisms in the intransitive realm account for the organization and style of Vermeulen's rhetoric. Intolerance of ambiguity and his neo-fascist arguments (for racial partition and violent means) are linked, through the conspiracy of ideology, in a dialogical and historical relationship with radical and liberal themes and styles of argument' (Durrheim, 1995: 231). This view of critical realism 'denies neither the Shotterian emphasis of the creative aspect of joint action, nor the Bhaskaresque/Parkerian emphasis on socio-economic-political structures' (Durrheim 1995: 213).

Concluding Comments

Having toured through the wider recent literature on social constructionism as well as the debate chapters of the present volume, peering at themes and arguments both common and contrary, this chapter proposed a central differentiation between anti-foundationalists and realists situated between and across the discursive–linguistic divide. Despite current differences, a case was made for an inclusionary approach recognizing merits of both across a divide which enables possibilities of explanation and critique. This involves a shift in the understanding of explanation and critique, from an endeavour based on empiricist grounds (truth–falsity; accumulated 'facts') to a rhetorical enterprise which defends or attacks discourse and practices in terms of their relational effects. In a world where 'truth' with some justification has been displaced, we may note yet another meaning of S–S in the context of a newly democratic country which still dares to have a Truth Commission.

References

Allport, G.W. (1954) *The Nature of Prejudice*. Reading, MA: Addison-Wesley.
Bhaskar, R. (1979) *The Possibilities of Naturalism*. Brighton: Harvester.
Bhaskar, R. (1986) *Scientific Realism and Human Emancipation*. London: Verso.
Bhaskar, R. (1989) *Reclaiming Reality*. London: Verso.
Billig, M. (1995) *Banal Nationalism*. London: Sage.
Billig, M. (1996) *Arguing and Thinking* (new edn). Cambridge: Cambridge University Press.
Burman, E. (1997) 'Differentiating and de-developing critical social psychology', in T. Ibáñez and L. Íñiguez (eds), *Critical Social Psychology*. London: Sage.
Collier, A. (1994) *Critical Realism*. London: Verso.
Danziger, K. (1990) *Constructing the Subject*. Cambridge: Cambridge University Press.
Danziger, K. (1997) *Naming the Mind*. London: Sage.
Dixon, J., Foster, D., Durrheim, K. and Wilbraham, L. (1994) 'Discourse and the politics of space in South Africa', *Discourse and Society*, 5: 277–96.
Durrheim, K. (1995) 'Rethinking cognitive style in psychology'. Unpublished PhD thesis, University of Cape Town.
Durrheim, K. (1997) 'Cognition and ideology', *Theory and Psychology*, 7: 747–68.
Durrheim, K. and Foster, D. (1995) 'The structure of sociopolitical attitudes in South Africa', *Journal of Social Psychology*, 135: 387–402.
Durrheim, K. and Foster, D. (1997) 'Tolerance of ambiguity as a content specific construct', *Personality and Individual Differences*, 22: 741–50.
Durrheim, K., Foster, D. and Tredoux, C. (1995) 'Conceptions of legitimacy as a variable mediating the relationship between relative deprivation and militancy', *South African Journal of Psychology*, 25: 106–11.
Eagleton, T. (1991) *Ideology*. London: Verso.
Edwards, D., Ashmore, M. and Potter, J. (1995) 'Death and furniture: the rhetoric, politics and theology of bottom line arguments against relativism', *History of the Human Sciences*, 8: 25–49.
Foster, D. (1991) 'Ideology', in D. Foster and J. Louw-Potgieter (eds), *Social Psychology in*

South Africa. Johannesburg: Lexicon.

Gergen, K.J. (1982) *Toward Transformation in Social Knowledge*. New York: Springer.

Gergen, K.J. (1994) *Realities and Relationships*. Cambridge, MA: Harvard University Press.

Greenwood, J.D. (1989) *Explanation and Experiment in Social Psychology*. New York: Springer.

Greenwood, J.D. (1991) *Relations and Representations*. London: Routledge.

Harré, R. (1986) *Varieties of Realism*. Oxford: Blackwell.

Harré, R. (1990) 'Exploring the human *Umwelt*', in R. Bhaskar (ed.), *Harré and His Critics*. Oxford: Blackwell.

Harré, R. (1991) *Physical Being*. Oxford: Blackwell.

Harré, R. (1992) 'What is real in psychology', *Theory and Psychology*, 2: 153–8.

Ibáñez, T. and Íñiguez, L. (eds) (1997) *Critical Social Psychology*. London: Sage.

Levett, A., Kottler, A., Burman, E. and Parker, I. (eds) (1997) *Culture, Power and Difference: Discourse Analysis in South Africa*. London: Zed Books.

McGarty, C. and Haslam, S. (eds) (1997) *The Message of Social Psychology*. Oxford: Blackwell.

Parker, I. (1989) *The Crisis in Modern Social Psychology, and How to End It*. London: Routledge.

Parker, I. (1992) *Discourse Dynamics: Critical Analysis for Social and Individual Psychology*. London: Routledge.

Parker, I. (1996) 'Against Wittgenstein: materialist reflections on language in psychology', *Theory and Psychology*, 6: 363–84.

Parker, I. and Spears, R. (eds) (1996) *Psychology and Society: Radical Theory and Practice*. London: Pluto.

Potter, J. (1992) 'Constructing realism', *Theory and Psychology*, 2: 167–73.

Potter, J. (1996) *Representing Reality*. London: Sage.

Potter, J. (1997) 'Discourse and critical social psychology', in T. Ibáñez and L. Íñiguez (eds), *Critical Social Psychology*. London: Sage.

Radley, A. (1991) *The Body and Social Psychology*. New York: Springer.

Sampson, E.E. (1993) *Celebrating the Other*. London: Harvester Wheatsheaf.

Shotter, J. (1993) *Conversational Realities*. London: Sage.

Spears, R. (1997) 'Introduction', in T. Ibáñez and L. Íñiguez (eds), *Critical Social Psychology* London: Sage.

Stainton Rogers, R., Stenner, P., Gleeson, K. and Stainton Rogers, W. (1995) *Social Psychology: A Critical Agenda*. Cambridge: Polity Press.

Ussher, J. (1989) *The Psychology of the Female Body*. London: Routledge.

Walkerdine, V. (1997) 'Postmodernity, subjectivity and the media', in T. Ibáñez and L. Íñiguez (eds), *Critical Social Psychology*. London: Sage.

Wilkinson, S. and Kitzinger, C. (eds) (1996) *Feminism and Discourse*. London: Sage.

Wilkinson, W. (1997) 'Prioritizing the political', in T. Ibáñez and L. Íñiguez (eds), *Critical Social Psychology*. London: Sage.

9

The Perverse and Pervasive Character of Reality: Some Comments on the Effects of Monism and Dualism

Maritza Montero

The chapters in this book are part of an old confrontation produced by human beings' reflection about their environment, their being in that environment, their relation with it and, consequently, their capacity to know, to comprehend that world while knowing and comprehending themselves. Two perspectives are opposed in these polemics, realism and idealism, as are two radically different views about the way knowledge is produced. Realism considers that it derives from characteristics of the world, pre-existent to knowledge, and reflected by it. Idealism presents knowledge as a production of the human mind. Two current versions of the confrontation are found in this volume: critical realism and social constructionism.

The chapters gathered here present explicitly and critically the problems that some interpretations of the realist and the social constructionist views of the relation between subject and world have posed. And also some of their excesses and errors, and some of their achievements. In doing so, they also demonstrate how, when submitted to critique and reflexivity, both warnings and complaints that may contribute to the study of psychology's epistemology and ontology, could be derived.

But a reading of the preceding chapters also reminded me of those specious problems that were so heatedly discussed in the Middle Ages by scholars: *Universalia*. *Universalia* referred to generic notions, abstract ideas and entities whose ontological status was not clear, meaning by this that their particular form of existence gave rise to many a discussion, some very byzantine. And indeed, in one of their more reducing and reduced expressions, these polemics between subject and object, between discourse and reality, the problem of truth and its criteria, sometimes seem to be a postmodern version of them.

My comments and reflections stem, as said, from that reading, and I organize them into the five following aspects that I consider central to the controversy and relevant to the preceding chapters: knowledge about reality and the adoption of a monist or dualist epistemological and ontological perspective; the empire of language; the problem of truth and of its existence;

authority, ethics and human interests; and the role of action in the relation between subjects and objects.

The Relation between the Knowing Subject and the Known Object, as a Problem

Is it possible to know reality? This question poses, the very moment it is formulated, a *dualist* position, according to which there is a knowing subject and there is a field or an object existing *per se*, separately, that could or could not be known. A possibility (knowing) and its contrary (not knowing) have been introduced, but that does not mean there is a difference between the latter and the former. In both cases, whether it is considered that there is a reality (whatever it may be) liable to be known by the subject, or whether it is considered that it is not possible for the subject to know it, one is assuming a dualist standpoint, and at the same time it means stating that reality does exist independently of that subject.

Within the first camp fall those theories that develop systems and procedures for comprehending and representing reality. In the second, those that consider a reality separated from the subject as not directly capable of being known, since it and the cognizant subjects are placed in different dimensions, and therefore the knowing processes people have would not attain it. On the contrary, those processes would generate circumstances that are assumed as reality, since actually they construct it. They are reality.

So, this is an absurd problem, albeit a tremendously important one. The sole statement of the non-existence of reality already is a recognition of it, and introduces it in our world. It gives objectivity to reality by relating it to the subject that denies it. Only what exists can be denied. What is non-existent is neither affirmed nor denied.

Miseries of Monism and Dualism

The adoption of a monist or dualist standpoint brings about the problem of exclusion. In both cases a scission that destroys totality is produced. That 'plurality contemplated as unity', understood as totality (Kant, 1781/1952: 43), is thus fragmented. Dualism recognizes the simultaneous existence of subjects and reality, separated in such a way that, as Ibáñez (1994: 40) points out, it produces, according to the sense of the polarization in the epistemological position adopted, idealistic or rationalist tendencies, in which knowledge derives exclusively from the subject, and empiricist or realist tendencies, that consider knowledge as deriving from objects and their characteristics, existing in reality, independent of the subjects.

In both cases, a close correspondence between what by epistemological definition has been separated, is supposed. That is, between subject and object, because otherwise the subjects' activity would not deal with reality and reality could not be represented in the subjects activities.

Ibáñez (1994: 41–2) also criticizes the interactionist resolution of this problem, based in the dialectics of subject–object as a realm for the construction of knowledge. As he poses it, not only knowledge, but also the validity criteria applied to it, are constructions. Moreover, subject and object are both the result of a construction process in which there is a strict separation of those two elements (Ibáñez, ibid.: 43). And invoking Kant, he points out how 'human beings cannot have the possibility of access to reality *such as it is*' (ibid.; emphasis added). But as I am indicating, a statement like that is a recognition of the existence of something responding to the name of *reality*. Be it capable or not of being known, it is there. And it seems that somehow we are left with the belief that we can know it, or that it is in some way (*such as it is*) that we shall never be able to know.

Ibáñez's analysis (ibid.: 43) points out the impossibility for knowledge to reflect reality or to adjust to it. That would imply the possibility of comparing the knowledge produced by the subject, and the reality represented, with independence between them. And this is impossible, because it would suppose the possibility of having a perspective external to the world where subjects and objects interact.

I think that impossibility derives from our being directly and totally involved, submerged, in the realm of the knowledge constructed by ourselves about reality, in which we elaborate our convictions and perplexities, in which we interact with success or with failures. And from wherever they may come, they pass through the sieve of our senses and of our capacity to understand, socially developed in a specific time and space.

Subject and object are on the same side, but not as contiguous entities in a realm that contains them as two separate units, but as that realm itself, constituted by both, inseparable, in continuous influence, construing their existence. There cannot be either a subject without an object, or object without subject. Reality is in both. Both are reality. The tangible world (with or without authority), and the subject defining it, conceptualizing, denying or affirming it, are real.

Lucubrations, theories and argumentations, too. Brown and Pujol with Curt provide an illustration of this point when they argue that 'the real owes its certain, ordered nature to the unfinished, unstable "hybrid" patterns-in-production of material and texts which labour within it'. Also Curts's notion of 'presencing practices' (quoted by Brown and Pujol with Curt) could be an example of this.

Therefore, reality exists, it is 'there' to be known, and it can be known because it is defined, re-defined, described once again every day by the subjects that belong to it and that are influenced by it while they create it. And from that unity derives the difficulty of conceptualizing it, and the illusion of describing it once and for all. Parodying Augustine (*Confessions*, XI: 17) when he referred to time, we could say: '*Quid est ergo realitas? Si nemo ex me quaerat, scio; si querenti explicare velim, nescio.*' (What then is reality? If no one asks me, I know; if I wish to explain it to one that asketh, I know not.)

That impossible character, that condition of the 'fatal object', as

Baudrillard (1991) would say, always in some way there, causing us to knock on authority or to be knocked by it, has been expressed in many ways, not only by exasperated scholars, but by poets, by 'ordinary' people, by cartoonists, by movie directors. Thus, Juan Gustavo Cobo Borda, a Colombian poet, finishes one of his poems (*Ofrenda ante el altar del bolero*) with this verse: 'Reality is superfluous', and an English-speaking one, T.S. Eliot, says in one of his quartets (*Burnt Norton*): 'Human kind / cannot bear very much reality.' Almodovar, the cinema director, has one of the characters in his motion picture *La flor de mi secreto*, say: 'Reality should be forbidden', but as someone else said: 'If reality would not exist, we should have to invent it.' Well it does, and we do.

What they express is the annoying character of reality. Its perverse character that fails once again to adjust to our plans. One of those abundant everyday life philosophers put a message the other day on the Internet, also expressing the discomfort or malaise caused by the existence of that knot of disarrangements that perversely resist our wishes, plans or values: 'avoid reality at all costs'. Perhaps social dynamics consist of that tension, that continuous strain between what is called the 'real' and the 'actual' (Willig; Brown and Pujol with Curt), between our constructions and those of other people, and of their effects upon life circumstances (another name for reality).

The current tendency to appeal to hybrid explanations combining a monist relativist epistemology with a realist critical ontology seems to respond to certain researchers' and practitioners' ethical need to provide their practice with grounds for engagement in certain activities and not others. And it also seems to derive from the criticism received by certain 'vulgar' constructionist perspectives that deny *tout court* the existence of reality. Since engaging in social transformation supposes there is a specific situation that needs to be transformed, the existence of such circumstances collides with such a denial. Such combination is logically impossible, since subjects and reality cannot be separated in a level of knowledge (ontology) only to be reunited in another (epistemology). The problem is not empirical, it is not in the practices. Actions and events happen daily. The problem resides in theoretical and ethical justifications.

The Empire of Language

The accusations made against social constructionism – of reducing everything to meaning and discourse, and discourse to language (Collier) – bring out another important aspect, related to the role played by discourse. We talk about reality, we invent it in our discourse, and produce discourses about it, we give names to it. Affirming or denying occur within it, and in fact, pronouncing or omitting the fateful name of reality – as, for example, instead of saying reality, speaking of 'the world', as do Burr or Brown and Pujol with Curt when they talk about 'cutting out the world' (is this a way to avoid a contradiction induced by the use of the word 'reality'?) – is a linguistic means to express something presented as if it were extra-linguistic.

Language has both a universal and a circumscribed character. Everybody uses a language to communicate with other people, and to convey meanings; those meanings establish linguistic modes specific to particular groups and to certain moments. This plural and omnipresent capacity of language is responsible for what could be called its imperialism.

By linguistic imperialism I mean that predominant character usually attributed to language, in its written and spoken forms. It appeals to some evident ways to express our ideas, but it is responsible for reducing the notion of text to one of its connotations (perhaps one of the more materialistic). As Stenner and Eccleston (1994) say, there is a de-textualizing process, the de-textualizing of texts in that reduction and in the centring in discourse as if it were the only or at least a privileged way to produce texts (Burr; Stenner and Eccleston, 1994: 98). Linguistic imperialism forgets that *actions* too are charged with meanings. They are also texts, and human beings can be a form of textuality. A great many criticisms levelled at social constructionism stem from this verbalist bias given to language and texts, when reducing them to only one form of expression.

But criticism of the verbalistic position attributed to constructionism is also directed to the privilege conferred in some of its expressions, to individualistic aspects (especially within linguistic constructions, that forget or leave aside its 'social' condition), avoiding the fact that constructions occur in social events, and create social events in which action and discourse achieve transitory accords about meanings. Social life has an 'anti-Babelic' orientation: to generate commonalties in order to counter the dissolving effects of individualism and dissidence. Babel and anti-Babel are part of the tension in construction, deconstruction and destruction happening in all societies. Language and action interrelate in the same realm, a realm usually called reality. The existence of language and of shared experiences show that that reality does not need to be either proved nor denied.

Authority, like God, is Everywhere

The argument that Potter calls 'death and furniture', directed against the usual criticism against the constructionist perspective about discourse and reality – object knocking and bringing into discussion the female genital mutilation carried out in some Muslim regions (yes, they seem to be universally used, I have witnessed several debates in very different places, where both examples were brought in as arguments) – is very impressive. But beyond Potter's ability to uncover the authority principle working in reactions and arguments that seem to proceed from generalized naturalization of certain modes of knowing, deeply embedded in common sense and in the field of science, I must confess the feeling of a certain vacuum sensation, a certain dissatisfaction.

Am I longing for good old authority that solves our doubts and confers on us a deceitful certainty, providing us with the Euclidean lever that enables us to move the world, perhaps achieving social change? Let us say that the rock used as evidence of reality in the arguments against social constructionism, its hardness, considered so real, certainly contains (atomic weight and organic and inorganic components apart) an authority argument. Yes, okay, but as any post-Galilean could say: *eppure non si muove.* Rocks do not budge by themselves. Rocks are there. And what bothers me is the fact that I feel that somehow we are jumping over the rock, or eluding it. There is authority and there is a rock. Both integrate many a relation, and I cannot let go of either of them. I need both.

I do not refute the fact that the rock is spoken of. The rock is said, defined, conceptualized, it is signified, and a certain conception of it is used as a criterion to argue, more or less convincingly, about a way to conceive reality. And criteria are constructions to be applied to rocks, to people, to everything. In this sense, the materiality of a rock is an authority argument, coexistent with its being there. But criteria reside in language, which is part of reality; and the objects referred to are also part of reality. Just as realists jump from solidity to the exclusion of the subject, when they separate rocks and persons and place them in two different spheres, Potter's argument is also jumping from the world of atoms and of the relativity in the definition of rock used to the criterion of authority, leaving aside its existence.

'Authority is the biz', and authority also seems to be *das Ding an sich* (with Kant's permission), the thing in itself. Arguing and meaning happen in a rocky world. We go on proposing to open and build roads in it, placing toll-gates and fences, not allowing some people in, dividing them, photographing them. The notion of authority and the process of authoring seem, at first sight, to be what in Kantian terms could be designated as a *category a priori*, that is, a 'knowledge we do not derive [. . .] immediately from experience' (1781/1952: 14). But instead of being an object of knowledge understood as an object of intuition, it seems to be an element of knowledge understood as doing, as a form of action. In such a sense it would not be, then, a proper category a priori as Kant defined it, since somehow there would be some previous experience of authority allowing recognition of that authority in the text. Then it is not 'pure knowledge a priori' (Kant, 1781/1952: 14), but *impure*, since it is mixed with some empirical elements (do I smell reality there?). In this sense, texts are part of reality, since they are intersubjective constructions, impossible outside a social frame.

Discourse is an element of doing (action), and of doing-in-relation, meaning by that the relation as 'the concrete existence' of the person (Moreno, 1993: 469). In discourse analysis, as in some detective novels where they have the saying '*cherchez la femme*', there could be said '*cherchez l'authorité*', since if we dig into texts (verbal and non-verbal), authoring shall be found, like the gem or the fossil hidden in the rock. Seek (de-construct), and thou shall find a fundamental concept that will allow us to know the sense of the text.

(My) Malaise with Constructionism, or Fear of Freedom?

My discomfort with the ambiguity found in some of the constructionist argumentations about reality could arise from the following issues. First, the pervasive effect of authority upon us. Being accustomed to knock, throw and kick rocks, I, for one, have difficulty in accepting them as a feature of language, or as something disappearing when one does not talk about them. Their materiality, authoritative or not, bothers me. Out of habit or out of bruises, there are rocks. It is like when someone covers his or her head from the sun, that act has a meaning for that person and conveys meaning to others. One does not need to say the word 'hat', or any other word meaning headcover, for the act of protecting one's head from the heat is enough in itself. Meanings and things cannot be separated. Meanings neither belong exclusively to verbal language nor to the quietness of things.

Secondly, in my case, commitment to community development projects directed to produce changes in slums in the outskirts of the city of Caracas, changes decided, planned and carried out by the dwellers of those sites, organized and in self-control of their decisions and actions. This commitment is part of a psychosocial practice that proposes a social and a community psychology oriented towards social transformation. But transformation of what? Of reality such as it is socially known and lived, representing a state of matters characterized by inequalities, unfairness and attacks on the freedom of certain social sectors? Of course, defining a field of psychology as a discipline oriented towards the production of changes in certain realities is not a proof of the existence of those realities, but it means that accordingly to certain ethical and political conceptions there is something that needs changing and it is affecting certain social sectors. Thus, my previous analysis and position about the problem. And my interest. Is this a bit of 'death and furniture'? But that ethical foundation provides me with grounds for action; even if we know it is a social construction.

Thirdly, the Marxian notion of ideology has led me, as many other social researchers, to try to understand how it is possible to develop social practices, both in action and in discourse, that hide the ways in which the interests of some groups are opposed and superimposed on those of other groups, in order to obtain benefits, by depriving them. This shows the influence of the 'philosophy of suspicion'. Influence reinforced by many a discourse analysis of political and economics texts that show how policies argued as beneficial for the population, or the nation, or economy, are harmful to certain groups, and attend to individual interests; and how those discourses can be de-populated (Billig, 1994) or how they can ignore certain social actors (Montero and Rodríguez, forthcoming).

As Potter says, discourse analysis has provided a valuable contribution to the study of ideological discursive structures. The deconstruction of methods and of truths claims can lead to the development of 'practices of resistance', and, as I have found in some community and psychopolitical studies, those practices produce planned changes carried out by active social groups, living in conditions of oppression. Thus, language and action not only serve to strengthen and keep in place a particular kind of social order, but also to construct a new one.

In this sense, the 'psychology of visibility' suggested by Brown and Pujol with Curt is very much like a psychology of ideology construction. Ordering, stabilizing and ensuring 'the repetition of the appearance of certain meaningful patterns' needs only a pinch of intention and interest to create an ideological process. The visible and the invisible are involved in each other. They are reciprocal. The sense of what is not visible is construed from what is visible, and vice versa.

Ethics, Politics and Human Interests

The previous considerations belong to the ethical plane. In that sphere we find accusations and refutations concerning the moral callousness and political irrelevance of social constructionism versus ethical and political involvement of critical realism. But ethical or political engagement does not derive automatically from the epistemological perspective adopted concerning the ways to produce knowledge. As I said, the work of many social constructionists tells us about their commitment to action, and ethical values. Social indifference and reactionary and ethically dubious positions are also found among realists. To suppose a direct and necessary relation between assuming or not one or the other perspective would be a gross simplification, easily leading to the dogmatism that Collier so strongly condemns.

The critical standpoint also commended by Collier, and widely accepted by all the other participants in this volume, provides a sound way to evade this peril, regardless of belonging to the constructionist or to the realist fields. On the contrary, non-critical attachment to a particular tendency considered as the best, or the sole possible way to produce knowledge, probably is the easiest way to become biased. This I know by direct experience. Having carried out my studies at a time when in my university militant Marxism and experimental behaviour analysis prevailed, fiercely opposed to a no less partisan psychoanalytic redoubt, I often heard authority arguments invoking St Skinner, St Marx or St Freud used to end discussion. Afterwards, as a teacher and as a researcher, some of my doubts and critiques about theoretical or methodological issues received as advice, from other academic sources, the recommendation to read Lenin's *Materialism and Empiriocriticism* in order to 'finish with those problems'. And I also did (Montero, 1976), as Collier does, absolve Marxism of its voids and flaws, on grounds of being 'too full' about other issues, agreeing thus, to be an accomplice of authority.

Personally, I find richer and fairer a relativistic perspective that considers notions such as that of ethical commitment as a 'process of becoming' (Brown and Pujol with Curt), since it acknowledges the dynamic character of social events, of life, of being, and allows me to correct my judgements, to evolve, to retract, and to contradict myself, freeing me from the fear of cognitive dissonance, and from rigidity. This does not mean that uncertainty is to be celebrated or deprecated. Uncertainty is inextricably tied to the production of knowledge. Recognizing its existence does not mean 'a celebration', actually for me it can be terrifying, but accepting the immovable character of a construed truth is something I find even worse. Ethical commitment, a critical perspective, constant reflection, and explicitly stating one's own interests sustain action.

Dogmatism, as certain widespread diseases that attack even within the 'best families', can take refuge within *any* epistemological, ontological, theoretical and methodological tendency. It is omnipresent. And I heartily agree with Collier that critique and reflexivity are the only antidotes to dogmatism (and, I should add, our only guarantee of freedom of thought and expression).

Human Interest and Authority

Talk of ethical considerations frequently include mention of values (and some of the chapters are an example of this). Nevertheless, I think values deserve a separate space, since they play an important role in most of the chapters by the authors contributing to this volume. Thus, Burr considers values and asks in whose name we should conduct our actions. What are usually called values (doubtless one of the most dissatisfying and undefined concepts used by social psychology) are always present in human behaviour. But does that mean that there exist certain fundamental, basic, universally shared values? Are there some values superior to other values? These questions reflect certain very dangerous ideas that lead to the consideration of the necessity to impose those that have a higher qualification. Human history is full of the sorry effects of such ideas, and how they deny the right to think and act in ways different from those derived from 'higher' precepts.

Intertwined with the concept of values as action-directing forces is the notion of interest. Whenever we talk about values, behind their defence are ethical, social, ethnic, economic, political, religious or personal interests. Habermas defines interests as 'basic orientations rooted in specific fundamental conditions of the possible reproduction and self-constitution of the human species, namely work and interaction' (1978: 196). Those are for him knowledge-constitutive interests. But interests also are linked to authority, and they tend to direct knowledge along certain lines. Again, a critical standing, as well as explicit recognition of the interests motivating us, are the sole protection to the biases they can introduce.

The Problem of Truth: A Problem of Interests

This is another thorny issue. Does absolute, universal, fundamental truth exist? Do multiple truths coexist? Is the truth we assume at a certain moment always true?

Burr acknowledges the importance of this issue when she brings forward the basic character of *the* truth due to the necessity (interest) of justifying advocacy for 'one view of the world over another'; for a certain 'organization of social life over another', or in order to not have to bear the smugness of those we consider wrong but who see themselves as right. As Burr proposes further on, the notion of truth provides a frame or gives support to moral choices. If that is the case, then we should recognize that choices respond to interests. Some have their justification in ethical considerations, some in economic ones, others are based on artistic or in religious precepts, and so on. But while considering truth as present only when certain interests are related to it can be very self-assuring and satisfying, it is just a way to construct a legitimating function for the notion of truth as defined according to some interests, and presented as essential. In that case, more than declaring certain reasons as true and others as false (that is, the case of 'false consciousness'), what we should do is to manifest the interests inducing us to make certain choices, to prefer certain modes of action and certain settings for them. A certain point of view can be considered good or bad according to the interests of a particular group. Besides, change is adjusted according to the circumstances affecting that group.

This would be what Ibáñez (1994) calls the use-value of truth or the practical conception of truth derived from social practices or, I should say, derived from the multiple, brief moments of certainty we have during our daily experiences. But not with a pragmatic or ethnocentric sense, since interests separated from reflexivity and critique may end up justifying anything – or, as the supporters of truth as a natural part of certain facts and objects, so much fear, jumping into the 'anything goes' wagon. Let us not then be paralysed by fear of commitment or by ontological insecurity, and let us engage with action and intervention in material or ideological struggles (but still recognizing and allowing the right of others to dissent).

The provisional character of all forms of knowledge should not be surprising. The history of science accounts for that. It shows how scientific truths are demolished every now and then. Expressing explicitly our political, moral or scientific standpoints and adopting a critical-reflexive perspective probably is the best antidote (although neither a definitive cure, nor the universal panacea) against paralysis and callousness. With respect to this, it is interesting to see how so many supporters of critical realism and of no less critical relativism, coincide in accepting the 'always ultimately provisional' character (as Willig puts it) of truth claims, stating that if the historical character of social phenomena is admitted, one cannot dispense with it, or with the notion of relativity. As Potter says: 'realism never quite turns timeless, solid and true; there is always an edge of scepticism and self doubt'. Likewise, relativists cannot do without the notion of reality, even when they jump from rocks to authority.

Doubt, as well as recognition of the social character of interaction, and therefore, of several perspectives, interpretations, beliefs, values and norms, according to the different events and accounts of it, is what makes me uncomfortable with Merttens's accounts which are used to prove the emergence of truth in stories, as the gem emerges (or is extracted) from the rock. Although very well told, and with the type of ending (first story) one loves (I sure do), or where one tends to take sides (with the boy oppressed by authority in the second one), her argument for the existence of an essential truth shows several biases.

The first one is to suppose that certain beliefs are of a superior kind. That is the case for 'the belief in the transparency of what we say or write', and the attainability of the 'aspiration to truth'. Beliefs are social constructions, historical, and therefore subject to changes and influences. We are not born with them. Transparency in texts is both an aspiration (what more could we wish?) and a belief (a very dear one) but, as hermeneutics has shown, usually nothing is less transparent than a text. And is there not a link, and an important one, between rhetoric and accuracy? Or is there a pre-determined, fixed, immanent accuracy to social events?

Moreover, as many a discourse analysis shows, authorial intention can be brought out and made explicit, since not always is it either easy to find or transparent. And that means relativism and constructionism are not only concerned with the constructions pertaining to the reader, the author's also need to be considered.

I do agree with Merttens's declaration of interest, about having certain beliefs and values considered fairer, more democratic, less cruel, more egalitarian than others. She calls them 'faith', a term I deem as very proper, but that does not mean that *the* truth is enshrined in them. Such a faith, something that people develop as a foundation for their deeds, is necessary in order to act. Perhaps even inevitable. But again, history illustrates the excesses of bestowing some of those beliefs and values with an essential truthful character. They can lead to oppression as well as to liberation. And again, a critical and reflexive perspective is necessary if we want to know what is to be done. Along with the recognition that even when we do not know it, we are going to do something, as Willig says, it is impossible not to act. Omission also is a form of acting.

Truth, as a foundation for action is but the brief, fleeting moment in which we find a meaning for events or for the relations between them; moments of certainty, often understood as *a* truth and not as atemporal certitude. Research and knowledge are therefore a voyage from uncertainty to certainty to uncertainty again, and so on. But not in circles, because through action (discourse and acts) we produce forms of knowledge where those truths are introduced, and also extracted. A knowledge that keeps transforming us, being transformed by us, and producing changes around us.

Actions, Discourse and Texts

At this point I need to place action in the conception of psychology's epistemology that I am referring to. The Discursive Action Model (Edwards and

Potter, 1992; Potter et al., 1993) acknowledges the importance of action focusing on 'action done through discourse' (1993: 389), and on 'how representations are constructed within, and constitutive of social practices' (1993: 390). I think those constructions give a textual character to those practices. Action too can be a text, and interpreted as a text. In everyday life we 'read' other people's behaviour, as well as our own, and interpret it, attribute different meanings to it, define and re-define it, deliberately or unintentionally ignore it, answer to it.

The notion of text should not be reduced to the discourse fixed by writing, as Ricœur (1986: 193–7) proposed. In relation to this, Shweder and Sullivan argue that intentionality 'makes it possible for the semiotic subject to react to any and every situation or object as a text or a symbol' (quoted in Much, 1993: 54). Action, in general, can be symbolic and textual, and I agree with Ricœur's consideration of human action as 'an open work, whose signification is "in suspense"' (1986: 197), but not because it is 'like a text' but because it *is* a text. Bhaskar (1989: 4) also makes a point about this with his statement about the wider realm of social practices and how those practices are not 'exhausted by their conceptual aspect'. There is more to life and knowledge than concepts. And that wider frontier is action.

Concluding Comments

Finally, I should like to comment that adopting a position about these matters certainly is not an easy task. Realist assumptions, critical or not, take the risk of losing the capacity to admit changes and, with that, remaining fixed to certain conceptions, to times and places and modes of relations that do not exist anymore, of ignoring the ways in which the world, and us with it, change. Relativism also has its risks: incertitude; having to find a compass inside ourselves and not knowing where the North is – yes, this has Kantian resonances: 'The starry heavens above, and the moral law within' (Kant, 1781/1952: 360).

Another cause for uneasiness is the fact that both relativism as well as realism keep their a priori or essential categories. Actually, declaring that everything is relative introduces an aporia that invalidates the very foundations of relativism, since the relative character of relativism leaves an open door for absolutism when it states that *everything* is relative. And that bothers me, although not to the point of leading me to consider that my truth is *the* truth, or is truer than other people's. And at the same time, this consideration does not stop me from engaging in specific political actions oriented by ethical norms, and from condemning others on the grounds that they suffocate liberty and seize the space and resources needed to express plurality in the beliefs about truth. And if this seems contradictory, it is perhaps because absolute coherence is the type of feature present only in absolutist, fixed texts.

References

Augustine (*c.* 400/1952) *Confessions.* Chicago: Encyclopedia Britannica and University of Chicago.

Baudrillard, J. (1991) *Las estrategias fatales.* Barcelona: Anagrama.

Bhaskar, R. (1989) *Reclaiming Reality: A Critical Introduction to Contemporary Philosophy.* London: Verso.

Billig, M. (1994) 'Repopulating the depopulated pages of social psychology', *Theory and Psychology,* 4 (3): 307–35.

Edwards, D. and Potter, J. (1992) *Discursive Psychology.* London: Sage.

Habermas, J. (1978) *Knowledge and Human Interests.* London: Heinemann.

Ibáñez, T. (1994) 'La construcción del conocimiento desde una perspectiva socioconstruccionista', in M. Montero (ed.), *Conocimiento, realidad e ideología.* Caracas: AVEPSO.

Kant, I. (1781/1952) *The Critique of Pure Reason.* Chicago: Encyclopedia Britannica and University of Chicago.

Montero, M. (1976) 'La clase social: sus derivaciones psicosociales', in J. Salazar, M. Montero, C. Muñoz, E. Sánchez, E. Santoro and J. Villegas, *Psicología Social.* Caracas: AVEPSO/Universidad Central de Venezuela.

Montero, M. (1994) 'Estrategias discursivas ideológicas', in M. Montero (ed.), *Conocimiento, realidad e ideología.* Caracas: AVEPSO.

Montero, M. and Rodríguez, I. (forthcoming) 'Discourse as a stage for political actors: an analysis of presidential addresses in Argentina, Brazil, and Venezuela', in C. De Landtsheer and O. Feldman (eds), *Politically Speaking: A Worldwide Examination of Language Used in the Public Sphere.* New York: Greenwood Press.

Moreno, A. (1993) *El aro y la trama (episteme, realidad y pueblo).* Caracas: Centro de Investigaciones Populares/Universidad de Carabobo.

Much, N.C. (1993) 'The analysis of discourse as methodology for a semiotic psychology', *American Behavioral Scientist,* 36 (1): 52–72.

Potter, J. (1996) *Representing Reality: Discourse, Rhetoric and Social Construction.* London: Sage.

Potter, J., Edwards, D. and Wetherell, M. (1993) 'A model of discourse in action', *American Behavioral Scientist,* 36 (3): 383–401.

Ricœur, P. (1986). *Du texte à l'action.* Paris: Seuil.

Stenner, P. and Eccleston, C. (1994) 'On the textuality of being: towards an invigorated social constructionism', *Theory and Psychology,* 4 (1): 85–104.

10

Psychology's Subject: A Commentary on the Relativism/Realism Debate

Bronwyn Davies

My task here is to provide a commentary on the debates around realism and relativism as they appear in this book. I have been asked to reflect on how these debates do or do not make sense from the standpoint of my own research. Briefly, then, my own research revolves around feminist issues, and more often than not takes these up in the context of schooling. While my first book (Davies, 1982) was located in an ethogenic framework, my later books (1989, 1993a, 1994, 1995) have used a post-structuralist framework, but with a clear indebtedness to that earlier engagement with ethogeny. The particular dilemma being examined here, that is, how psychologists might position themselves in terms of the binary relativism/realism, is not one that has any currency in the various contexts in which I generally work and write. While I imagine it is unlikely that I would be called a 'realist', the only person who has cast me as a 'relativist' that I am aware of is Rom Harré, who expressed complete astonishment when I said I did not think the term had any relevance to my understanding of what I was doing in my research and writing. If a 'relativist' is one who believes that there can be no way of arguing the superiority of one view over another, then I am certainly not a relativist. So I come as an outsider to these realist/relativist debates (from my point of view) but as one who can apparently be read as unquestionably 'relativist' by at least one of those engaged in the debate.

It seems to me that there are three central nodes of conflict in the debates as they are presented in this book. The first, and most fundamental, is the relative importance of and the relationship between *the individual* and *discourse*. If discourse and discursive practices are taken to be constitutive of individuals, of their patterns of desire, of agency and so on, then the essentialist construction of persons so central to the discipline of psychology has to be revised (Fuss, 1989). What that revision actually entails seems to be both a point of resistance and of misunderstanding. The second node of conflict is what can and cannot be accomplished through deconstructive acts. The chapters contain both over-claims and under-claims about the power of deconstruction. The third issue is the psychologists' role in relation to social change. The writers gathered together here are those who have a shared commitment to some kind of critical engagement with the social world. Yet there is a moral/philosophical debate which casts doubt on each other's capacity for commitment which overlaps with and interrupts the debate in curious ways. Rorty observes, in an interview with Sayers, that:

> Around the world, liberal democratic intellectuals share a sense of common purpose. They want peace, prosperity, social justice, equality, and end to racial and gender prejudice – all the usual things. Most of the issues that divide political philosophers are pointless technicalities compared to the consensus among them about what kind of world they want. (Sayers, 1997: 32)

It is possible to read the disputes here as just such technicalities, which get in the way of an examination of just what psychology is capable of in relation to that common purpose.

The Location of Constitutive Force in Discourse and the Implications for Psychology's Subject

Understanding the constitutive force both of structures and of discourses is a perilous task for psychologists. Their field of play is the individual subject. Traditionally, psychology's subject can be subjected to many forces which (mis)shape it in any number of ways, but in its ideal form, psychology's individual subject is *the* central constitutive force both in its own life and in the shaping of society. As I have observed elsewhere (Davies, 1993b) it is the failure to remove this essentialized being from centre stage that leaves psychologists unable to take full advantage of the possibilities opened up in the discursive turn. Those who still hold on to the essentialized subject as the subject of psychology inevitably see the attention that others pay to discourse as a waste of time.

Part of the problem, from a post-structuralist standpoint, with the way the binary realism/relativism is being used by some of the antagonists here is that they are not understanding that what they are engaging in is a *discursive act of categorization*. Rather, they are treating the terms, either explicitly or implicitly, as *referring to essential properties of psychologists or of psychological action*. The implicit essentialist positioning here means that falling into either side is dangerous: the relativism side because it contains an inevitability of non-action, and the realist side because lurking within it are the inevitability of positivist practices and assumptions. The writers' attempts to undo the binary, or to have a piece of both sides, for example by calling themselves critical realists or ontological relativists, is largely undone by this implicit essentialism. Each time they adopt one of the terms that might enable them to straddle the binary, they become uneasy about the fact that they might well slide back into one side or the other, as if the sides were real places they might fall into, and as if there were only two possible ways to fall. But it is an easy trap to escape from if 'realism' and 'relativism' are understood as categories which may or may not be useful in promoting understanding. Once this is taken as given, the binary realist/relativist becomes one among many category systems through which we might make sense of who we are and what we are doing. It can also be seen as one which, when used to prevent understanding, can be used with powerful effects. This is not to say that there will not be times when our actions or writing may usefully be described as 'realist' or as 'relativist' where these categorizations help to clarify the particular meaning-making we are engaged in. But as long as realism/relativism is understood as the only, or even the primary, binary then its capacity to generate obscurity is vast.

Language is littered with binaries or category systems which may or may not be more useful (or obfuscatory) in any particular context or time. We can describe what we are doing as structuralist or post-structuralist, British or non-British, masculine or feminine, white or black, essentialist or non-essentialist. The important question to ask is, what is achieved by each of these apparently innocent descriptive acts? That is, how have we constituted each act of speaking or writing in so naming it? How has that constitutive act been read by the various speakers and writers, listeners and readers? My point here is that if we play with the different constitutive acts we might engage in, we can see that none of us is essentially realist or relativist. (I use the word play here to give a sense of lightness to what it is we can do with language. There is a heaviness about the debates here, with the exception of Potter's chapter, which means that the richness of meaning-making we can engage in, as we move within and across discourses, is likely to be missed.) We can nevertheless always be constituted as realist or relativist in a discourse which makes these terms relevant, particularly one which is intent on proving the moral superiority of being on one side or the other. But any set of categories is only relevant to the being of the speakers for the moment(s) and in the contexts in which it is being taken up and read as meaningful. No more and no less. But if each binary is understood not as constitutive, but as descriptive, then it is *not possible* to straddle the binary and have a bit of each, as the force of the binary will hold the opposition between the terms in place (and thus the impossibility of moving, in any satisfying way, between them or beyond them).

Julia Kristeva's (1981) article, 'Women's time', enabled me to first make the conceptual leap from a central focus on being *someone* (that someone being revealed by my ways of speaking) to a focus on *discourse* as something which can be used in particular ways with particular powerful effects (one of which might be the constitution of 'me' as a particular kind of person). Kristeva shows how each of the competing feminist discourses have been generated over time, partly in reaction to the problems encountered in the one that went before. These discourses oppose and contradict each other in quite fundamental theoretical ways. Yet they are each still necessary, she argues, as they can each achieve quite different and important things. Liberal feminism, for example, is the most appropriate discourse to use when overturning rules of exclusion, since the assumption of 'equal human rights', inherent in liberal discourses, is least likely to be rejected as a shared premise for action. Radical feminism is a more useful discourse to adopt in redressing the effects of oppression on individuals and groups. The celebration and re-naming of those who have previously been downgraded is appropriate activity when the intention is to enable the participants to locate themselves in a discourse which undoes some of the effects of oppressive discourses. Kristeva argues that even though each feminist discourse makes different and competing claims, each is still necessary, as each has different potential from the others to counteract oppressive patriarchal discourses.

If this shift is accepted, then instead of using discourses as a means of defining the user (e.g., since I use liberal feminist discourse then I must be a liberal feminist), the discourse can be used to achieve what it can achieve to bring about desired changes (e.g., I want girls to have rights to the same schooling as boys so I will use liberal feminist discourse to secure those rights). It is quite liberating not to be limited by the label liberal feminist just because I use that discourse when it is most appropriate to my purposes. If someone were to call me a liberal feminist now, I would say: no, it is simply one of the discourses I have access to and which I find useful on occasion. The only meaningful 'I am' statement would be: I am a user of liberal feminist discourse when it suits me, and I am also a user of discourses which are quite contradictory to liberal feminism when it suits my purposes (discourses such as radical feminism and post-structuralist feminism). This does not mean that I should not also responsibly examine the discourses I use for any unintended negative effects. I am not advocating a utilitarian approach which entails an irresponsible attitude to all other issues, other than my immediate purposes, but rather to draw a distinction between discourse as something that has effects and discourse as a means of identifying the 'real nature' of the speaker. It is also true to say that what I am capable of imagining myself to be, or what I am capable of saying, is bounded and constrained by the discourses I have access to and the discourses those others whom I interact with have access to.

Is it possible for psychologists to make this shift? That is, to abandon a concept of the essential self and move to a constituted self with the focus on language? Or does this possibility become instantly muddled with 'moral relativism' because the only 'moral being' imaginable is one who has an essential self, who is, by definition, not a moral relativist? Is there another binary trap here which is going to disallow the take-up of this point, because the reader does not want to be on the wrong side of that particular good/bad binary? A moral relativist seems to be constituted by some of the writers as one who cannot make up his or her mind to act or to recommend action, since he or she has no stable moral base which allows a choice to be made. The evidence for this seems to be pseudo-empirical in the form of a vague reference to specific unnamed others who are incapable of commitment. This is probably the weakest and yet most complex point in the arguments put forth. For my part, freedom from the essential self and an understanding of the constitutive force of discourse has enabled me to become far more capable of action than I was before. The teachers and students I have worked with would make the same claims for themselves. I agree with Rorty when he says:

there is no such thing as 'how things really are'. There are simply various descriptions of things and we use the one that seems most likely to achieve our purposes. We have a multiplicity of vocabularies because we have a multiplicity of purposes. (quoted in Sayers, 1997: 32)

The subsets of binaries that seem to be tied into the arguments about relativism and realism that I found (for the most part) in Burr's chapter are mapped out in the list below. Each is sometimes treated by the writers as an unquestionable binary in the sense that it is taken to be self-evident that something must be one or the other, and that there is no third space into which something could be said to fall, nor any other binary or discursive strategy which would enable the thing in question to be seen in any other terms. The cluster of categories on the left is generally associated with a realist position, and is more often than not seen to be superior, and the cluster on the right is generally associated with relativism and is seen to be negative or at least problematic.

Realism/relativism (or idealism)

Definitive categories / Difference and diversity
Sharply drawn lines / Bewilderment
Authoritative answers / No answers
Power / Powerlessness
Advocacy for the powerless / Conservatism
Agency / Paralysis
Us (the powerful) / Them (the powerless)
Individuals / Discourse
Action / Discourse analysis
Moral being / Moral relativist

The effect of these discursive strategies in Burr's chapter is that although she sees the logical force of the relativist arguments, she has no choice but to commit herself to realism. Some of the problematic assumptions she and other writers build out of these binaries, or combinations of them, are as follows:

1   Discourse analysis of itself is not and cannot *be* or *lead to* powerful action. By focusing on 'interpretative repertoires' you lose the capacity to act. By locating relations of power in discourse rather than in individuals you lose the capacity to talk meaningfully about individuals engaging in powerful action.
2   Categories such as 'race' and 'gender' cannot be used for political purposes once you have drawn attention to the way in which the use of that label obscures the differences between the disparate groups within the category.
3   A discourse analytic approach leads to or implies moral relativism, or an inability to take up a moral position.

The trouble that these assumptions get Burr into are revealed in her summing up. She constructs reality and discourse analysis as on opposite sides of a complex binary divide. Then, in her conclusion, she argues that this dichotomy is false, and that like Brown and Pujol with Curt she sees reality and discourse as inseparable and argues that the separation between ontology and epistemology is no more than a realist device. She then argues that the supposed difference between realists and constructionists, namely that realists can engage in action and constructionists cannot, is false. She observes that social constructionists are equally able to adopt moral positions and 'appear to be just as committed to defending their own moral and political choices as are realists'. But in a final startling shift, Burr then claims that 'it still seems to be the case in practice that constructionists and discourse analysts, afraid of reifying any particular constructions, remain "observers and commentators", leaving the action to others'. She even goes so far as to accuse them of irresponsibility. Her position seems to be, then, that the social constructionists have an important and legitimate set of arguments, which she fully grasps, but for moral (not rational) reasons, realism must be adopted so that psychology can maintain its power to influence action. This is so since (unnamed) social constructionists are irresponsible when it comes to action. Her underlying binary logic, then, is more powerful than her ability to enter into the possibilities opened up by discourse analysis. The underlying binaries in her language drag her back to a realist position even though the weight of her argument would seem to lend itself to a preference for relativism.

What is and is not Accomplished through Deconstructive Acts

The conclusion of those writers who position themselves as realists seems to be that fiddling with discourse is an individual, self-indulgent act with no real effects (though they also exaggerate the effects by declaring, for example, that a category such as race is unusable for political purposes once it has been rendered problematic by discourse analysts). Such claims underestimate what hard work discourse analysis is. They also underestimate the necessity for ongoing discourse analytic work, made necessary both by the sheer complexity of discourse and discursive practice, and by the power of dominant discourses to reassert themselves, and to erase partially or override the deconstructive work that has been done. But underestimating both the constitutive power of discourse and the extraordinary difficulty and fragility of deconstructive moves is, I suspect, an inevitable side-effect of maintaining the individual as the central conceptual device of psychology.

Let me give a simple example of the ways in which a category which is made real inside a dominant discourse can be impervious to deconstructive moves made on it within other discourses. Take the binary Australian/non-Australian. For me, 'I am an Australian' will go on being a meaningful statement, no matter how multicultural and diverse Australia recognizes itself to be, and no matter how much, on occasion, I might want to distance myself from being an Australian (e.g., when John Howard is the Prime Minister). There is a dominant legal discourse which makes it difficult for me to sustain any claim that I should be read in another way. The 'fact' that 'I am Australian' appears on my passport, which I need for entry and exit to many of the countries I want entry to, including my own. The men and women at the barriers squint at my photograph and squint at me, deciding, yes, she is Australian, she looks like 'an Australian' or she looks like the person in this photograph. If I had a sex change, and in some contexts was regarded as one who looked like a male, they would, presumably, still squint at me and at the photograph, making up their minds that I really looked like a female, because that's what it says on my passport.

But what if I were Swiss, a decade ago, and then married an Australian? I would suddenly have found, whether I liked it or not, that I was no longer Swiss, because the dominant legal discourse in my country (that was no longer my own) no longer categorized me as eligible to belong in that category. What 'I am' would become, in the legal discourse of 'my' country, Australian, even though I might have no sense of what that might mean in practice, and even though I might have no sense of identification with 'being Australian'. What 'I am' is constituted through multiple discourses, some of them more intractable than others, some with more immediate and evident effects than others.

At the same time, I and many other Australians are engaged in recognizing the diversity of 'Australians', and many of us are learning not to make sweeping statements about what an Australian is, based on our own specific experience of the term. This work is particularly important for those of us who have privileged access to powerful speaking and writing positions. To continue to speak as if all Australians are white and middle-class would be irresponsible, since to do so actively undermines the capacity of our readers/listeners to hear those who are different from us as having something equally legitimate to say, particularly when it contradicts what we have said, and particularly when they are members of marginalized groups. That work of destabilizing or deconstructing the category does not undo the force of the legal discourse which says I am or am not Australian. Further, that work would not, or should not, preclude me from using the term 'Australian', when I find it necessary to use the term to achieve the particular ends I am setting out to achieve (one of which might be to increase understanding of the diversity of people included in the term). In other words, deconstructive work does not make a category useless. In some conversations, where the focus is on deconstruction, the term Australian might be rejected as one which obscures and erases difference. In other conversations, the same players may come together with a common purpose and unite their action under the flag of the very term they set out to deconstruct in the previous conversation. Putting a concept under erasure does not obliterate the term. Derrida puts a cross through the word he is deconstructing in such a way as to leave the word visible, readable. The cross signals that the word is under erasure. The visibility of the word signals that it is still a word we need to use, as we do not know how to proceed without it. By putting it under erasure we can signal that it is problematic, in need of deconstructive work. That deconstructive work may eventually lead to the production of a different way of talking, of making sense of who we are or what we are doing. Even so, the original term will most likely go on being used in some contexts, and with powerful effects, as if that deconstructive work had never happened. Deconstruction, then, *is never complete.*

Clearly, from what I have written so far, I find the idea that a 'relativist' cannot/does not make recommendations for action, or cannot/does not act, quite strange, even frustrating. There are several parts to my frustration. One is to do with the meaning of 'cannot' or 'does not' and another is to do with the meaning of action. In all cases the accusations of unwillingness or inability to act are unclear in their reference. If the writers are referring to specific individuals whom they have observed as unable or unwilling to act, then I have no comment to make as I do not know who they are talking about or what is considered to be inaction. I have not come across any of these people in my own work. If, on the other hand, the writers who make these claims are making a generalized 'logical' argument, then the only way in which 'cannot' makes sense is if we assume that each person only ever operates inside of one discourse at a time, and that within that one discourse they do not engage in contradictory acts. Since neither of these is a feature of people in the everyday world, then 'cannot' only makes sense in a world dreamt of by philosophers. The slippage between that ideal philosophical world and the empirical world psychologists generally inhabit is a serious problem in many of these chapters.

In my book *Power/Knowledge/Desire: Changing School Organisation and Management Practices* (1995), I have included a lengthy set of recommendations for action. To me, the implications for action seemed self-evident, and did not need to be spelled out. Anyone who read the book could surely work them out, I thought. But the people with whom I was working on that project thought that recommendations would be useful for them and the activities they were engaged in, and so I included them. I did not find this remotely contradictory. The text is written as a multivocal text such that the voices of the teachers and of the principals and of the students are all there, often in violent conflict with each other, each with very different agendas, positioned very differently and making very different assumptions about what the study is about. I refused, in my writing, to arbitrate and say, see the teachers are right, or the students are wrong, or the principals are right or wrong. What I set out to make visible was how it is that their actions make sense to them. Each of the participants has a different lived history, a different sense of their own embodiment, different positioning in relation to each other, different access to and familiarity with a range of discourses. Each makes a different set of assumptions, those assumptions being closely tied to their positioning within the institutional contexts in which they find themselves. Each was differently located in relation to each of the events being analysed or spoken about in the project. What the participants in my study produced was not a random plurality of readings, but a plurality of meanings that made sense. Once the plurality of readings has been recognized as legitimate, communication across readings can take place, not in order to agree upon 'what really happened' but to comprehend how readings other than one's own can also be read as legitimate. Further, I can quite legitimately say to the reader, *if* you are concerned about gendered practices in schools, and *if* you can understand the things that are said in this book, *then it follows* that you will be able to see the need for the following kinds of action. I do not say, or want to say, here is a truth about schools and that truth dictates that x, y or z should happen. I say, given certain commitments and understandings, then x, y and z could well be very useful activities.

Another thing I find difficult is that I cannot get a clear sense of what the action is that the 'relativists' have failed to engage in, or what the action is that the 'realists' need their authoritative psychological discourses to facilitate. It is my experience that deconstruction in and of itself can produce very powerful effects.

A good example of such powerful effects was a student I worked with when I was teaching a course on post-structuralist theory in the USA. She was, when she came to see me about dropping out of the course, in a state of extreme agitation and anxiety. As we talked, it became evident to me that she was caught up in a complex set of competing discourses, all of which seemed to require specific and conflicting action on her part. Her inability to know what she should do, that is, the 'correct' action to adopt, filled her with a sense of inadequacy and helplessness. Her four-year-old daughter, she told me, had been sexually abused by her partner, the man she loved and had been about to marry. The police said her daughter had to be interviewed by them. The psychiatrist said such an interview would damage the daughter. The state law said the partner should be gaoled. The psychiatric discourse said he was disturbed and needed her understanding. The romantic discourse said she was unloving for having reported him. The state law declared that failure to report could have led to the removal of her daughter from her care. Her parents' religion dictated that he could only be seen as the devil incarnate and with whom she must immediately cut off all contact.

When she came to see me she had been painting in the kindergarten room as a way of releasing her stress and maybe finding some direction for herself. She was looking for some clue to how she 'really felt' so that she could know how to act. Needless to say she could not find any clear sense of what she really felt other than total confusion. We talked about each of the discourses she was caught up in, and we talked about which ones she was in a position to refuse, and which ones she had no power over at this point in time. I suggested she go ahead and write her essay, but use the essay as a space in which to clarify her positioning in relation to each discourse. We spent some time examining each discourse and making it clearly visible as such. Through this conversation it became evident to her that she could not, at this point, change the law. The consequences of defying the law, by refusing to have her daughter interviewed, were not, when all the detail was examined, in the best interests of her or of her daughter. So compliance, at this stage, seemed to be the best option open to her. The psychiatric discourse, on the other hand, which was being put to her by her partner, she could refuse. She could simply say, each time he telephoned her, I do not want to enter into that psychiatric discourse right now. The psychiatric discourse being put to her by her own counsellor she could use differently, not as an oppositional force to the legal one, but as one which would give her some assistance in gauging how to minimize the harmful effects of the police interview. By recognizing and analysing the relative power of each discourse she could re-position herself, not as crazy, nor as irresponsible, but with a set of tasks to do and a set of choices to make about what she would choose to do. Later she could decide what commitments she might make in the future as a result of this experience. For example, she could set about changing the relevant laws so that they would not have the same effects on others as they had had on her.

Once she had written the assignment she was calm and had a quiet and positive energy about her. She was amazed at how easy it was to refuse to enter into discourses which she saw as optional and counter-productive for her or her daughter, and equally surprised at how relatively painless it was to comply intelligently with non-optional discourses once they have been understood as non-optional.

Social Change and the Discursive Power of Psychology

Gathered together in this book are a group of psychologists who recognize, in varying ways, the constitutive force of discourse, and almost all of them worry, in one way or another, about the implications of that recognition both for the subject of psychology and for the power psychologists have to bring about change. They recognize, for example, that they themselves become authoritative individuals through their 'psychological' knowledge about individuals. Some see this as a power they must not risk losing, since it is a power they can use for the greater good. Others see it as a power they cannot divest themselves of, even if they try, since their views are, too often, read as carrying greater weight than those of ordinary mortals.

In its alignment with positivist science, psychology has gathered a great deal of status in the everyday and scientific world. With the discursive turn, such alignments are recognized as problematic and the constitutive force of psychology as a discipline makes morally-aware psychologists uneasy. The original task of psychology was not to shape the world through attempts to describe and analyse it, but authoritatively to tell it as it really was. The discursive turn makes visible that the constitutive force of those scientific 'descriptions' was in some cases both oppressive and harmful. For the authors gathered here, the apolitical stance of traditional psychology is rejected. They understand their social, constitutive power, and they want to use it to good ends. Yet if psychologists are to bring about social change through the good use of the powers they have as psychologists, they might be foolish, some argue, to risk losing the authoritative status they have as psychologists by undermining the discipline's taken-for-granted right to make truth claims.

The difficulty for those wanting to adopt this position is that it is largely through the discursive turn that they are able to turn their critical gaze on psychological truth claims and to see that they are constitutive of the thing it has taken itself to be describing. Further, those who adopt the position of the traditional truth-telling positivist psychologist also strongly maintain the importance of remaining apolitical. They are thus even less comfortable fellow travellers than the supposedly inactive relativists. How might psychologists position themselves in this new and contradictory discursive space?

Potter points to the subtlety and sophistication of people's everyday practices of 'fact construction', and shows how social constructionism raises important questions about social scientists' own factual constructions. The 'we' whose action should not be impeded in Burr's chapter is shown up as a potentially morally compromised being. Potter's conclusion is that social constructionism's, or relativism's, political contribution is that it 'supports freeing up from established systems'. And of course psychology, as that term is traditionally understood, is an established system. It is something psychologists cannot entirely free themselves of and yet retain the power that comes to them by virtue of being positioned as legitimate players in that particular system. Potter is willing to go further than any of the other players gathered together here, in running the risks of calling that established system into question.

Resistance to shifting the locus of constitutive force from individuals to discourse seems to come from psychologists who see themselves as at risk of *losing their subject* (both the people they make authoritative claims about as well as the subject psychology itself). So the question becomes, can we both understand what the discursive turn has to offer, incorporate it insightfully into our discipline, and proceed with the task of being psychologists? The risk in this is a superficial incorporation which stops short of genuine understanding of the constitutive force of discourse.

Merttens writes about the widening gulf between theory and practice, about her immersion in theory at night, which she uses to make sense of her data, and her immersion in 'practice' during the day. She believes the gap must be bridged but that this is very difficult because (she assumes) the theories of Foucault and others are necessarily relativist and make it impossible to recommend one line of action over another. The partial solution she presents in her chapter is the use of stories which *of themselves* will instruct the teachers. In listening to the stories, she argues, they will take them up as if they were their own experience. Although each one will hear the stories differently, the stories nevertheless appear to convey the ideas the researchers wish the teachers to understand. Merttens thus avoids adjudicating between truths, recognizes the plurality of readings and yet successfully conveys the message she wants to convey. This appears to me to be an unnecessary sleight of hand. She has actually made a decision about what she wants the teachers to know, but is creating a situation in which they *apparently* have the power to come to know in their own way. I'm not surprised that she feels uneasy. She is treating her teachers as objects to be manipulated, not according them the respect she accords herself. At the same time, she is underestimating the extent to which teachers get locked into struggles over power and control and cannot easily remove themselves from those struggles, even when they are able to see them as such.

Brown and Pujol with Curt weigh into the argument optimistically with a claim that the representations of social constructionism, which constitute it as relativist and unable to connect with action, can be readily dismissed: 'only in its crudest formulations does social constructionist work come to resemble such linguistic neo-Platonism'. What they argue for is a 'relativist ontology'. While 'ontology' takes its original meaning within a binary ontology/epistemology (the study of being/the study of knowledge), Brown and Pujol with Curt are attempting to deconstruct partially that binary by retaining the terms but showing the dependence of one on the other. Thus they place 'the assemblages of relations at the centre of the analysis, with the implication that the real owes its certain, ordered nature to the unfinished, unstable "hybrid" patterns-in-production of materials and texts which labour within it. Unfinished organizings take on the character of stable entities via the mediation of practices which order, stabilize and moreover ensure the repetition of the appearance of certain meaningful patterns. . . .' Their definition of ontological relativism centres on 'this quality of continual variation or becoming [which] is affirmed as within and ultimately carrying off the real'. In other words, 'the real' is reclaimed as a useable term in so far as it refers to the powerful and actual effects of the ongoing work we do to achieve it. This is not very different from Collier's opening line: 'the nature of language and practice is such as to support realism . . .', but it moves in a different direction. While both claim the term 'real', one uses binary logic to prove his case and the others make a deconstructive move on an underlying binary to find a way to recognize the coexistence of the orderly world we achieve and the unstable shifting patterns that are also there if we choose to look. As a result of his argument, à la Lenin, Collier finds structures as there and as constitutive, while Brown and Pujol with Curt find both organizations and selves to be achieved as (always revisable) effects of practice.

Willig also enters the debate, announcing the apparent contradictoriness of her two positions, one as social constructionist and the other as revolutionary socialist. She uses her version of critical realism to argue that these positions are, after all, not contradictory. She says 'I take for granted the unavoidability of ultimate epistemological relativism as well as the permanent ontological contestations among individuals and groups in society.' An important contribution that Willig makes to the debate is to point to the paralysing effect realist arguments can have. But her underlying philosophy seems to be of the kind that 'life is nasty, brutish and short' and that groups must organize as best they can to gain what power they can. Since all ontological positions can be overturned, 'political interventions must be coherent and mutually reinforcing and cannot be left to individual, context-dependent moral-political choices'. In other words, individuals who think they can make a difference on their own, need to realize that it is only as part of a larger organized group which shares a coherent discourse that power will be able to be used. (The implicit moral in her story for the disputants in this book is to stop arguing with each other and agree on a shared discourse if they want to have powerful effects.) Like several of the other writers, Willig finds the social constructionists guilty, presumably since without them her desired coherence would still be in place. She says the constructionists (like Burr, not naming names) are reluctant to make recommendations for improved practice, indeed, they even engage in 'absentionism' which is 'unhelpful' and 'dangerous'. She cites Parker et al. (1995) as one exception.

Reading the chapters in this book is like watching some strange shadow-boxing match where the identity of the people being beaten up is always kept a mystery. In the final event, none of the disputants are in any doubt about the power of discourse, though they cannot agree on what the implications of that understanding are for practice. Nor are they in any doubt about the power they gain from being constituted as psychologists. All agree they should act in socially responsible ways. All are caught up in the binary realism/relativism in one way or another, some using it to cement their own legitimacy as realists, others both trying to remove themselves from it by deconstructing it, yet failing, finally, to do so, as they do not succeed in negating its power to define who they are and what they are doing.

References

Davies, B. (1982) *Life in the Classroom and Playground: The Accounts of Primary School Children.* London: Routledge and Kegan Paul.

Davies, B. (1989) *Frogs and Snails and Feminist Tales: Preschool Children and Gender.* Sydney: Allen and Unwin.

Davies, B. (1993a) *Shards of Glass: Children Reading and Writing Beyond Gendered Identities.* Sydney: Allen and Unwin; Cresskill, NJ: Hampton Press.

Davies, B. (1993b) Review of J. Crawford, S. Kippax, J. Onyx, U. Gault and P. Benton, *Emotion and Gender: Constructing Meaning from Memory, Australian Women's Book Review*, 5 (1): 33.

Davies, B. (1994) *Poststructuralist Theory and Classroom Practice.* Geelong, VA: Deakin University Press.

Davies, B. (1995) *Power/Knowledge/Desire. Changing School Organisation and Management Practices.* Canberra: ACT Department of Education and Training.

Fuss, D. (1989) *Essentially Speaking: Feminism, Nature and Difference.* New York: Routledge.

Kristeva, J. (1981) 'Women's time', *Signs: Journal of Women in Culture and Society*, 7 (1): 13–35.

Parker, I., Georgaca, E., Harper, D., McLaughlin, T. and Stowell-Smith, M. (1995) *Deconstructing Psychopathology.* London: Sage.

Sayers, S. (1997) 'Is the truth out there?', *The Australian Higher Education Supplement*, 18 June: 32.

11

Constructionism and Realism: How Are We to Go On?

Kenneth J. Gergen

In important respects the drama of social constructionism was born of its opposition to a form of realism embodied in the dominant order of positivist/empiricist science. There was sweeping plausibility in the view that scientific claims to knowledge were effectively uncontaminated by culture, history and ideology – that indeed they were the crowning achievement in the human attempt to understand nature and self. Constructionist critique – emanating from the history of science and sociology of knowledge, gaining breadth and depth through contributions from critical theory, feminism, literary theory, rhetoric, and more, and then spilling across the disciplines – flew in the face of the acceptable, and thereby the drama that still colours the present colloquy.

The simple crossing of paths has now become a mottled terrain of conflict. Constructionist critique was enormously appealing to many groups whose voices had been marginalized by science, and to all those whose pursuits of social equality and justice were otherwise thwarted by existing authorities. Such critique not only served to level the playing field of discursive competition, but also opened the door to broadscale political and moral critique of existing authority structure. Constructionism and culture critique walked hand in hand – for a time. Slowly, however, those engaged in social change began to find that the constructionist axe turned back to gash the hand of the user. There was no power structure, race and gender oppression, poverty and so on that was not itself constructed. A new schism emerged, one more directly reflected in the pages of the present volume.

The complexity of the conflict has further intensified: first, many engaged by social construction wished to press on to document its character. Research was mounted on issues of conversation and discourse, and soon there was an investment in precisely those empiricist canons of rigor that constructionism had been at pains to subvert. Constructionists desirous of distancing themselves from empiricism grew cold at such research. Further, humanists, phenomenologists, and cognitive constructivists, who welcomed the constructionist emphasis on language and its critical challenge to positivist hegemony, soon found that many of their own icons – intentionality, agency, experience and cognitive construals – were brought low by deconstructionist efforts. The scholarly atmosphere is now striated with conflict. How, then, are we to go on?

It may be useful to situate this problem in a more general context. Conflicts of this variety are virtually endemic to scholarly life. And, in significant respects, conflicts within the academy bear a similarity to altercations within the broader society – for example, between political parties, religious factions, and unions and management. In all cases we confront differing conceptions of the real, the rational, and the good, along with commitments to congenial patterns of action and particular arrangements of material. As many commentators have also noted, societal conflict has become an increasingly commanding feature of the contemporary cultural landscape. We not only confront increasingly prevalent cleavages in terms of racial, economic and gender differences, but as well on issues of sexual preference, environmental protection, abortion, pornography, religious fundamentalism, vivisection and more. Elsewhere (Gergen, 1991) I have attempted to link this pandemic explosion of grass-roots activism to the emerging technologies of communication. As technologies enable persons of like disposition to locate similar others, to declare group consciousness, and to generate agendas of change, so do we find an increasing profusion of value-based enclaves. So pervasive is the resulting conflict that at least one commentator, James Davison Hunter (1991), has proposed that western society is essentially immersed in 'culture wars'.

In what follows I wish to treat the realism/constructionism antinomy within this broader context of societal conflict – viewing our present controversy as tissued to the society, and in turn, possibly bearing on its future. If we have created a sea of struggle within the academic sphere, how are we to proceed? Is there anything in our mode of comportment in this case that bears on the broader societal potentials? Are there any insights to be garnered from our interactions that harbour promise of broader implication? My particular way of treating these questions is certainly informed by social constructionist dialogues of which I am a part (see especially, Gergen, 1994). However, the treatment is not uncongenial to the realist, and many of the conclusions could have been reached via this route as well. Essentially, I wish to absent the antinomy itself and 'view it through a different lens', or more formally, embark on a metadiscourse. This is to step out of the agonistic and ingurgitating modes of argument in which we have been suspended, and inquire into our actions themselves. From a broader historical or cultural standpoint, for example, we may ask why we are at loggerheads, what is at stake for us, and what alternatives exist or could be created?

The present analysis is composed of three parts. First, I wish to consider the potentials of solving the issues through elimination by conflict. Secondly, I shall raise questions concerning the ways in which we situate ourselves within the competing discourses of realism and constructionism. Finally, given what I hope will be a softening of difference, I shall turn to some of the broader implications of the analysis.

Animating Animus: The Pleasures of Eradication

In major respects the course of developments in the realism/constructionism debate are quite familiar. They largely recapitulate the form of academic conflict in which most of us have been involved from the beginnings of our professional lives. There is high drama to be derived in commitment to an ideal, set against the backdrop of an inimical other. Failure to participate in that drama is to miss one of the greatest pleasures of scholarly life. Nor did most of us have to wait to embark on scholarly careers to participate in this cultural ritual. It was long there – as we defended our sandcastle against wicked intruders, an intimate friend from calumnious gossip, or a beleaguered minority group against unjust policies. In a certain sense, we are all 'Christian soldiers . . . marching to Pretoria . . . and we shall overcome'. Given the glories of championing the good in the face of evil, what are the central options deposited by our traditions at the doorstep of the present?

In many respects our most congenial option at this juncture is isolation and subterranean warfare. It is simple enough to divide ourselves into fragmented, hostile and self-satisfied enclaves. We may enter our minuscule groups of the like-minded, declare the intellectual and moral high ground, circulate our truths within the journals and conferences protected by our kind, and locate ways of undermining the investments of colleagues and institutions outside the fold. Such is largely the condition of relationship now existing between empiricists and constructionists. It is an emerging state among those groups set against empiricism – discourse analysts, feminist theorists and culture critics among them. It is a state that threatens now to divide all those who otherwise search for alternatives to what we blithely characterize as the dominant discourse.

How can we view this state as anything but unfortunate? It is not simply that we thus herald a condition of all against all. It is also a condition that deadens those within the contentious enclaves. Because this option thrives on separation, on forms of solipsistic self-gratification that only succeed over time in strengthening the internal structure of beliefs and values, there is little means of resolving conflict, no catalytic confrontation that might press the issues forward or offer new insights and potentials. Further, the structure of signification within the separate circles continues to feed upon itself. Consider, for example, experimental social psychology, a discipline that has virtually insulated itself from all of the major intellectual and social debates sweeping the academy and society in the past decades. This embattled, self-preoccupied group has sustained virtually the same set of research interests – cognition, attitudes, prejudice and aggression among the primary – for almost half a century. In effect, we find a freezing of assumptions within the enclaves, a diminution in catalytic creativity, and, one must suspect, over time a growing ennui.

Further, we must ask, what are the societal implications of this self-satisfying and self-affirming option? If we are concerned with what is communicated by the scholarly profession to the society concerning the nature of difference, we should do well to close our doors. Not only has the anguish of political correctness, for example, suggested that scholars are little more than bickering back-biters, but we in turn suggest to the society that where culture wars are concerned, we have little to offer. Culture wars are us.

There is a second option animated by the existing animus, which is that of direct confrontation. Again we are fully prepared for this ritual, and in certain respects our mode of combat is exemplary. We have acquired the capacity to replace the force of arms with a war of words. Thus, we can pursue debate, drawing the battlelines more sharply and clearly in hopes that, over time, the superior paradigm will win. We avoid the torpor of solidification and move towards a superior level of comprehension. In certain measure, essays within the present volume express such a tendency. Collier's spirited defence of critical realism, as against 'discursive and pragmatic idealism' is exemplary. Although less bellicose in posture, Willig's desire to replace the incipient conservativism she discerns in postmodern constructionism with an activist realism is also apposite. On the other side, Potter's offering frequently adopts an aggressive posture.

Yet, *pace* Mick Billig, I have severe doubts in the potential of argumentation to yield compelling solutions in such cases. There are several major shortcomings relevant to the present case. First, both realism and constructionism operate as foundational ontologies. They cannot properly be compared within the terms of either position, because the very presumptions of the standpoint from which one would be arguing would automatically foreclose on the alterior intelligibility. For example, the realist cannot convince the constructionist by pointing to evidence of, let us say, 'a real material nature', for such evidence has no currency within a constructionist ontology. Further, the constructionist cannot use rhetorical pyrotechnics to compel the realist, because the recognition of 'mere rhetoric' would disqualify the arguments.

There are further reasons why the stalwart combatants need never capitulate. In open dialogue one can continue indefinitely to remain secure in his/her beliefs – unaffected by counter-argument – because the very structure of dialogue ensures this possibility. The chief reason stems from the essential undecidability of meaning. One may voice an argument, but whether these words are granted meaning, and the particular meaning they are allowed to convey, is not determined by oneself but by one's audience. One's utterances stand as an open text, subject to appropriation from virtually any standpoint. And, just as one's arguments always stand vulnerable to the adversary's reconstitution, so are the adversary's utterances subject to a reciprocal appropriation. In effect, each interlocutor confronts a situation in which 'I cannot control your interpretation of what I say, but I am positioned so as to grant (or deny) intelligibility to your reply, or to bend your words to my interpretive designs'. Under these conditions of interdependent intelligibility, protagonists are free to block or transform all communiqués that might otherwise threaten their differing positions. The means for destroying the other's intelligibility are as vast and varied. Sentences may be lifted from context, concepts altered through recontextualization, arguments pressed to absurd extremes, examples transformed through parody, insidious intentions imputed, and so on. With sufficient experience in the ways of meaning making, another's arguments may always be dissolved.

And why shouldn't all stops be pulled in such disputes? The metaphor of argument as war virtually ensures that neither party will be willing to admit the superiority of the other. To do so would not simply carry the ignominy of defeat. To give way to the other's arguments would – in the western cultural tradition – invalidate the originary essence of the self. Or, more broadly, one's words are robbed of authority; one is no longer cast in the likeness of God, king, hero, and father, but returns to the status of errant child – now corrected by a knowing parent.

In terms of the broader society, argumentation may be a significant improvement over isolated antipathy. However, there is little hope that argumentation can ever reduce the intensity of the struggle. From the present standpoint, we might anticipate just the opposite: galvanized opposition and intensification of antagonism. This is certainly the typical case within the academy. Unless there is strong agreement on the grounds of argument, and what counts as rationality and evidence, arguments are seldom settled through rational interchange. As Thomas Kuhn (1970) remarked, too often such struggles are dissolved only through the expiration of the opposition.

Realism and Constructionism: What is at Stake?

Given the problems inhering in both indirect and frontal modes of antagonism, what options remain? Perhaps a more promising possibility is to consider both realism and constructionism as forms of discourse – again a stance that both realism and constructionism can embrace. Rather than viewing these intelligibilities either as expressions of individual minds or as transcendental logics, for the present let us simply consider them as forms of speaking or writing – composites of words and phrases used by people on various occasions. In this way we can consider the dual discourses as cultural resources, modes of intelligibility that exist alongside an enormous panoply of other cultural expressions. If this seems reasonable, we may ask a number of pertinent questions concerning the situated utility of the discourses. This analysis, in turn, may yield a new range of insights into what is, or is not, at stake in the present debate.

First, let us suppose that all the protagonists in the present colloquy possess both of the discourses ready at hand. We might presume this dual capacity simply by virtue of willingness to engage in the debate. One would scarcely wish to plump for one side of the binary without any familiarity with its contrasting number. Most of the entries into the present volume, in one form or another, manifest this dual familiarity. Given the broad availability of these discursive resources to the parties to debate, let us further suppose that there are occasions on which the various protagonists are likely to use them in earnest. That is, the users would wish to have others treat these words seriously, as representations of their own thoughts or beliefs. Thus, the most ardent constructionists would wish to teach their children, 'This is a dog', and 'that is a cat'. And if the constructionist screamed, 'Run, there's a fire!' he or she would not wish others to look with suspicion and retort, 'Oh, that's just your construction.' Similarly, those who embrace tenets of realism may often draw arrows from the quiver of constructionism. Would the most committed realist wish to delete from his/her repertoire such conversational moves as, 'That's just your story', 'This is a cultural myth', 'They are making it up', 'This news report is slanted in favour of the government', and 'The way you are putting that is oppressive.' Even the unreconstructed empiricist, blind to constructionist theory, will wish to say, 'Given their theoretical commitment, I can see why they would draw that conclusion', or, 'Physics, biology and psychology are simply different ways of conceptualizing the world.' Whether these dual capacities pose any particular dilemma for the individuals involved is moot; however, in light of the work of Billig and his colleagues (1988) on multiple and competing discourses, we should scarcely be surprised by the present case.

Given the sharing of both realist and constructionist discourses by all protagonists, we might also suppose that there are occasions on which virtually all would agree on which discourse is applicable or appropriate. That is to say, most of those engaged in realist/constructionist debates would join together in the harmonious use of a similar vernacular. Because most of us share a cultural history, and because we have been exposed to similar systems of education, and occupy similar positions of privilege, we will tend to converge in preferences and conventions – from tastes in food and drink to standards of scholarly excellence. I suspect under these conditions that most all of us would stand fast against neo-Nazis, the Mafia, Islamic terrorism, smuggling heroin, cliteroctomy, and Tory policies on higher education. Using a compelling discourse of realism, we would point to multiple failings and immoralities. Further, in fine constructionist form, we would be happy to demonstrate how such groups could – through the circulation and verification of discourse within their midst – come to find their actions reasonable and right. By the same token, most of us would fight fiercely against such groups when they used either constructionist or realist discourses to achieve their goals.

With ample possibilities for agreement on discourse use, let us press the present case to its ironic conclusion: those who typically champion constructionism might employ a realist discourse to throttle the realist, and the putative realist might adopt constructionist arguments to subvert constructionism. While this may seem improbable, closer inspection suggests that such tactics are not uncommon. It has long been recognized as a forgivable irony that social studies of science scholars, attempting to demonstrate the constructed character of scientific knowledge, will employ traditional ethnographic data to secure the case. And how often have constructionists been confronted by realists clamouring to point out that constructionist arguments are themselves constructed. In the United States, the charge of 'political correctness' is essentially a form of constructionist discourse (originally used by critical theorists to demonstrate the ideological underpinnings of the dominant discourse), employed in this case by realist conservatives to defend their traditions against constructionist attacks.

Following this line of argument, we see that it is useful to separate speaker from speech – identity from discourse – and view the discourses or realism and constructionism as available to us all for situated purposes. In this sense there are no realists or constructionists *per se*, but cultural participants who adopt these and other discourses on various occasions as conversational exigencies prevail. In this sense what we write about these issues in the academic arena may have little to do with our discursive habits in other locales. More important, I suspect that none of the parties would, on serious deliberation, wish to eradicate the alternative discourse. This is so philosophically, because each of the discourses gains intelligibility by virtue of its opposition. In that meaning is born of binary structure, so do realism and constructionism require each other as a means of rendering themselves intelligible. It is so pragmatically because of the enormous range of contexts in which these discourses often prove serviceable – including, as means of defending themselves against the other.

In the societal arena, there is much to be gained through this separation of persons from discourse – of seeing language as a vehicle for relating as opposed to a conveyor of foundations of the real and the good. On the one side, this enables us to remove the one-dimensionality of various political, ethnic and religious groupings, and to appreciate the potentials of all participants for inconsistent accounts and multiplex forms of action. We can avoid being drawn into the tendency to see discourse as a reflection of unified psyches, or as reflecting a personal essence. On the other side, we can begin to sense the limits of discourse in establishing social order. We can at last put reigns on the vain hope – from the Ten Commandments to charters of Universal Human Rights – that some particular arrangement of words will guarantee the replacement of pain and anguish with happiness for all. As implied by the preceding, the very attempt to secure The Word may itself ensure that such hopes are never met.

Beyond Argumentation

If realist and constructionist discourses are viewed as cultural resources – not unlike styles of art or architecture, forms of cuisine, or modes of dress – then we may ask whether it is necessary to set them against each other. For what reasons would we wish to submit them to the traditional rituals of argumentation in which one must subdue the other? If we do not wish to destroy one of the languages, why should we promote a war of words? If this is simply a matter of defending threatened egos, enlarging academic turf, or responding once again to the excitement of mock battle, the world would be better served

by other choices of scholarly activity. In the end it is the actions that are ratio-
nalized by meta-theory rather than meta-theory itself that will make a
difference. A greater flourishing of these potentials – on both realist and
constructionist sides – would be far more telling in its effects than another
round of metaphysical fisticuffs.

Yet, this proposal still leaves open the question of antagonistic activities.
Putting the meta-discourses aside, what if we object to certain activities ratio-
nalized by a given discourse – for example, experimental manipulation as
warranted by realist discourse, or arid argumentation analysis as favoured by
constructionism? Or more broadly, what does the present analysis have to say
to actions that we index as racist, sexist, unjust, intolerant, and the like?
Thus far the suggestion is that treating these matters on the level of theoretical or conceptual warrant has major limitations. Polarization, galvanization
and undecidability are followed by our failure to appreciate the ways in which
many of the discourses embedded in these pursuits are employed for causes
we might otherwise embrace (including our very attacks on these forms of
activity).

It is at this point that we are poised to enter a new domain of dialogue. As
we move through the space of critique and counter-critique, and then reflect
on the form of our antagonism, we begin to confront a new range of questions. How are we to go on – in academic life or society more generally –
when we embrace mutually unacceptable forms of life? If traditional modes
of critique and debate are flawed, how else can we proceed? And, can we
bracket our differences in the pursuit of common answers to these questions?
In some degree, features of such pursuits are already prefigured in this discussion – both in the present analysis and the chapters of this book more
generally.

In the present analysis are embedded three such avenues of common depar-
ture. As just outlined, we are first drawn into a search for *non-confrontational
modes of action*, modes of opposition that are not so acutely condemnatory,
or intensifying of conflict. Secondly, an argument was put forward for the
separation of persons from discourse – for seeing the latter not as an expression
of the former's essence, but as a communal tool. In this way we open a space
in which we can also separate persons from forms of life. More broadly, we
can begin to see racial epithets, batterings, or metro bombs as modes of intelligibility shared within communities. We move away from the presumption of
an 'inner evil' which can be altered with the infusion of alternative words, or
eradicated through the incarceration of individual beings. Further, because
we can begin to see the potentials in all for multiple and situated discourses,
we are moved to consider means of inter-mingling intelligibilities. We begin to
seek situations in which new audiences can be addressed, thus bringing forth
different modes of speech and other actions. Thirdly, we are led in the present
analysis to consider *explorations in commonality*. We can appreciate the possibility that the vast share of activity in which any of us are engaged is shared
by any group that we might oppose. Other than the specific actions we
oppose, the remainder of life may be highly congenial. In many cases, one

might even locate economic and political interdependencies – for example, participation in the same tax structure, or opposition to strong governmental control. With increased focus on that which is shared, the lethal edges of opposition might be blunted and new forms of relationship invited.

Other chapters in the present collection also enrich the possibilities for moving beyond confrontation. Many of the chapters, for example, rely on *polyphonies* – the use of multiple and competing discourses. Both Burr and Willig carry out an open dialogue between the opposing positions, thus locating the argument 'within' themselves as opposed to attributing the positive position to self and the negative to others. Merttens recognizes the competing voices and, avoiding the combative option, simply *shifts the discursive register*. Her focus on narratives also serves as a unifying metaphor, as it allows her to employ a constructionist trope ('the story') while simultaneously using the story in the service of political realism. Brown and Pujol with Curt make excellent use of what might be called *inter-interpollation*, that is, employing discourse fragments from both constructionist and realist registers to generate a vision of future potentials. Potter develops what might be seen as a *trickster motif*, first fragmenting both the forms of discourse and the argument itself so as to reduce the sense of 'a unified, hegemonic front'. His humour also invites the audience to take part, to join as opposed to 'being educated'. This same diminution of distance is achieved by following a censuring of Ros Gill's attack, with a celebration of her efforts.

In conclusion, we can locate within these many offerings a new stage of development – a festering antithesis giving way to a promising synthesis. Yet, the synthesis is not singular in this case, but multiple. We find here intimations of a new range of relational forms, forms that are redolent with potential – not only for our intellectual and practical/political lives together, but for the societies that establish the very possibility of our endeavours.

References

Billig, M., Condor, S., Edwards, D., Gane, M., Middleton, D. and Radley, A. (1988) *Ideological Dilemmas: A Social Psychology of Everyday Thinking*. London: Sage.
Gergen, K.J. (1991) *The Saturated Self*. New York: Basic Books.
Gergen, K.J. (1994) *Realities and Relationships*. Cambridge, MA: Harvard University Press.
Hunter, J.D. (1991) *Culture Wars*. New York: Basic Books.
Kuhn, T. (1970) *The Structure of Scientific Revolutions*. Chicago: University of Chicago Press.

Index